Stop Your Stinking Overthinking
Table of Contents

The Stinking Overthinking Trap
Table of Contents

STOP

YOUR STINKING

OVERTHINKING

Strategies for Quieting the Busy Mind, Letting Go and Staying Present

BARBARA HEAVENS

Stop Your Stinking Overthinking

Strategies for Quieting the Busy Mind, Letting Go, and Staying Present

Barbara Heavens

Introduction

Author Fyodor Dostoyevsky (1864) once wrote, "Thinking too much is a disease," and I can't agree more! What's odd about it is it's almost addictive. Once you enter a cycle of overthinking, you get stuck there, and your brain keeps at that subject until it exhausts itself. Like having a popcorn kernel stuck in your teeth, it's irritating, yet simultaneously entertaining. The kernel's not good for you, but your tongue keeps toying with it. Likewise, the spiral of continuous contemplation is harmful to your physical and mental health, yet your mind keeps spinning it round and round.

Overthinking is aptly named. It occurs when you think about a particular thing over and over and over for long periods of time. You might venture a little sideways sometimes, but you never steer completely away from the main subject.

Like, it rained the other night at my house with lots of big lightning strikes and loud rolls of thunder. Well, my dog is scared of thunder. He has PTSD from a few years back when lightning struck one street over and broke a water main six feet under the ground. None of us humans were home at the time, so that had to be terrifying for him! So anyway, it was storming, and the dog was shaking. If anyone in the house moved, he'd shadow them and stick like glue to their heels. I picked him up to snuggle and comfort him, and that sent me down a rabbit hole of lightning strikes. I got to wondering how they worked and why they happened. I thought of photos I'd seen of spectacular hits that branched out in all directions. I remembered all the lightning rods on just about every building in a nearby theme park, and that got me contemplating the number of times those have been struck—the answer is many, by the way. All these ruminations were set to the words of an old Fleetwood Mac song that says, "Thunder only happens when it's raining" (Nicks, 1977), and that got me thinking, *Does it?* And so down that track I went, trying to prove Stevie Nicks wrong. Meanwhile, the storm passed, and my dog jumped down, but I was still sitting there, lost in thought, hearing thunder rolling in the distance but seeing no rain outside my window.

Some people believe overthinking is a good thing. They believe that if they think about a certain problem, situation, or conflict enough, they'll eventually find the solution. The opposite is true, though. The more time you spend pondering an idea, the less time you have to develop it and put it into action. On top of that, the longer you dwell on the topic, the less likely you'll be to accept any solution as the *right* one. So what happens instead is that you end up mentally and physically exhausted. Instead of, say, creating world peace, you deplete yourself of any semblance of peace at all.

Psychologist and author Dr. Susan Nolen-Hoeksema detailed the research she performed in her book, *Women Who Think Too Much: How to Break Free of Overthinking and Reclaim Your Life* (2004), stating that women are a little bit more likely to overthink than men, but not by that large of a margin: women 57% and men 43%. Nolen-Hoeksema also reports that younger adults are more susceptible than older ones, with 73% of 25–35 year olds succumbing to the habit, 52% of 45–55 year olds, and just 20% of those aged 65–75. Though the numbers differ, it's apparent that too many people think too much. This is a dangerous trend because rumination leads nowhere good. It often results in depression, anxiety, and even alcoholism.

If you're not careful, overthinking can be chronic, but it's not incurable. With a bit of humor and a lot of insight—and with a little humility and loads of encouragement—you can pull yourself free from its grip and turn it into something you can monitor, manage, and manipulate if not entirely eliminate.

Stop Your Stinking Overthinking: Strategies for Quieting the Busy Mind, Letting Go, and Staying Present will equip you with tools to manage and reduce overthinking and help you achieve a healthier state of mind and a more present life. In these pages, you will discover

- tools and techniques to regulate your nervous system.

- strategies to retrain your mind to new and empowering habits.

- tips to manage and reduce overthinking and enhance your overall well-being.

- personal anecdotes and real-life examples that illustrate the negative effects of overthinking.

- ways to put a stop to your stinking overthinking.

You are not doomed to overthink for eternity—or even for the duration of your existence on this planet. But you are destined to free yourself from this burden of excessive thoughts and to stop letting rumination steal your joy in the *now*.

I didn't prove Stevie Nicks wrong; I didn't come to any conclusion at all. *Does* thunder only happen when it's raining? I may never know, no matter how much I crank the gears in my brain, and they're tempted to start spinning again...

Instead of getting back on that rollercoaster, let's buckle up, get ready to laugh at the brain's most ridiculous antics, and learn practical steps to stop that stinking overthinking!

Chapter 1:

Understanding

Overthinking

Amit Ray, an Indian author and philosopher, taught, "Overthinking is not a disease; it is due to the underuse of your creative power" (Ray, n.d.). Wait a minute! Dostoyevsky said it *is* a disease, so is it or isn't it? Yes. No. Both!

Overthinking is not a psychological disorder, nor is it a physiological ailment. However, if allowed to dominate your mind, it can result in mental health conditions like anxiety and depression, which, *if allowed to dominate your mind*, can lead to physical maladies like heart conditions, diabetes, and hypertension—in other words, disease.

When you overthink, you're certainly utilizing your imagination, being innovative, and creatively attempting to think yourself out of the box your rumination has put you in. When you overthink, you trick yourself into believing the solution is just one idea away. But when you get there, that concept isn't right either; the real answer is just one *more* idea away. So the cycle rolls on and on, and you get stuck in this pattern until Ray's notion proves true: An underuse of your creative power keeps you locked in the box.

Why Do We Overthink?

Overthinking occurs when you excessively analyze situations or potential outcomes. However, since you don't arrive at a solution, you often end up distressed by your indecision. Sometimes, an event or thought can trigger this loop of analysis and make you spiral out of control. For instance, if someone sends a short text message, you might spend hours guessing what it means. *Did they mean to be rude? Are they upset?* This process of worrying can consume your mind and distract you from more important tasks.

Why do we overthink in the first place? Oftentimes, it's due to one of these issues:

- **Your brain has no off switch:** You keep replaying the events or conversations you're worried about, thinking of every "if only" and "what if" and contemplating different scenarios. When you go to bed, those thoughts may still be swirling. You glance at the clock and realize several hours have passed—you're still awake, and then you dread the next day at the office because you're sure to be exhausted from not sleeping, and you think about how that's sure not gonna help you resolve that awkward situation with the boss—you're reminded of what you said to your boss the day before, and then you're back to the beginning again... Sigh. Normal thoughts can sometimes process for a while, but you eventually come to a conclusion—you hit the off switch—but overthinking only has a snooze button. It's like how time ticks to eternity; you might prolong the start of your day, but eventually, it resumes.

- **You're indecisive:** Have you convinced yourself that the longer you think about something and the more effort you put into it, the more angles you will cover and the more perspectives you'll consider? It would be okay if you stopped right there and accepted a decision, but what happens instead is that you obsess and overanalyze until all those options become barriers. Research suggests that extended contemplation delays decision-making, and that it's not until you have a distraction from that thought process that your mind can actually assess the information and come to a conclusion (Strick et al., 2010).

- **You second-guess every decision:** Overthinking often begins innocently enough with the good intention to solve a problem or fix something that went wrong. It might even be something fun, like where to plan a vacation. Rumination's not picky. It'll even bring up that day in middle school when you and your best friend argued over who would wear the one and only tiara to the dance, and you fought over it until it broke, and now you're trying to figure out what you could have done differently. But I digress. You're actually spinning your wheels on whether you should go to the beach or the mountains. Should you take the kids or leave them with Grandma and Grandpa while you and your special other have a little getaway? You could make great family memories at the beach, learning to surf, collecting shells, and hunting ghost crabs, but your son's not a strong swimmer, and your daughter hates the sand, so maybe you should stay in a cabin by the lake. You can make great memories with your spouse there, cuddling by the fire, sipping coffee on the deck as the sun rises over the trees, and rowing out on the water to catch some fish... but you are terrified of snakes, which are definitely in wooded areas, and your partner couldn't catch a fish to save their life, and... No decision is *right*.

- **You are not focused on solutions:** You might begin with a problem that needs a solution, but once your mental wheels start spinning, you quickly end up far off the beaten path, trying to figure out what it was you were trying to figure out in the first place. Overthinking means dwelling on the problem, not focusing on a solution. Remember the thunderstorm I mentioned in the introduction? I was *dwelling on the problem* of lightning, thunder, and heavy rain.

I was not considering any options to lessen my dog's fear (aside from holding him), doing anything to quiet the noise, or providing him with a comfort blanket or toy. Those things would have been *solutions*. If my mind had tracked that course, my time would have been productive. As it was, I didn't achieve anything; I just humored my imagination.

- **You replay thoughts or rehash conversations:** Raise your hand if this is you! (Me, me, me!) I can't count the times I've done this after a disagreement or an embarrassing moment. The scene runs through my mind over and over, and each time, my face flushes red again. *I said what? I should have said [fill in the blank]! Next time, I'll say it [this way], and I won't sound so dumb/silly/foolish.* Or I'll think of the perfect comeback at like 3 a.m., when it's way too late to text that person what I meant to say, and way too much time has passed since I said that, and if I bring it back up now, I'll just be embarrassed all over again.

- **You struggle with stressful situations:** Stressful situations like job interviews, arguments with friends, or even changes in routine can all trigger overthinking. Perfectionism, fear of failure, and certain other psychological patterns you rely on exacerbate overthinking. A perfectionist might replay every detail of a presentation—similar to what I mentioned in the previous section—fearing they did not do it perfectly or realizing things they could have said to make the presentation more effective. When you overthink, you become consumed by that one thing to the detriment of everything else. What if you are rehashing that presentation—which probably was a success—when you should be moving forward with putting that proposal into action? You waste your time and mental energy on something that's in the past and cannot be changed, and you fall behind in the progress you should be making.

Did you find yourself in any of those examples? If you're like me, you identified with more than one, and that's normal. We all tend to overthink sometimes; it's only problematic when it interferes with your daily life. Whether at work or home, recognizing this habit and being aware of the triggers are essential steps toward overcoming overthinking. Putting a stop to overthinking frees you to be more productive in all areas of life. Let's talk more about this and get a better understanding of what we're dealing with.

Emotional Reasoning and Its Impact

Emotions are quick and often imprecise responses to situations. In the 1970s, American psychologist Paul Eckman identified six key emotions all humans experience: happiness, sadness, disgust, fear, anger, and surprise. Psychologist Robert Plutchik later arranged those emotions in pairs opposite each other, similar to a color wheel. This "wheel of emotions" has since been further developed to place many more complex emotions—such as embarrassment, shame, or pride—in various areas of overlap (Cherry, 2024).

Emotions influence the way you engage with people and affect how you live your life. Some emotions alert you to danger; others comfort you with feelings of security. All, however, have the potential to lead to poor decision-making if you allow them to dominate your reasoning process. For example, if you feel sad, you might fixate on other sad things and fall into a spiral of negativity.

This is why emotional reasoning (ER) is intertwined with overthinking. ER distorts your perceptions. When you engage in emotional reasoning, you believe something is true just because you *feel* it to be true. For instance, you may feel angry that a friend canceled plans because you think this means they don't value your friendship. You're using emotions as evidence instead of relying on logic or observable facts.

If unchecked, this behavior can ruin relationships and create problems that aren't really there. Overreliance on emotions can worsen anxiety and lead you to make decisions without support for your conclusion.

To better manage emotions, you need to distinguish between your emotional mind—a more reactive and impulsive state—and your rational mind, which is logical but can seem cold. A balanced approach, according to Emma McAdam of Therapy in a Nutshell (2024), is to cultivate what is called the wise mind. The wise mind acknowledges emotions while also considering logic and reason.

One effective way to recognize emotional reasoning is through cognitive behavioral therapy (CBT) techniques, which encourage you to challenge your thoughts systematically. For example, instead of letting sadness dictate your belief about your friendship, examine the situation logically. Your friend probably had a valid reason to cancel that had nothing at all to do with you. We'll discuss CBT further in a later chapter. For now, let's focus on some things you can do to jumpstart your overthinking recovery.

Strategies to Combat Overthinking

One practical method to combat overthinking is to slow down your reactions. There's plenty of time between a stimulus and your response to take a thoughtful pause. Take that moment to breathe, count, or simply reflect on the situation so you don't make a rash decision.

Predicting emotional triggers can also be incredibly helpful. For instance, there's a family gathering coming up, and you don't get along with your sister-in-law. Just the thought of being in the same room with her sends your mind into a loop, overthinking, rethinking, and emotionally thinking about that thing she said last Christmas that insulted your mother, sent your niece running for cover, and drove a wedge between you and your brother. As the scene starts to play in your head, and the reels whip through your brain like an old drive-in filmstrip, you fall down, down, down into the pit of anger and hostility, contemplating all the things you're going to say to her the moment you see her, *overthinking, rethinking, and emotionally thinking* through them again and again until you're exhausted. Your sister-in-law is a trigger. Be aware of that and plan accordingly. You might ask your spouse to give you a subtle signal if they notice you're getting frustrated, and it will remind you to step back and calm down before returning to the conversation.

In some situations, you can take the opposite action of what your emotions tell you to do. If the emotional response is urging you to shout in anger, speak softly instead. If you feel the urge to overthink, the opposite—underthinking—probably wouldn't be very helpful either. In this case, don't ruminate—proactivate! Okay, I made up that word, but what you need to do is proactively consider the subject. Don't just spin your wheels; give purpose to your thoughts.

Another practical approach is to write down how to handle such situations better next time. This helps to solidify your understanding of your emotional responses and creates a strategic plan for future instances.

Understanding Intrusive and Automatic Thought Patterns

Intrusive thoughts are unwanted mental images or ideas that come into your mind without warning and cause distress. Some can be disturbing, like sudden thoughts of violence or inappropriate situations, and are commonly associated with anxiety, obsessive-compulsive disorder (OCD), and post-traumatic stress disorder (PTSD). People dealing with these issues might experience intrusive thoughts more frequently because of their predisposition and end up in a cycle of worry that impacts their daily lives.

Automatic thought patterns differ from intrusive ones in that they are not interrupters. They are the unconscious beliefs you hold about yourself and the world around you. For example, if you got turned down for a job promotion, you might unconsciously believe you are unworthy of success. Such assumptions can influence how you respond to situations and shape your perceptions and emotions, even when there is no real evidence to support them.

Shift Your Perspective

Cognitive fusion occurs when you become entangled with your thoughts and lose sight of the present moment. It can be detrimental and lead to increased stress and anxiety. To counteract the impact of intrusive and automatic thoughts, you need to change the way you view them. Instead of letting thoughts control you, learn to observe and analyze them. Below are some ways to achieve this goal:

- **Cognitive defusion:** In contrast to cognitive fusion, cognitive defusion involves detaching yourself from your thoughts and emotions rather than letting them dictate your actions. To practice cognitive defusion, examine your thoughts as if they are merely passing words in a stream. Instead of engaging with negative thoughts or trying to suppress them, acknowledge their existence and choose whether to focus on them or let them go. This approach helps reduce the burden of negative thinking and fosters psychological flexibility.

- **Acceptance and commitment therapy (ACT):** Cognitive defusion is often utilized in combination with ACT to help you accept your thoughts and feelings while committing to actions that align with your values. As you focus on what truly matters to you, you begin to let go of the power that intrusive and automatic thoughts hold over you. Identifying core values and engaging in activities that reflect these values can bring more meaning to your life and diminish the grip of negative thoughts.

- **Mindfulness:** Set aside a few minutes each day to practice mindfulness, which can help train you to acknowledge intrusive thoughts without letting them control you. Keep a thought journal and review it regularly to identify thought patterns and become more aware of your thought processes. Build a supportive network around you and seek professional guidance.

Productive Reflection vs. Destructive Overthinking

I mentioned previously that many people mistakenly believe that overthinking is beneficial, that the more they analyze a subject, the more perspectives they'll get on it, and the better able they'll be to make an informed decision. That would be considered *productive* thinking, which would be fine; however, overthinking just stirs the concoction of possibilities into a big pot of murky mess!

Personal reflection—an act of productive thinking—involves taking the time to thoughtfully consider and analyze your thoughts, experiences, and actions. It's a process of self-examination and introspection that helps you gain insight into your emotions, motivations, and values. Through personal reflection, you can better understand yourself, improve self-awareness, and make positive changes in your life. It's a self-assessment from which you arrive at an actionable conclusion.

Destructive overthinking refers to the excessive and harmful habit of constantly dwelling on negative thoughts and scenarios—when you focus on the downside of a situation instead of the positive. It can lead to feelings of pessimism, hopelessness, anxiety, and stress and make it difficult to make decisions or take action. This type of overthinking can be detrimental to your mental and emotional well-being and may hinder your ability to function effectively.

Catastrophizing is a form of destructive overthinking that refers to the tendency to perceive a situation as considerably worse than it actually is. It's when you magnify the importance of negative events, expect the worst imaginable outcome, and live as if that's the reality of the moment. Naturally, when you're in this state of cognitive distortion, your anxiety skyrockets, and your distress plummets.

Let's say you were in a tizzy this morning because you overslept—slammed that snooze button five times, to be honest—and put yourself in a crazed rush to get dressed, out the door, and in the office within 45 minutes. You plop down at your desk and wonder *Did I turn off the coffee maker?* You glance at the insulated mug in your hand and remember emptying the pot into it. *If the burner's still on, there's nothing in the carafe to warm. It'll just keep heating the glass, but there's nothing in it! And I left the dish towel right there on the counter beside it. If the machine keeps running, the glass will overheat, it will explode, and the towel will catch on fire! That will spread to the window curtain, and the walls, and the cabinets. My whole house is going to burn down before lunch!* You can't call the neighbors to check. The ones you do know are at work now, and no one has a key to your house anyway. All morning, you worry away. *Surely, the fire department would call if my home caught fire, right? But how would they know how to reach me?* The report you just handed your boss was interspersed with reminders to double-check things and buy a fire extinguisher, and somehow, "Give my neighbor Cindy a key to my house" was worked into the final paragraph. It's noon when he knocks on your office door with a really puzzled look on his face, but no sound comes from his mouth because he's whiplashed by your mad dash outside to your car. He's left there blinking in confusion as you race home—*gotta beat the firetruck there!*

Was that personal reflection, looking back on your peaceful morning to ponder the delicious coffee you brought to work with you? No. It was down and dirty, destructive, catastrophizing! You didn't just wonder; you worried, feared, and then convinced yourself of the most disastrous possibility. The thoughts going through your mind were not helpful in any way. They did not give you new perspectives or help you reach a logical conclusion. Instead, they set your anxiety off like fireworks and compromised the quality of your work.

Take heart! There are several ways to challenge negative thinking. Here are some tips that may help:

- **Seek professional help:** Consulting a mental health professional such as a therapist or counselor can provide you with the necessary support and guidance. They can help you understand your emotions, identify triggers, and develop coping mechanisms.

- **Build a support system:** Reach out to friends and family members for support. Talking about your feelings and experiences with trusted individuals can provide emotional relief and help you feel less isolated.

- **Practice self-care:** Engage in activities that promote self-care and relaxation, such as exercise, bubble baths, or hobbies that you enjoy.

- **Cognitive restructuring:** This is a therapeutic process that involves identifying and challenging negative thought patterns and replacing them with more constructive, rational beliefs that improve mental well-being and enhance decision-making skills.

- **Mindfulness techniques:** Meditation and deep breathing, can help bring awareness to negative thought patterns, restore you to an accurate sense of the present moment, and promote a more positive mindset.

- **Establish a routine:** Create and stick to a daily routine to add structure and stability to your daily life. Prioritize healthy habits, such as regular sleep patterns, balanced nutrition, and staying physically active.

- **Challenge negative thoughts:** Cognitive-behavioral therapy techniques can help you challenge distorted and negative thinking patterns that contribute to depression and anxiety. Learning to reframe your thoughts in a more positive and realistic manner can make a significant difference.

- **Set realistic goals:** Break large tasks into smaller, achievable goals. Reaching small goals can build a sense of accomplishment, boost your confidence, and contribute to a more positive outlook.

- **Limit stress:** Identify sources of stress in your life and develop strategies to manage or minimize them. You could set boundaries, delegate tasks, or practice relaxation techniques.

Be patient and compassionate with yourself as you work through these strategies.

Oh, Stop It!

Wouldn't it be nice if you could just tell your mental gears to quit spinning? While stopping your stinking overthinking might not be quite that simple to stifle, effective management of those tendencies comes down to "engaging in daily actions that will train you not to overreact and remain in control from the inside out." To accomplish this retraining, try the following tips (Mara, 2024):

- Identify your triggers.

- Recognize when you start to overthink.

- Rein in those thoughts and put them to work finding a solution; don't just let them spin.

- Understand that the problem is not the problem, but overthinking is.

- Consider if the thing you're pondering will still be worth considering in a week. If not, let it drop.

- Allow yourself to stop at "good enough" and don't pursue the perfect answer.

Author and well-being coach Shira Gura (n.d.) promotes an "unSTUCK" method:

- **S**top: Pause to separate your thoughts from the emotional reaction that has arisen to them.

- **T**ell: If strong emotions are attached to your thoughts, get them out in the open and acknowledge them.

- **U**ncover: Investigate your thoughts and give validity to truthful ones.

- **C**onsider: Replace illegitimate thoughts with truthful ones.

- **K**indness: Be kind to yourself! Don't beat yourself up for your struggles; allow yourself to feel and to heal.

Keep these suggestions in mind as we move ahead. In the next chapter, we'll explore the mind-body connection and get a better understanding of how overthinking impacts your overall well-being. We'll also discuss strategies to combat mental stress and learn about grounding techniques.

Chapter 2:

Understanding Your Mind-

Body Connection

In the previous chapter, we talked a lot about how overthinking can increase stress and how that heightened anxiety can lead to physical discomforts, ailments, and diseases, like heart conditions and diabetes. In this chapter, we're going to flip that flop and consider how your body's *physical* condition can impact your *mental* state.

The terms "mental health" and "emotional health" both refer to the function of your mind and are often used interchangeably. However, the two have some important differences:

- **Mental health** refers to how we think, solve problems, and make decisions. It is the more physical aspect of the mind and involves brain processes, mental disorders (like chemical imbalances), and behavior and personality changes.

- **Emotional health** has to do with feelings and how we experience and manage them. It deals with insecurities and fears as well as joy and satisfaction and also moderates social skills and self-regulation.

Both aspects, however, are interrelated when it comes to the mind-body connection.

A recent study from the Washington University School of Medicine (2023) revealed that the mind and body affect each other in physiological and not just abstract ways. Researchers claim their findings confirm a literal link within the brain's physical structure between these two components of the human being that were thought to operate separately. They state, "Parts of the brain area that control movement are plugged into networks involved in thinking and planning, and in control of involuntary bodily functions such as blood pressure and heartbeat." We tend to think that thoughts and feelings are distinct from bodily functions and movements, but this demonstrates that the two parts (mind and body) work together, not independently.

In the pages that follow, we will focus on the body-mind connection, learn about how some of your negative and strong emotions can be stored deep down in your body, and understand how that physical emotional storage affects not only your mental well-being but also your physical health.

Mind-Body Connection: How Emotions Affect Health

The study mentioned above has helped researchers understand *why* anxiety has accompanying physical symptoms, *why* vagus nerve stimulation relieves depression, and *why* regular exercise can lead to a more positive outlook. Though such correlations have long been known, science is just now starting to discover the links that connect these networks. It's enabled them to explain how the mind and body have a back-and-forth communication track such that the one affects the other and the other affects the one.

This is why meditation, yoga, and deep breathing calm the body *and* the mind, and it is why high anxiety stresses the body *and* the mind. As Professor Evan Gordon of the Mallinckrodt Institute of Radiology explains (as cited in Washington University School of Medicine, 2023):

> We've found the place where the highly active, goal-oriented "go, go, go" part of your mind connects to the parts of the brain that control breathing and heart rate. If you calm one down, it absolutely should have feedback effects on the other (para. 4).

While it's not new information, this revelation provides a tangible approach to something previously considered only in philosophical—and in more recent centuries—psychological circles.

The ancient Greek physician Hippocrates and those who studied under him are thought to be among the first people in recorded history to attempt to understand emotions. In their work, they pulled from ancient science and philosophy as they explored the endocrine, nervous, and immune systems, as well as structural parts of the body, in search of the inner workings and their connection to disorders and diseases.

Hippocrates and his followers developed "the theory of the four humors," which assessed a person's health based on the "humors" of blood, phlegm, black bile, and yellow bile. They concluded that when those four were in balance, a person was in good health, but if any was unbalanced, disease prevailed. Their prognosis aimed to restore the balance by improving the patient's diet, increasing their amount of physical activity, and managing the body's excretions of urine, feces, blood, and perspiration.

Greek physician Galen, who lived about 500 years after Hippocrates, based his practice on Hippocrates' humoral factors but expanded his diagnostic skill to include monitoring the pulse. In this case, he was often able to discern between organic ailments and those traced to the emotions.

Twelfth century physician, Moses Maimonides, took Galen's ideas a step further, attributing "passions of the psyche" to "changes in the body that are great, evident, and manifest to all," and he advised they be kept in balance as the topmost priority. Later scholars suggested that the imagination also contributed to nonphysical ailments by inciting the emotions, which then disrupted the body's physical condition. "Vivid ideas" were even thought to cause "monstrous births," a persistent concern that lasted well into the 19th century (Frontiers of the Mind, 2023).

A shift occurred in the 18th century, when they study of anatomy became the foundation of pathology. Physicians at this time concluded that disease resulted from what they called "lesions," or parts of the body that were susceptible to ailment, rather than emotional or humoral imbalances. As the 19th century rolled around, inventions like the stethoscope led to improved patient diagnostics and furthered the promotion of anatomical conditions as the primary explanation for disease, drifting away from mental or emotional influence.

At about the same time, study of the nervous system was developing and quickly became a dumping ground for things that couldn't be explained away by faulty anatomy. Hysteria and insanity were said to result from "a considerable and unusual excess in the excitement of the brain" or "violent emotions or passions of the mind," and many conditions, like epilepsy, were even considered to be imaginary complaints of people who were seeking attention (Frontiers of the Mind, 2023).

Throughout the 20th century, advancements in medical equipment allowed audio and visual glimpses inside the body and the study of tissues and cells at microscopic levels. This, combined with the growth of the psychology field, which began in the late 1800s with such pioneers as Sigmund Freud and Joseph Breuer, further distanced the notion of psychological influence over health and disease and separated the two areas of science.

The wheel seems to be turning once more toward acceptance of the mind and body connection, and it has influenced the development of integrative medicine, a field of medical science that bases diagnosis and treatment on the condition of the whole person, taking into account both mental and physiological states.

Strategies to Use Physical Wellness to Combat Mental Stress

Many of those early theorizations from Hippocrates, Galen, and others were on the right track. They understood that there was a mind-body correlation, but they could not seem to find concrete evidence. Hence, their theories eventually lost momentum in favor of tangible scientific "proof." Today, we have the benefit of learning from both camps—emotional study and anatomy—and can get a more complete picture of how the mind and body philosophically *and* physiologically work together to achieve overall health and wellness.

Director of the U.S. Office of Disease Prevention and Health Promotion, Dr. Paul Reed (2021), notes the sort of catch-22 loop. Ill physical health yields ill mental health; conversely, optimal physical health yields optimal mental health. Reed says, "What's good for the body is often good for the mind," and recommends the following tips to keep both physical and mental health in tip-top order:

- **Get moving!** Moderate to vigorous physical activity wards off all sorts of illnesses and ailments and improves your cognitive functions. Exercise has specifically been shown to increase the amount of norepinephrine, a neurotransmitter that helps the brain deal with stress. In fact, 50% of the brain's norepinephrine supply is located in an area involving emotional responses (*Working Out Boosts Brain Health*, 2020). The U.S. Department of Health and Human Services (2018) promotes the following physical activity guidelines for adults:

  - Move more; sit less. You will benefit from any movement that is moderate to vigorous.

  - Do moderate to vigorous muscle-strengthening activity at least two days a week.

  - Get 150–300 minutes of moderate or 75–150 minutes of vigorous aerobic activity throughout the course of each week. Get more benefits from additional cardio work.

- **Have a mental health screening.** Request this from your healthcare provider regularly as a preventative measure and to moderate existing conditions. If necessary, seek therapeutic benefit from professional help.

- **Take in ample nutrition.** Fuel your body well to give it the healthy sustenance it needs. Include foods that boost your brain power, too, for improved overall well-being.

While physical activity cannot substitute for mental health treatments, it can contribute to sustained mind *and* body wellness. This statement concisely sums up the mind-body connection and the importance of keeping both parts of your being functioning well (*Working Out Boosts Brain Health*, 2020):

> The cardiovascular system communicates with the renal system, which communicates with the muscular system. And all of these are controlled by the central and sympathetic nervous systems, which also must communicate with each other. This workout of the body's communication system may be the true value of exercise; the more sedentary we get, the less efficient our bodies are in responding to stress (para. 7).

It kind of reminds me of the old "bones" song to teach children the skeletal system. You know, "The head bone's connected to the neck bones. The neck bones' are connected to the backbone. The backbone's connected to the hip bone..." Maybe we could borrow the tune but change the words to, "The cardiovascular system's connected to the renal system. The renal system is connected to the muscular system. And they're all controlled by the nervous system..." But I don't think it has the same catchy ring.

Where Deep-Seated Emotions Are Stored in the Body

Emotions can be uncomfortable, especially the negative ones; although, pleasant experiences can be overwhelming too. When you feel something too much—if it's too scary to confront, if it hurts too much, if you fear the trauma will happen again, if you worry the repercussions will be too severe, if you've overthought too much and it now feels catastrophic— you may try to push those emotions deep down inside to a hidden place where they're no longer in your face. Instead of tackling those feelings head-on, you bottle them up. The problem is that whenever you avoid processing your emotions, you keep yourself in perpetual inner conflict.

According to Sean Grover of *Psychology Today* (2018), repression feeds fear and triggers psychosomatic symptoms. He describes 10 areas of the body in which these stuffed-away emotions are stored. You might experience these symptoms individually, but they can also occur in combination, depending on your emotional state:

- **Hurt:** A broken heart is not just a thing of fairy tales and sappy movies. The heart is your natural center of love, devotion, and deep-seated sentiment. When someone hurts you, and you don't fully process it all the way through to a place of healing, you may feel tightness in your chest and, yes, pain in your heart.

- **Anxiety:** Approximately 40 million American adults are affected by anxiety disorders each year. That's more than 19% of the population! I'll admit I'm one of those 40 million (*Anxiety Disorder—Facts & Statistics*, 2022). Though I have a magic power of being super calm in the middle of crises, I don't handle stress very well in general. Anxious feelings often manifest in breathing difficulty—in various forms like shortness of breath, shallow breath, or rapid breath—and are sometimes accompanied by lightheadedness and potential incidents of passing out.

- **Loss of self-identity:** When you feel like your life is in flux, when major changes have occurred and turned life upside down, and you no longer identify the you that you thought you were—even if it's a good experience, like building your personal growth—you'll likely experience sleep disturbances like insomnia, frequent wakings, or trouble getting back to sleep once you are awake.

- **Fear:** This is a very common effect. It definitely happens to me! When you are afraid, your stomach may cramp or roil, and you may feel the need to purge. Gut complaints are closely linked to conflict and being afraid of the outcome (or a fear of not knowing what will happen next). It can be fear of physically dangerous things or situations or personal confrontations and disagreements.

- **Anger:** "Oh, my aching back!" If you haven't said it yourself, you've likely heard it on TV during a comedic moment when one character is frustrated with another. In reality, lower back pain is not a laughing matter, so try to work through and resolve frustration whenever you encounter it.

- **Loss of control:** If you are strong-willed, if you are a control freak, or if you feel like your plans have all gone wrong, you could develop a headache. Control tendencies can make a situation worse, which, in turn, can make you feel worse and develop migraines or some of the other symptoms in this list, like back pain, neck tension, or anxiety.

- **Trauma:** Trauma can be a physical incident in which you were injured, threatened, or experienced a severe loss, but it can also occur from anything that impacts you intensely on an emotional level. If these feelings are not worked through early on, you risk becoming numb to your feelings so that you don't feel that critical harm again. You deaden your feelings to eliminate vulnerability.

- **Oppression:** You have the right to be heard! But perhaps, instead, you've been stifled. Persistent silencing creates an inner conflict of wanting to speak up but fearing either harsh consequences or having your words land on deaf ears. The resulting tension can constrict the muscles in your throat and make your voice hoarse or raspy.

- **Resentment:** When you resent someone, you give them power over you—in your head. You don't hurt them at all, but you do continue to wear yourself down. As an overthinker, you probably know this already! Reliving conflicts, confrontations, arguments, and uncomfortable or frustrating situations is exhausting, isn't it? Fatigue results when you're busy hashing out all that blame and anger inside your mind.

- **Burden:** Shouldering too much responsibility—even if you've unnecessarily placed it upon yourself—can really be a pain in the neck. When you feel overburdened, your neck, shoulders, and upper back can tighten up with a lot of tension and lead to headaches, jaw displacement, and spinal shifts, increasing the discomfort you already feel in your upper body.

Not all ailments are psychosomatic, of course, but because the mind and body are connected by emotion and physiology, you may literally feel your feelings.

Learning to Deal With Strong and Overwhelming Emotions

Doctors often advise their patients to reduce the stress in their lives, but is it really possible to reduce stress? I'm not so sure! What you can do, however, is deal with it.

You might be in the middle of a stressful situation, and it may come to a resolution. However, does that mean the stress is gone? Not necessarily. Something could be worked out but still be difficult, especially if things didn't go your way. What you really need to do—and the only way to minimize the effects of stress on your life—is to learn how to *manage* stress.

Below are some strategies to use your body to calm your mind and progress toward getting your overthinking under control:

- Allow your emotions to brew, but limit the time you dedicate to them to no more than an hour a day. As you grow accustomed to scheduling contemplation (or overthink) time, shorten it in increments until you give those thoughts only five minutes a day.

- Ground yourself with techniques like sensory awareness exercises. The 5-4-3-2-1 exercise is my personal go-to! It's simple and very enjoyable, and it can be done anywhere at any time. Situate yourself in a quiet place where you won't be disturbed. Then, run—actually, no, walk slowly—through each of your 5 senses, listing 5, 4, 3, 2, or 1 of the things you sense around you. For example, start with 5 things you can hear, then 4 things you can see, 3 things you can touch, 2 things you can smell, and 1 thing you can taste. Go through them again, but change up the senses and try 5 things you can smell, 4 things you can touch, and so on.

- Practice breathing exercises. Qigong is a healing art that was established in ancient China and involves controlled breathing and movement as well as meditation. Allison Lim of the Traditional Chinese Medicine World Foundation (2022) explains that the practice targets specific parts of the body and the stressors that are affecting them. For example, heart qi balances peace and harmony throughout the body, while liver qi manages anxiety and stress, and lung qi processes grief. If you're not familiar with qigong, the 4-7-8 breathing technique is a good one to get you started. Again, find a quiet place and eliminate interruptions. Sit in a comfortable chair and keep your back straight with your feet flat on the floor. Inhale deeply for a count of 4 seconds; hold that breath for a count of 7 seconds; then slowly release it for a count of 8 seconds.

- Do yoga. Yoga is a wonderful practice to relax both the mind and the body—and those connectors that keep both aspects bumping off each other. Traditional yoga can be done at beginner, intermediate, and advanced levels to suit your abilities, and chair yoga has become a popular method for seniors or those with mobility or other health issues that prevent them from performing the full range of movements.

- Walk with intention in a mindful manner. Mindfulness—which we'll discuss in depth in the next chapter—is the practice of allowing yourself to embrace your feelings in a nonjudgmental way that pulls your focus off your troubles and centers it in the present moment. There are many ways to practice mindfulness, but sensory walking is a great way to use your body to relieve your mind. You walk every day, so it's not a sport or a skill you need to learn. Just extend it to lengthier efforts, like doing a lap or two around your neighborhood, and focus on the sensations you encounter on the journey. *Hear* the bird songs, *feel* the sun's warmth on your cheeks, and *breathe in* the fresh, clean air. What other sounds do you hear? What scents blow in the breeze? Did you feel the flutter of the butterfly that brushed your arm? Did you see that cat scamper under the fence?

Other ways to relax your nervous system and pacify your mind include doing light exercise, getting an emotional support pet or engaging more with the pet you have, replacing negative thoughts with positive ones, establishing and enforcing boundaries, tending to self-care, and picking up a hobby.

Healthy coping skills like the ones we've discussed here help you calm your mind and body from the effects of stress without repressing your feelings or avoiding the issues. When you're ready, you'll be more able to think with purpose, arrive at actionable conclusions, stop ruminating, and quit running your mind and body ragged.

Chapter 3:

Mastering Mindfulness

Stress is your body's way of telling you it can't handle what you've got going on. You can't really avoid it. Even if you were a hermit, you might still worry about your provisions, your health, or what would happen if some developer bulldozed your location to build the next megamall.

Your body is designed to react to stress. It's meant to keep you safe from harm. Stress responses can be positive or negative, but both help your body adjust to new experiences. If you're that hermit gathering firewood in the forest, and you turn around and greet a grizzly face-to-face, stress will be a good thing because it will trigger your fight-or-flight response and jumpstart your body to do what it needs to survive. If, however, you get stuck in lengthy overthinking sessions every day wondering what it would be like to live alone in the woods... *Would I prefer a cabin or an earthen structure? Would I have to cook everything over an open fire? Can a hermit have modern amenities? I mean, they're not necessarily going off-grid. They just want to get away from people. Would online orders still get delivered? What about pizza? Do they even have phone service or the internet? What if I were a hermit, and I came face-to-face with a grizzly while gathering firewood? What do you do with grizzlies, run away? No, I think you play dead. No problem, I'd probably pass out anyway. But then, it might think, "Yum!*

Fresh meat!" and *have a go at me. And being a hermit, no one's around to hear me holler for help. Forget what happens when a tree falls in a forest; if you scream during a bear attack and no one's around to hear it, do you make a sound?* ...you'd find yourself stuck in critical fight-or-flight tension with nothing to actually fight or flee from.

You would've wound yourself up for no reason at all. That kind of stress is harmful. It increases your heart rate, makes you breathe rapidly, and releases cortisol, which, since it doesn't have a real job to do—like boost your metabolism and ready you to throw punches or run like lightning—just builds up in your body. Persistent cortisol release brought on by the stress you place yourself under when you ruminate and obsess over your stressors can greatly increase your risk of developing heart disease, obesity, anxiety, lung issues, and other physical ailments.

Aside from excessive contemplation, numerous other life factors contribute to high levels of stress. Everyday worries like work duties, family responsibilities, paying bills, and even going on vacation—yes, it's true—can result in any or all of the three types of stress:

- **Acute:** This is short-term, positive, or negative stress that comes and goes, like angst before a job interview or the trill of a roller coaster's fist drop.

- **Episodic:** This is recurring acute stress that you encounter regularly so that you don't have time to recover from one incident before being plunged into the next. First responders often experience this.

- **Chronic:** This is prolonged stress that lasts for weeks or months. You might feel this during a health crisis or during a difficult relationship.

You might have an acute stress response if you occasionally overthink, episodic if you do it a few times a week, and chronic if you ruminate daily, especially multiple times a day or for long periods at a time. And you might start to notice some of those psychosomatic symptoms we discussed in the previous chapter. Reliving harsh confrontations may keep hurting your heart, rehashing fretful what-ifs might keep your stomach tied in knots, and constantly worrying over responsibilities can keep your shoulders hunched up to your ears.

What can you do to relieve all this stress and reduce its effects? In Chapter 2, we gave you some strategies for putting your body to work to restore peace of mind, and we touched on mindfulness practices as one of those techniques. Mindfulness offers so many options and provides so many benefits that we are devoting this entire chapter to it.

Buddhist monk Thich Nhat Hanh (n.d.) wisely observed, "With mindfulness, you can establish yourself in the present in order to touch the wonders of life that are available in that moment." So let's learn what mindfulness is, dispel myths to discern what it's not, discover how it differs from meditation, and learn how to start practicing this technique.

What Is Mindfulness?

Did you know that your brain is plastic? It's funny to apply that term to such a complex organ, but it comes straight from the Latin *plasticus* (minus the suffix), meaning "of molding," and the Greek *plastikos*, meaning "to mold or form" (M-W, n.d.). In essence, your brain can be shaped and changed—it actually is every day by the act of neuroplasticity. By adding the Greek *neura* or *neuron* to the beginning, we specify that we're talking about "nerves," as Galen interpreted it from the original meaning of "sinew" or "string" (Online Etymology Dictionary, n.d.).

Neuroplasticity

Dr. Richard Davidson, a psychologist, researcher, and professor at the University of Wisconsin-Madison, is known for his studies on the effects of meditation on neurological conditions, specifically in regard to the brain's ability to morph throughout the course of life (neuroplasticity, if you weren't paying attention, wink-wink). Traditionally, Western science has considered the brain static, but Davidson challenged that theory when he hotwired some monks' brains.

Davidson chose to examine Tibetan Buddhist monks because they are "masters of the art of dispassionately observing the inner workings of their own minds," and so determined they, of all people, would be the best subjects for his inquiry. His study linked states of consciousness to the central nervous system's electrical activity and revealed that the strong neural activity associated with meditation takes place in the left prefrontal cortex and amygdala (Weil, 2006).

What Davidson discovered was that the long-term practice of meditation altered not only the function of the monks' brains but their structure as well, including the growth of new neurons and the establishment of new connections within the brain's circuitry. Davidson and his team were able to observe these changes, the impact in the prefrontal cortex brought on by visual stimulation, and circuitry changes in amplitude and frequency with the use of functional magnetic resonance imaging (fMRI), quantitative electrophysiology, and positron emission topography—basically high tech machines that can see into your mind (Davidson & Lutz, 2008).

Davidson's studies led the way for further research, such as that more recently conducted by Dr. Lisa Feldman Barrett, a psychology professor at Northwestern University. Feldman Barrett's studies challenge the notion that the brain has dedicated circuits for the fight-or-flight response. Basing her conclusions on much stronger fMRIs than what are standardly used (seven-tesla magnification as opposed to three-tesla), which can see deeper into small, localized regions of the brain—the periaqueductal gray

(PAG), in particular—her team has been able to observe the amygdala—the part of the brain often referred to as the "home of fear or emotion"—and has noted that changes in PAG activity occur even when you are placed in nonthreatening situations or are attending to mundane tasks like comparing alphabetical letters to each other on a computer screen.

Predicting Uncertainties

Feldman Barrett theorizes "that we don't go through life constantly detecting threats and reacting with flight-or-fight circuits. Rather, brains operate mainly by prediction, not reaction." What she says really happens is that, instead of your brain choosing to fight or fly, it assesses the situation, compares it to what it already knows or establishes new biases to base future assessments on, and provides you with the best actionable solution, which *could be* to fight or to fly (Feldman Barrett, 2024).

To put that in perspective, when you overthink, you put your brain in a perpetual state of heightened alertness. This rewires your connections, reroutes brain messages, and trains your brain to continually search for solutions to innumerable unknowns. Understandably, this process of constantly reducing uncertainty is mentally and physically exhausting, and it can be a very costly expenditure of your metabolism, pulling vital resources away from body systems that regulate mental and physical health and reallocating them to futile contemplation. Hence, those nasty psychosomatic symptoms pop up along with potentially dangerous diseases and disorders.

Your emotions play into this as well. Some of the things you overthink are not as frivolous as a theoretical hermit life; many are reenactments of past traumas and fears of future catastrophes. You might even start off with a pleasant mental ramble about the serenity of living alone in the wild but end up dreading that if you choose that lifestyle, you'll be the only human left on the earth after the inevitable global destruction that's already starting to occur and that began when your boyfriend left you and how you hated him after that, but once the world ends and you find yourself very literally single, you'd give anything to have even that big, stupid jerkface back... You'll feel everything from peace and joy to fear and anguish, and you'll keep your mind and body in a constantly jacked-up state.

Training Your Brain

Dr. Amishi Jha, an associate professor of psychology at the University of Miami and director of contemplative neuroscience at the school's UMindfulness initiative, brings the conclusions of Davidson's and Feldman Barrett's work together by assuring us that, because the brain is malleable, yes, it gets changed by our thoughts and feelings, but it can also be transformed for the better. She says you can take matters into your own hands to intentionally train your brain to rewire its neural pathways—you *can* stop overthinking.

Jha explains that emotions can have a detrimental effect on brain shape and function. Worries can keep you awake, fears can prevent you from taking progressive action, and the sum of all feelings can lead to debilitating disorders. However, consistent mindfulness equips you with powerful tools to identify negative thought patterns and emotional triggers—as well as inhibitors—and enables you to actively shift your focus away from them, helping you reclaim the power those problematic emotions have taken from you.

Some research suggests that mindfulness may even be able to improve age-related cognitive degeneration. Jha explains that the thicker the brain material is, the healthier it is. As you age, your brain tissue naturally thins, resulting in frequent forgetfulness and difficulty learning new skills. Jha points out that mindfulness prevents this thinning and says that long-term practitioners' brains actually look healthier and younger than those of their non-practicing peers.

In addition to retaining brain thickness, a group at Harvard found more density in the gray matter of the hippocampus (responsible for emotional control and memory storage) and less gray matter in the amygdala (responsible for fight-or-flight, stress, and fear management), resulted from the prolonged mindfulness study they conducted. The "good" section of the brain got bigger and thicker, and participants who reported feeling less stressed showed shrinkage of the amygdala! This means that mindfulness can keep your mind sharp *and* lessen the weight of your burdens. You don't have to eliminate external life stressors in order to reduce stress—although I'm sure that helps—mindfulness can do it for you by tempering the brain region that handles your reactions to them (Seaver, 2023).

What It Is

Mindfulness can lead to better cognitive control, which can help regulate all those emotions, tensions, and memories that your overthinking stirs up, and it can level out your mood too. So what is this magical method?

Mindfulness is "an intentional state of focused, nonjudgmental awareness of the present moment" (Seaver, 2023). Much like a gym session exercises your muscles, mindfulness methods effectively work out your brain, improving memory, attention, and emotional regulation. And, like regular physical exercise makes your body parts more accustomed to and more capable of performing certain actions, regular mindful workouts help your brain learn what to expect from various circumstances and be better able to handle all the uncertainties it encounters throughout each day.

Many mindfulness techniques require you to focus on the moment, notice what you experience, and redirect your focus if it strays. Jha equates that to a brain pushup. Now, I'm no gym rat, but I have seen the effects of regular physical activity on my body; regular mental motions like "brain pushups" can only yield positive results.

When you practice mindfulness on a consistent basis, your mind is literally changed. The moral of the story is this: Practice mindfulness techniques to shape your brain into a better-functioning, better-prepared, better-at-predicting outcomes, more efficiently responsive tool that can assess any situation without having to spin its wheels round and round in overthought to the point of mental and physical exhaustion.

In the next sections, we'll learn more about this impactful activity and put a mindfulness plan in action.

Common Myths and Benefits

Before I really looked into it, if someone suggested mindfulness to me, I brushed them off. I thought it was some new-agey thing, and I wasn't interested. I admit I bought into a bunch of the myths and misconceptions and cast judgment before I educated myself. What a mistake! There's nothing mystical or mysterious about it; to the contrary, it's very practical, convenient, free (for the most part), and, most importantly, effective.

Let's bust some myths and conquer your doubts about this beneficial practice:

- Myth #1: Mindfulness is no different from meditation.

    - Truth: Meditation is just one possible activity. The goal of mindfulness is not to silence the mind but to make it aware of your present experience. This can be achieved in a number of ways, like while walking, while sitting and breathing, *or* while meditating.

- Myth #2: Mindfulness is a Buddhist practice that conflicts with other religions.

  - Truth: Though taught by Buddha, no spiritual ideologies are involved in mindfulness. The goal, again, is to calm the mind, to be attentive to your circumstances with an air of care and concern.

- Myth #3: Mindfulness means clearing the mind of all thought.

  - Truth: While that can be incorporated into the practice, it is not what mindfulness aims to do. You will still have thoughts, and you will still hear mental chit-chat, but that internal talk will be sharply focused and highly concentrated in an effort to keep the mind on the topic of your present surroundings and the situation you are in at that very moment.

- Myth #4: Mindfulness means instant happiness.

  - Truth: Not necessarily. As Toni Bernhard of *Psychology Today* (2014) puts it, "The present moment is not always a pleasant moment." If your "right now" is right after you were reprimanded by your boss or had an argument with your spouse, the present moment may not be a happy one, but it can provide you the opportunity to make peace with the current state of your life, whatever that may be.

- Myth #5: Mindfulness is just taking time to relax.

  - Truth: You will likely be more relaxed after a mindfulness session, but there's more to this technique than just propping your feet up in a recliner. This myth is comparable to saying yoga's just the stretch and yawn you do when you crawl into bed. Like yoga works the body, mindfulness *works* the mind. During mindfulness practices, you actively and intentionally focus on the present moment, capture and proactively redirect wandering thoughts, and learn to recognize your thought tendencies in order to better manage them in the future.

Mindfulness benefits anyone who practices it, from daycare workers to emergency responders and from test-taking college students to new moms. In fact, recent studies have shown the benefits of mindfulness extend from pregnant moms to their babies, who "later showed less negative social-emotional behavior than the babies of less mindful women" (Hendriksen, 2018). What benefits can you expect to receive from this practice? Let's find out below:

- **Less stress and anxiety:** Chronic stress-induced anxiety is a growing concern, but researchers have confirmed that mindfulness reduces this angst without the worries of pharmaceutical side effects, is cost-effective (usually no costs at all), time-effective (takes little time and can be done whenever you want, no appointments necessary), and has little stigma surrounding it (unlike seeing a therapist or taking medication).

- **Fewer depressive symptoms:** Not only does mindfulness reduce depression, but it also helps prevent future episodes from occurring. Mindfulness-based cognitive therapy (MBCT), a combination of cognitive behavioral therapy (CBT) and mindfulness-based stress reduction (MBSR), is an eight-week program that particularly effective in this area—as effective as antidepressant medications (Kuyken et al., 2015).

- **Improved overall well-being:** Consistent mindfulness practice has been shown to improve the effects of type 2 diabetes, rheumatoid arthritis, lower back pain, psoriasis, and fibromyalgia (Cash et al., 2015). It also helps you deal with illness and move on post-recovery. It can be a catalyst to motivate you to get regular checkups, pursue physical activity, and improve health habits.

- **Better emotional regulation:** Because mindfulness helps you identify your feelings, it also helps you be more aware of the feelings you experience at any given moment, thereby enabling you to rein them in and manage them effectively.

- **Stronger memory:** Mindfulness may improve your memory. As we discussed earlier in this chapter, it physiologically thickens the gray matter in your brain's hippocampus, which is the region responsible for memory storage. And as we learned, the thicker the brain, the healthier it is! So the next time someone calls you thick-headed, take it as a compliment.

- **Improved relationships:** Mindfulness is a practice of acceptance without casting judgment. As you learn to acknowledge and accept aspects of your own self, you also tend to apply this to other relationships and become more welcoming of others' flaws.

- **Sharper cognition:** Mindfulness requires the active participation of several cognitive abilities, including focused attention, redirecting thoughts, and dismissing interfering thoughts. As Dr. Jha noted in her research, practicing these things regularly actually trains your brain to do them better, and as Dr. Davidson proved, such persistent practice shapes and reshapes your brain to improve its functionality.

- **Less overthinking:** When you practice mindfulness—when you do Dr. Jha's brain pushups—you focus, notice, redirect. This trains your brain to pay attention to the thoughts cycling through it, alert you to ones that are unhealthy or unhelpful, and cut those destructive thoughts off and throw them in the trash before they get the chance to spin in circles.

Before we dive headfirst into mindfulness mind workouts, let's clear up some confusion about mindfulness and meditation.

How Mindfulness and Meditation Differ

Mindfulness and meditation are both effective means to calm your mind, settle your emotions, and improve mental focus, but they can be used together; these are two distinct concepts.

Let's start with basic definitions:

- **Mindfulness:** We've already mentioned that mindfulness involves intentional focus on the present moment. One of its most well-known proponents, Jon Kabat-Zinn (2023), defines it as "the awareness that arises through paying attention, on purpose, in the present moment, non-judgmentally." The key term here is "present moment."

- **Meditation:** This is a practice in which you focus your mind on a specific thought, or perhaps an activity or event, "to train attention and awareness, and achieve a mentally clear and emotionally calm and stable state" (Shapero et al., 2018).

The main difference between mindfulness and meditation is that, while mindfulness arrives at a calm state, that's not its primary intent; that is, however, the end goal of meditation.

A few other variances are also worth noting:

- Mindfulness does not necessarily include meditation. There are many other means of achieving mental awareness in the present moment.

- Meditation often incorporates repeated mantras that are not essential to mindfulness methods.

- Mindfulness can be practiced regardless of religious orientation and is not specifically a spiritual activity.

- Meditation, most closely associated with Buddhism, can be utilized in other belief systems by centering your focus on your spiritual devotion.

- Mindfulness can be done in a variety of ways, many of which are loosely structured and can be practiced in almost any setting.

- Meditation usually takes place in a structured setting with less flexibility than mindfulness sessions.

- Mindfulness helps you arrive at a state of mindful awareness.

- Meditation aims for a state of steadied peace.

Mindfulness and meditation can be practiced independently of each other. However, both benefit your mental and physical health and improve your overall well-being.

How to Start and Sustain Your Mindfulness Practice

Ed Halliwell, a leading mindfulness instructor in the UK, softens the straightforward definitions of mindfulness we've discussed so far. He describes the practice as a way to tune in to what we experience in mind and body "with a warm-hearted curiosity and learning and acting on what we discover—with the intention to live life as fully, wisely, and compassionately as possible" (Pattemore, 2022).

I like that! It kind of gives me the warm fuzzies. That reminds me of my psychology teacher from high school, Mr. Nelson. He was a hoot! And he could read his students as if he'd written our stories himself. When we studied the work of psychotherapist Claude Steiner and learned about stroking egos, giving people the cold pricklies, and receiving warm fuzzies, Mr. Nelson wore a special tie for each lesson. The strokes tie was light brown and had a picture of a dog being petted; the cold, prickly one had all these blue, gray, and white spiky, ice balls all over it set on a silvery background; and the warm fuzzies—my favorite—had a peachy background that was covered in smiling, furry little critters in browns and oranges that looked like they could jump right off the tie and snuggle with you. I always hoped Mr. Nelson was wearing that tie when I passed his classroom on the way to dreaded chemistry because it always perked me up and chased away the cold pricklies that awaited me in *that other class*.

Warm fuzzies are sentiments, actions, and behaviors that bring you peace and joy. They help you forget about those nasty old cold pricklies that make your heart race, fill you with fear, and chill you to the bone. For some reason, it seems the cold pricklies are the ones that capture our attention when we overthink. The good news, though, is that mindfulness can help you restore that tranquility once again.

Jon Kabat-Zinn, PhD, is the founder of the Center for Mindfulness and its Stress Reduction Clinic at the University of Massachusetts Medical School. He is known as one of the most influential teachers in the mindfulness movement, and his nine pillars or nine attitudes of mindfulness set the standard for all forms of this practice (Kane, 2024):

- **Be nonjudgemental:** Observe what's in your mind and what's happening around you without deeming any portion good or bad. Whatever you notice simply is as it is.

- **Have a beginner's mindset:** Look at the world with the eyes of a child and the fascination of seeing it for the first time. Find amazing in the ordinary.

- **Let go:** We tend to want to hold on to warm fuzzies and dump the cold pricklies. That's only natural; however, once the good and the bad have been acknowledged, they both need to be released and just observed for their having been.

- **Accept things as they are:** If you desire to change something, you must first accept it for what it is. Only then will you be able to move beyond it.

- **Be patient:** Things rarely happen according to your desired timeframe. Change, growth, and healing all take time, and you need to allow those moments to pass—or arrive—when they will.

- **Be non-striving:** Forcing things won't make them happen any faster. Hold your intention— your goals, your mindfulness, your meditation—without trying to take matters into your own hands.

- **Trust:** Have trust in yourself and in your intuition. Maintain boundaries but honor your feelings and rely on your instincts.

- **Be generous:** Give freely of yourself and devote time and energy to the welfare of others.

- **Have gratitude:** The old saying to "have an attitude of gratitude" may seem cliche, but it is sage advice that withstands the test of time. Grateful people tend to have less stress, lower anxiety, fewer bouts with depression, and general satisfaction with life. It's great to celebrate the big things in life, but don't overlook the little things, as they can add up to great joy.

Embrace one of the above attitudes and start your mindfulness practice. The list is in no particular order, and it doesn't matter which pillar you choose because they are all interconnected. Choose one you'd like to work on, and it will have residual benefits on the rest.

Mindful meditation, journaling, and yoga are some simple activities to get you started. Here's a good overview of these three options:

- **Mindful meditation:** Meditation involves focused reflection or contemplation about a particular subject, thought, or emotion. When partnered with mindfulness, it utilizes breathing techniques, stillness, and sensory awareness to become more in tune with your body, mind, and soul. Mindful meditation is known to enhance sleep, increase attention span, reduce cognitive decline, lower anxiety, lessen depression, manage weight, and improve chronic conditions.

- **Journaling:** Writing down thoughts in a journal is a good way to process experiences. By writing them out, you mentally work through them. It can help you release things you've been holding onto, and it can also help you track your triggers.

- **Yoga:** Many people choose yoga for its low-to-no costs, relative simplicity, adaptability, and convenience. There are many variations to accommodate different body types and agility factors. One method you can even do while sitting on a chair! Yoga is known to relieve anxiety—and the nervous system in general—tame the fight-or-flight response, strengthen the respiratory system, and promote relaxation.

When you commit to mindfulness practice, don't feel like you should master it right away. It's called a "practice" for a reason. Allow yourself time to get used to the exercises, and soon enough, they'll feel natural.

Practices to Try

If you are new to mindfulness practices, you might feel a little awkward focusing so much attention inward and upon yourself, but it's okay. Be gentle with yourself. Be kind and patient with your progress. Acknowledge what you feel. That's part of the process!

First, commit a specific block of time to mindfulness each day. Maybe begin with small sessions that last only 10-15 minutes and gradually increase to about 30 minutes a day over a 2-week period. Don't pressure yourself; that would be counterintuitive.

Below are several beginner-level exercises for you to try. Give each one a whirl to see which seems right for you:

- **Body scan:**

  - Lie down on your back in a quiet space where you won't be disturbed.

  - Starting at your crown and slowly working your way all the way to the tips of your toes, notice the sensations your body experiences. Stay on each area for one full minute before moving on to the next.

- **Mindful walking:**

  - Put on your comfiest cross-trainers and head outside.

  - You don't have to walk fast but move at a steady pace, taking in everything your five senses pick up. What do you smell, see, hear? And how does this physical motion make you feel?

- **Mindful meditation:**

  - Sit in a chair or on a cushion with a good but relaxed posture in a quiet place where you won't be disturbed.

  - As you breathe, notice each inhale and exhale, feel your lungs expand and empty, and hear the sound of air moving through your nose or mouth.

  - Soften your visual focus. Let your eyes lower, but don't close them. Simply allow whatever is before them to exist.

  - Notice your arms. Let your arms hang loosely by your sides, or place your palms on your thighs.

  - Notice your legs. If you're on a chair, place your soles flat on the floor; if you're on a cushion, fold your legs comfortably in front of you.

  - If your mind wanders, don't make a sudden attempt to stop it, but gently rein it in and direct it back to what you're feeling in the moment.

  - When you're ready, end the session by lifting your gaze and slowly taking note of the sights and sounds around you. Notice what thoughts you are experiencing and what your body is feeling.

- **Alternate nostril breathing:**

  o Sit comfortably with your legs crossed on a cushion on the floor.

  o Take your right thumb and press it against your right nostril. Then, inhale deeply and slowly.

  o Release your thumb and press your left ring finger against the left nostril. Exhale slowly and deeply, taking longer to exhale than to inhale.

  o Keeping the ring finger on the left nostril, inhale slowly and deeply.

  o Release the ring finger and place the thumb back on the right nostril. Exhale slowly and deeply, again taking longer to exhale than to inhale.

  o Repeat several times until you feel calm, less stressed, and more present.

- When you're done, press your right hand against your right knee and then your left hand against your left knee.

- **Engage the five senses for five minutes:**

  - Sit in a comfortable place, like on your front porch or in a neighborhood park.

  - Set your handy timer for five minutes.

  - Look, listen, smell, touch, and taste all the things that are around you. Attune to the present moment.

- **Mindfulness-based stress reduction (MBSR):**

  - This practice combines mindfulness meditation and yoga and varies by the individual participating in the activity. It follows no set steps and is not scripted but is performed in a manner that best suits you. It focuses on

    - commitment to the requisite lifestyle change that is necessary for dedicated mindfulness practice.

    - emphasizing individual effort, motivation, and regular

meditation practice even when you don't feel like doing it.

■ perceiving the experience as a challenge and not a chore so that it is done in a spirit of adventure in living, not as work (Ackerman, 2024b).

Positive Psychology published the following mindfulness schedule as suggested by Dr. Amit Sood, chair of the Mayo Mind Body Initiative (Ackerman, 2024a):

- **Monday:** Pay attention throughout your day to things you are grateful for and express that **gratitude** in your journal or meditative contemplation.

- **Tuesday:** Notice those around you who may be hurting in some way and show them **compassion** as you encounter them.

- **Wednesday:** Accept yourself for who you are and extend that **acceptance** to others without trying to change them.

- **Thursday:** Consider your life's **purpose** and generate awareness of where or in what you find **meaning**.

- **Friday: Forgive** yourself for anything you've been begrudging yourself for, including perceived failures and what you think are illegitimate fears, then extend that forgiveness to others for any wrongs they have committed against you.

- **Saturday: Celebrate** all the joy in your life—however big or small—and celebrate the lives of others too.

- **Sunday:** Through awareness, meditation, or prayer, spend time in **reflection**, looking back over the past week, month, or year, or perhaps on some other specific period of time.

A recent study found mindfulness practices—MBSR in particular—to be just as effective for treating anxiety disorders as the popular pharmaceutical antidepressant drug escitalopram (Hoge et al., 2022). If your habitual overthinking has pushed your anxiety, stress, and patience to your limits, put some mindfulness practices to the test and provide your mind and your body with a natural way to restore and improve your overall well-being.

Chapter 4:

Rewriting Your Mental

Scripts

Overthinking is not a disorder, disease, syndrome, sickness, short circuit, neurosis, psychosis, or figment of your imagination. It is all in your mind, though. Well, sort of. Your thoughts are definitely internal, and they tend to stay that way unless you choose to audibly express them. But that doesn't mean overthinking is an imaginary problem. It is, however, a habit. Believe it or not, you are able to control it, just like any other habit you want to make—or break.

Establishing something as a routine requires continuous work and practice. Putting an end to one also takes intentional, persistent effort.

One way to challenge overthinking is to develop a conscious awareness of your thoughts. When a thought comes to mind, and your mental gears start spinning, stop to consider if that thought is productive. Will following that train take you to a destination or merely send you in circles? If it's intrusive, consider what evidence you have to back it up. Is it valid and worth your time to ponder it, or is it a falsehood and distraction? Training your mind to question these thoughts interrupts the cycle and shifts your focus. Over time, you can replace the habit of rumination with more constructive thinking patterns.

In this interactive chapter, we will explore different tools and techniques you can use to find your calm, become fully immersed in the present moment, and regulate your nervous system.

What Is Your Inner Dialogue Default?

Until just a few years ago, I thought everybody heard voices in their head or at least *a* voice—their own. I've always been able to hear my thoughts. I *thought* that's what *thoughts* were. As I type this, I hear myself reading it inside my head. My lips aren't moving, and no one can hear me. I'm *thinking*. But not everyone has this ability!

According to Dr. Kyle Killian (2023) of *Psychology Today*, only about 30–50% of people can hear their thoughts. That means the majority of people either don't have this internal dialogue at all or only encounter it on rare occasions. My mind was completely blown when I first learned of it. *How do other people think?* I wondered as I began to wander down rabbit holes. I could not imagine a silent mind. *That must be blissful! They don't rehash awkward conversations, awaken themselves at 3:30 a.m. with what they* should have said *to someone the day before, or get stuck on a song. Luckies! But, again, how do they think?*

Killian explains that many rely on visual imagery and memories of events to fill that quiet void, and others may think out loud, either speaking audibly or moving their lips silently. In his more than 40 years of study, Dr. Russell Hurlburt, a professor of psychology at the University of Nevada, Las Vegas, "concludes that inner speech is just one common form of thought, along with inner seeing, feeling, sensory awareness and unsymbolized thinking— in which a concept isn't necessarily attached to words or other symbols." He suggests that most people utilize a combination of thought forms when internally contemplating something (Williams, 2022). Everyone processes information, works out problems, and makes plans all in their minds too; it's just not necessarily done with internal words. That got me wondering further: *Does everyone have an inner voice?*

Your inner voice—not to be confused with inner dialogue—is essentially what you think of yourself. Imagine if you could step outside of your physical being for a moment and observe "you." The judgments you would make on those observations are your inner voice. It's supposedly an objective perspective, but it's rarely an accurate one.

Your inner voice—also referred to as your inner critic—can be nice. It can act like a loving friend, reassure you of all your positive attributes, and tell you how pretty you are. Or it can be mean. It can beat you down like a bully with insults, tell you how stupid you are, and convince you that you're doomed to failure. Dr. Małgorzata Puchalska-Wasyl of John Paul II

Catholic University of Lublin, Poland, categorizes the inner voice into four characteristics (Williams, 2022):

- **Faithful friend:** This voice is thought to be the most common. Caring and kind, it encourages you with positivity and gives you virtual pats on the back.

- **Proud rival:** This one is a competitive spirit that high-fives you but coaches you to do better.

- **Ambivalent parent:** This one's tough because it packs a punch of criticism into each offer of love and support.

- **Helpless child:** This is the most negative, often leaving you feeling powerless and desperately seeking support and encouragement.

Experiments performed by Hurlburt and Dr. Charles Fernyhough, a professor of psychology at Durham University in the UK, utilized fMRIs to compare deliberate inner speech—thoughts you are aware of "saying," like adding and subtracting numbers while trying to balance your bank account—to spontaneous inner speech—unintentional internal messages, like, "You're not good enough to get that job promotion," that your inner critic may hurl at you. They found that deliberate thoughts originated in the brain's left hemisphere, which is where speech production takes place, and spontaneous thoughts occurred in regions of auditory perception. In other words, when we "hear voices," we are listening rather than talking (Hurlburt et al., 2016).

This is why, when the negatives "speak" louder than the positives—in whatever form you "hear" them—it weighs you down with undue stress. So your inner critic may say things, but your inner self is taking it in and believing it like a child soaks up whatever their parents say to them (good or bad). It actually increases rumination because you constantly question those assessments and worry that they're true, and it can lead you into a downward spiral of belief that you have no worth.

Yes, even people who don't hear their thoughts can still be prone to both a negative inner voice and overthinking. They may replay scenes in their minds or picture events happening as if watching a film on a movie screen. Anyone can be plagued by the *habit* of thinking, rethinking, ruminating, wondering, and mentally wandering after a topic and its tangents to the point of mental and physical exhaustion.

How do you gain control over your inner voice and rewrite the script of that internal dialogue or mental screenplay? Puchalska-Wasyl advises that you pay attention to those thoughts, identify the dominant voice, and observe how its messages make you feel. She suggests that knowing which voice is guiding you can help you understand how to reframe your thoughts.

Results of the Hurlburt-Fernyhough study support Pchalska-Wasyl's idea, as they indicate that "turning spontaneous thoughts into a deliberate, more positive

[one] may help turn an inner critic into an inner coach, by transforming passive opinions into more active advice" (Williams, 2022). That's a complicated way of saying it will help you turn that frown upside down!

"That sounds great," you say, "but how do I actually *do* that?" I'm glad you asked!

1. **Listen intently:** Whenever you catch an unintentional thought popping up, stop what you're doing and tune in. If necessary, excuse yourself from a meeting, politely remove yourself from a conversation, or tell your spouse you have to go to the restroom. Go somewhere quiet with no interruptions, and pay attention to what you hear. You may need to practice actively listening to other people before you master this technique with your inner dialogue.

2. **Be curious:** Don't just hear with your internal ears; follow the trail to see where it takes you. When you reach a destination, stop and analyze what you've observed and resist the urge to overthink. Question its relevance. Determine if it was truthful. Was it just an illusion? What feelings did you experience?

3. **Write it down:** Journal the internal discourse you experience. Record the thoughts, the times and dates when they occurred, and what was happening in your life at the time. Then, write

down the answers to the questions posed in the previous step.

4. **Take a step back:** Take a breather. Practice mindfulness. Do some yoga. Take a walk. Clear your mind.

5. **Review the discussions:** Open that journal and read what you've been experiencing. Create a chart that lists positive chatter on one side of the page and negative speech on the other. For each positive, add another encouraging thought. For each negative, write down a counter-truth.

6. **Refute with truth:** Next time you hear positive inner dialogue, embrace it, but the moment something derogatory enters the conversation, stop it in its tracks. Pick up that chart you created in the previous step, and replace the lies or the hurtful statements you just heard with the ones you wrote down to counter them.

7. **Refuse to be a victim:** Resolve not to allow your inner voice to rule your life. Your mental and physical health—and your relationships, by extension—depend on it. It may sound strange, but you need to establish boundaries with your self-talk and take ownership of your thoughts, words, and actions.

Journal It

Cathy Hutchison of Your Visual Journal (2023) says journaling should be purposeful, and the way you go about it should be determined by what you want to get out of it. For self-improvement, you may ask yourself questions, set goals, and record what you learn. Therapeutic journaling should include freewriting, exploring feelings, and contemplating the reasons for feeling those emotions.

Journaling is great for those overthinking moments when you rehash a conversation or project how scenes would have gone if you'd said *this* instead of *that*. Just write it down like an actual script, recording the banter between you and your "characters." Hutchison says journaling is also an effective way to rewrite your internal dialogue. In this case, the part of you is your listening ear, and the other "character" is your inner voice. Jot down what you hear and what you say back. With practice, the conversations will become more fluid and congenial.

Cognitive Restructuring

This therapeutic technique helps you recognize negative thinking patterns that interfere with daily life, disrupting relationships and discounting achievements. These thoughts can often lead you into overthinking cycles, but cognitive restructuring (CR) puts a halt to that by deconstructing those harmful thoughts so you can reorganize them in a more accurate way.

CR is a key technique in cognitive behavioral therapy (CBT), which has proven to be a successful treatment for anxiety, depression, and personality disorders, among other conditions. Often, people who participate in such programs experience cognitive distortions, which are skewed ways of viewing the world, such as catastrophizing, black-and-white thinking, and overgeneralization. CR helps you transform such maladaptive thoughts into helpful ones by changing the way you view circumstances, enabling you to change how you feel toward those events. CR requires you to monitor your inner self, question your assumptions, and gather evidence to support or dispute those thoughts. Once you assess these aspects, you can generate alternative viewpoints that will provide a more positive outlook and a less critical inner critic.

Avoid Self-Sabotage

Self-sabotage is a nasty way to treat yourself. It often occurs when you're looking forward to doing something, but you have big doubts, shaky nerves, or a vicious inner voice telling you you've made a bad decision. What happens is you get ready, and you take the classes, buy the equipment, or learn to dance—whatever this new opportunity requires—and then you don't do the homework, get the wrong tools, or spin yourself into a tizzy on the dance floor till you're too dizzy to twist the night away at the People Without Partners community center old-fashioned sock hop.

Or worse. You've got 10 minutes to perfect your presentation before you present it to the board, but instead of sharpening your speech, you offer that valuable time to the overthinking gods and spend those final 10 minutes catastrophizing. It probably started when your proud rival inner voice said, *You can do this! Someone else could do it better, though.* The more it rambled about what could be better, the stronger points you should have included, and the great reception it could have if you had only researched the information more thoroughly, the deeper into fear and panic you fall as you become certain you're doomed to fail. *I mean, yours is fine, but if you'd put this line in there instead of that one, the chief shareholder would probably jump for joy instead of fall asleep leaning on his hand.* Then, just like that, you're called to the meeting. Because you *didn't* prep for the previous 10 minutes, and you *did* overthink, you sabotaged your potential and flopped the performance.

Speaker and author Alyce Cornyn-Selby (n.d.) defines self-sabotage concisely: "Self-sabotage is when we say we want something and then go about making sure it doesn't happen." And the funny thing is, you usually try to blame someone or something else for the occurrence. In the board meeting example, you might think the members were just a bunch of closed-minded jerks, or perhaps your assistant didn't edit the PowerPoint well enough, or the boss didn't give you enough time to prepare. While outside factors may have played some role, it comes down to what you did yourself to lock in your missteps, and you need to own that responsibility.

There are a number of reasons for self-sabotage:

- You have self-imposed limits on how much success and love you allow yourself to have, so you set yourself up to fail when you reach that limit.

- You're humble and don't want to take all the glory for yourself, so you fail in order to allow someone else to have success. Ironically, this works out to be more prideful than generous: You think so highly of yourself that you *know* you'd do a knock-their-socks-off job, so you offer it to someone else who "needs a chance."

- You have low self-esteem and don't believe you deserve success or good things.

- You fear the changes success brings, even though they're good things that you actually want.

When you face decisions, you have a very brief amount of time to choose between self-advancement or self-sabotage. Since it's common to run on autopilot, you may not even realize the choice you've made until you're in the middle of the mental action. To give your brain a fighting chance at choosing the right path here (which would be the one leading away from destruction), take some time to challenge your beliefs.

Look at that list above. Can you relate to any of those descriptions? Can you add to the list? These views could be what's holding you back and what's keeping you from achieving the success you not only seek but also deserve.

Visualization Is a Powerful Healing Tool

Walt Disney (n.d.) was right when he observed that "imagination has no age," and his contemporary, Albert Einstein (n.d.), understood that "imagination can take you anywhere." Visualization is a mental exercise in which you *imagine* some future happening the way you want it to as if it were happening right now, today. To participate in this practice, you can be a child or a child at heart! We talked earlier about your inner voice; consider this your inner eye. Look at your situation through the lens of your deepest desires, and *see* those dreams fulfilled.

Visualization involves each of the five senses to direct your subconscious toward the desired result. When used consistently, this practice can train your brain to view that end goal as having already been achieved. You do this in two parts: envisioning the desired outcome and envisioning the steps you must take to get there. The theory is that what you focus your attention on and proactively work toward is more likely to become your reality (Moe, 2021). It can work positively—say, to acquire a job promotion—or negatively—as with the board meeting presentation example in the previous section.

Cognitive behavioral theory, the foundational basis for cognitive behavioral therapy, postulates that thinking influences behavior and vice versa. It actually incorporates feelings into a middle position between the two. While feelings do not get changed directly, they are affected by how the thoughts and behaviors impact each other. Visualization is a source of manipulation to bring the three aspects into a balanced and desirable alignment that will help you reach your goals, attain what you desire, and improve your mental well-being.

Below are the basic steps to practice visualization:

- Engage all five senses and write down in full detail what it is that you want. Some people like to create a vision board and either draw or paste images that represent those desires. Set this board in a prominent place where you will see it frequently throughout each day. Also, write your goals on index cards and read them when you wake up each morning and before you go to sleep each night.

- Think about how you would feel when that vision becomes reality. Referring back to cognitive behavioral theory, involving your feelings will manipulate your thoughts and behaviors into cooperation and make you more likely to act.

- Learn all you can about your goal and the steps required to get there. You may need to take a class or do some research to enable you to physically work toward the desired result.

- Understand that there may be setbacks. Don't be defeated by them, but learn from them and grow.

- Set aside at least 10 minutes twice a day to practice visualization. Just close your eyes and imagine what you desire as if it were the present reality. See it, hear it, smell it, taste it, and touch it in your mind and fully engage your subconscious.

Another visualization technique is color breathing, in which you assign a color to a positive emotion and while performing deep breathing exercises, envision that color washing over you and filling your body, washing away all negativity. Guided imagery is also helpful. For this exercise, you sit somewhere comfortable and quiet, close your eyes, and, while performing deep breathing exercises, imagine yourself in a place where you are calm and at peace. Engage your senses; feel a soft breeze or smell fresh meadow air. Imagine peace as you inhale and expel tension with each exhale.

Visualization is a simple but powerful method you can use to boost mood, improve decision-making abilities, progress toward your goals, and break the overthinking habit.

Make a Habit of Gratitude

Visualization helps you embrace future achievements as if they were today's reality, and mindfulness keeps you centered in the present moment. Maintaining a "now" mindset enables you to acknowledge and appreciate what you have and reduces the frustration caused by contemplating what you lack. It replaces envy and greed with humility and generosity and opens your heart to gratitude.

Maintaining a consistently grateful mentality and regularly expressing gratitude bring peace of mind, relieve anxiety, reduce depression, increase optimism, improve relationships, and elevate overall well-being. To make gratitude your habit—and possibly replace that nasty habit of overthinking—anchor yourself in the present moment, look for good in the little things, work through each of your senses and notice something to be grateful for, and breathe deeply and clearly as you bring joy in and send dissatisfaction out.

Keep a running log of the positive things you observe each day. Place the list beside your bed and read through it morning and night. Express gratitude to your loved ones and to others you encounter. Keep it at the top of your to-do list, and make sure you check that box every day.

Chapter 5:

Embracing the Present and Letting Go

A lot of overthinking is done over the difficult experiences you've gone through in your past. Whether they are the result of ancient or recent history, emotional scars reopen easily, and when you dwell on them, they remain raw and exposed. Every time you cycle back through an emotional injury, you hurt yourself. Even if the person who inflicted the harm is no longer in your life, when you ruminate about the situation, you allow the offender to keep causing you pain.

Putting the past in its place is a choice—so is holding on to it. It's time for you to choose to move forward, acknowledge what has happened, but ultimately let it go. It's the only way to truly heal.

Putting the Past in the Past

Everything that has happened in your past has contributed to the person you are today. Both the good and the bad have shaped you and influenced your cognitive, social, and emotional development. How you handle what you've gone through determines whether you stagnate or grow. The best way forward is by learning from your experiences without getting stuck on them and without reliving them in your head.

Think of the process as keeping your mental car in drive but periodically glancing in the rearview mirror. You want to be aware of the dangers that lurk back there, but you want to stay ahead of them and not let them overtake you again. Keep moving forward; don't get stuck in the historic muck, or you'll become immobilized. Your wheels will spin, but you'll get nowhere.

It's challenging, and it may take a heavy emotional toll, but letting go of past pains releases burdens you don't need to carry anymore and leaves you with a sense of freedom and a newfound hope.

Here's what you need to do:

- If you haven't already done so, distance yourself physically and emotionally from the person who inflicted the harm.

- Give yourself permission to address those old wounds. Allow yourself to face them, but limit yourself to the amount of time you spend there. You want to recognize what they are without reliving the moment.

- Permit yourself to feel. This exercise will likely stir up emotions you've shoved aside. You might become upset, but it's okay. Let them flow out of you so you can stop holding them inside.

- Be kind to yourself. Do not beat yourself up or get angry with yourself for not having gone through this process before. Don't think you *shouldn't* still feel the things you do or that you *should've* done [fill-in-the-blank].

- Allow yourself to forgive the offender. Forgiveness does not mean forgetting what happened. It simply means drawing the situation to a close and freeing *yourself* from continued pain.

- Accept that you may never receive an apology from the other person. Your healing does not depend on their actions. What matters is that you put the event in the past and move forward.

- Bring yourself back to the present. What happened is over and done. It is no longer going on right now.

- Be grateful for the experience. This is a hard one, but like I said before, going through this helped shape your "you-ness." Growth is always a good thing, even if it took great difficulty to get there.

- Surround yourself with a solid support system who will encourage you, prop you back up if you stumble, and keep you moving forward.

- Seek professional counseling if necessary. There is no shame in needing help! Some past experiences may be too traumatic to fully process on your own. Therapists are trained for this. Let them give you the boost you need.

Know that healing takes time. Be patient as you work your way through each step. Celebrate the small victories as you achieve them and find joy and hope in every tomorrow.

Strategies to Improve Present-Moment Awareness

As we discussed in Chapter 3, the brain physiologically changes when you practice mindfulness. It grows new neurons whenever you learn new skills, drop old habits, or develop new ones, and heal from the emotional injuries of your past. Every challenge, every lesson, every experience rearranges the brain's synaptic connections. When you say you feel "wired" after something exciting happens, you mean it literally!

Because of this neuroplasticity, you can train your brain to respond differently to various stimuli, including the habit of revisiting old, hurtful memories. Instead of feeling overwhelmed, distraught, angry, or confused when something triggers these reminders, you can teach your brain to become relaxed, calm, clear, and relieved. It just requires some enhancements to your mindfulness practices, like those listed below:

- **Body focus:**

    o Lie down in a quiet place where you are comfortable and won't be disturbed.

    o Pay attention to how the bed, sofa, or floor feels and the way it supports your back, head, and legs. Notice the touch of the fabric on your fingers. Is it soft, rough, or smooth?

    o Now, take one slow, deep breath in and out.

    o Focus on the top of your head and work your way to the tips of your toes. This differs from a body scan in that you're working and releasing muscle groups rather than noting sensations.

    o Intentionally contract the muscles of your scalp. Hold the tension for a few moments and then release it. Work the areas around your ears and along the back of your neck as well.

- ○ Move to the face. Tense and relax each group: forehead, eyebrows, eyes, cheeks, mouth, lips, jaw, and front of the neck.

- ○ As you work your way down, feel the tingling sensations and be reminded of the work every part of your body does throughout the day. Try to leave each muscle group relaxed. Return to the ones that are resistant.

- **Listen to autonomous sensory meridian response (ASMR):** ASMR videos have become quite popular on social media, and they're easy to search for on YouTube. Their purpose is to encourage pleasure and calm by inciting a tingling sensation in the head, spine, and limbs brought on by distinct sounds. It's often mundane tones that we usually tune out that bring us to this state of relaxation, but the audio is hyperfocused on them, excluding background noise. For example, a video creator may simply open the plastic wrapper on a piece of candy and crinkle it between their fingers or phonetically zoom in on the buzz of an electric razor trimming a man's hair.

- **Feel the beat of your heart:** Sit somewhere quiet. Take a slow, deep inhale and exhale, and then locate your pulse. Use the index and middle finger of one hand and feel the inner wrist of the opposite arm, or place them on the carotid artery in your neck just under your jaw. Tune out the noise around you and focus on your heartbeat. It may seem to grow louder as you listen more intently. Continue to take slow, deep breaths in and out, and listen to your body's rhythm for as long as you like.

- **Write down what you've done:** At the end of the day, make a list of your accomplishments. They don't have to be big ones. In fact, the smaller they are, the better because it will help you see that you have been productive with your time, and there are lots of positives to be grateful for. Some days, just getting out of bed on time can be the biggest feat of the day! Congratulating yourself on getting things done can relieve a lot of anxiety and help you be mindful of how you spend your time.

These practices can remind you of the mind-body connection and promote a more grounded, conscious way of living that improves the well-being of both the mental-emotional and the physical states of your being.

Learning to Embrace Uncertainty

Fear of the unknown is a great paralyzer. And let's face it, everything beyond this very moment is unknown. You can plan all you want, and you can prepare for every thinkable outcome, but you can never know for sure what will happen next. Depending on your current situation, that can be terrifying. Actually, even if you're in a relatively stress-free time of life, you may still be nervous about tomorrow.

It's not healthy to constantly fret over what is to come, but that's precisely what many overthinkers do. *Think* about it: If you rehash an awkward conversation, you plot what you'll say *next time*. If you're up in the air about a vacation destination, you're contemplating where you *will go*. If you worry about encountering a grizzly if you *become* a hermit, you're anticipating a future event too.

A great way to overcome this tendency is to embrace uncertainty. Here's how to find the positives in any situation and discover the silver linings that are hidden in life's experiences:

- **See the glass half-*full*:** Be optimistic. Be hopeful. See the positive potential in your circumstances. Laugh off embarrassing moments and mistakes. Celebrate your successes instead of pouting bout perceived failures.

- **Demonstrate compassion and kindness:** Open yourself up to helping others. Don't focus on your own discomfort; concentrate on lifting someone else up.

- **Adjust your faulty beliefs:** Maybe you've convinced yourself that you'll fail at every new thing, so you're better off not even trying that *uncertain* new thing. Assess your current mindset and restore truth to your convictions.

- **Remind yourself of past success:** You really haven't failed at everything, have you? And I bet you have loads of talents and abilities to tackle innumerable obstacles. Look back on the things you've done well to reassure yourself of what you can do with whatever comes your way next.

- **Be curious and courageous:** Be excited about the unknown. There's lots to learn there. You might even find things you like if you are brave enough to step forward.

- **Challenge your competitive side:** See uncertainty as an opportunity to show off your strengths and build new skills.

- **Remove "what if" from your vocabulary:** "What if" will do you in. It's the ultimate dream destroyer because it works hand in hand with catastrophizing. *Hey, I have a great idea! But what if [fill-in-the-blank-disaster] happens?* And there go all your hopes down the drain.

- **Do what makes you happy:** Fill your life with joy! Go to the spa, get coffee with a friend, or read your favorite book three times in a row! Overwhelm yourself with positivity, and there will be no room for fear or doubt.

Uncertainty is inevitable, but it doesn't have to be defeating.

Learning to Set Realistic Goals and Priorities

Do you make New Year's resolutions? *I'm going to exercise every day this year! I'm going to lose 20 pounds by June. I'm going to be more organized, go out with my friends more often, write the great American novel...* How many of those have you followed through with? If you're like 80% of people, you give up by Valentine's Day (Emde, 2023). So many people fail because they either set unachievable goals or don't properly plan them out.

You've had a lot of birthdays, right? What do you do when you blow out the candles on your cake? Make a wish. Wishes require no effort. Wishes are just magical happenstance and hopes granted by genies and fairies.

Unfortunately, many people approach goal-setting like those birthday wishes: They state the thing they want the most and wait for it to happen.

If only! Sure, goals are things you really want and maybe things you need. Oftentimes, they're events or actions you want to participate in or would like to see happen in your life. Unless you're just mean-spirited, I think it's safe to say that you set goals with positive intentions, like earning a job promotion or purchasing a new home and achieving or acquiring something for your betterment—or putting an end to your overthinking habit.

It's going to take work to get there.

When you set goals, they need to be balanced. The achievement of any one goal should not be to the detriment of another aspect of your life. For example, career advancement should not sacrifice family engagement. On the contrary, they should complement each other; spiritual pursuits should enhance personal growth.

When you write down your goals,

- be realistic; choose things you are actually capable of doing.

- assess your needs; decide how this goal benefits your life and your family.

- understand your purpose; consider why this is important to you.

- get a clear vision of what you want to accomplish; imagine attaining the desired end result.

Once you have your list ready, write down the action steps necessary to achieve those aspirations. Set due dates for completing each step, and check them off along the way. As you progress, periodically reassess your goals. Make sure they still align with your vision and the action steps still apply. Reset dates if necessary, but don't give up.

With persistence and dedication, you can let go of the past, embrace your future, and move forward into a healthier, happier you.

Chapter 6:

Strategies for Long-Term

Success

They say the definition of insanity is doing the same thing over and over again but expecting a different outcome. Overthinking does involve repetitive thought, and it can drive you crazy, but it is not a mental health condition. Yes, you are sane, but no, you are not achieving different outcomes—you're reaching the same non-actionable conclusion every time.

As Albert Einstein (n.d.) keenly understood, "We can't solve problems by using the same kind of thinking we used when we created them." So, constantly thinking about something can't solve the problem of *constantly thinking about something*.

In this chapter, we're going to focus on self-observation: the skill of reflecting on your choices, attitudes, beliefs, and behaviors in an effort to bring awareness to your self-defeating habits. These are the things that aggravate your anxiety, compound your stress, and send your emotional state into overdrive, confusing cognition and contributing to poor physical health. We'll give you techniques to discover what is driving you, and then we'll explore ways to calm the nervous system back down and achieve a satisfying equilibrium in life. You'll find that rewiring your mindset and regulating your emotions and nervous system are the secrets to reducing, controlling, and getting rid of anxiety, catastrophizing, and overthinking.

The Healing Art of Self-Observation

Self-observation is an individual activity. No one can lead you through it because no one else is inside your mind. You and all the marvelous facets of you are the only inhabitants there.

As we talked about in Chapter 4, you have an inner voice, and it can sometimes speak with numerous intentions that contradict each other. Yes, you may have an argument with yourself inside yourself. It may not be internally audible; you might sense a conflict of emotions or battle indecision. When you observe yourself, you give no one and nothing but yourself your full attention while you listen to and watch your mindsets and behaviors to discover what drives your compulsive patterns.

All you need for this exercise is space, stillness, silence, and you.

One article I read compared self-observation to bird-observation, or bird-watching. Birds are anxious little critters that don't stay in one place too long. They're pretty boisterous, and they definitely don't hesitate to speak their minds or act on impulse. I honestly don't know if they think at all, but they do go through the same motions all the time, much like you do when you overthink.

Like old-time photographers used to say, "Watch the birdie!" My neighborhood is home to a pair of sandhill cranes—we affectionately call them Lucy and Ricky because they're redheads like Lucile Ball. I say it's "home," but they act like they own the place. They casually walk down the middle of the street. Sometimes, they stroll along the sidewalk, but if they want to cross to the other side, they take their grand old time. If a person, animal, or vehicle approaches, they jump and flap and squawk at them, and whoever or whatever it is has to back off and wait for the birds to go on their way. Though the cranes are not an apex species, they continuously behave like they are. Lucky for Lucy and Ricky, they're protected in this state, but if they weren't, I have a feeling their jump-flap-squawk dance would rarely end happily. Laws keep these birds safe, but you must learn to rein in your repetitive thoughts and behaviors in order to stop your mind from putting itself in the street of harmful habits.

Below are five simple steps for practicing self-observation:

1. **Ssshhh.** Be quiet. In your busy life, finding a moment of silence can be challenging, but you need to carve out time for quiet reflection. Tell your inner voice to shut up! Turn off the radio, television, devices, and anything else that makes noise, buzzes, or jingles, and isolate yourself in a room apart from people, pets, or other

distractions. Find a space where you can be alone. If you can't find a quiet space in your home, try a peaceful corner of a library or a secluded bench at a park.

2. Once you have found your quiet space, **let go** of what you would normally be doing, and don't allow yourself to think about what else you *should be* doing. This right now is what you *should be* doing, nothing else. It is time to let go of anything else that might be occupying your mind. Letting go doesn't mean ignoring responsibilities; it means prioritizing your well-being. Allow yourself the freedom to relax and just be. Just settle down and allow yourself this moment.

3. **Do nothing.** Don't fidget. Don't squirm. Don't force yourself to think on any particular topic. This may seem daunting initially, especially if you are used to being continually active or engaged. Close your eyes so you have no visual distractions, and just tune in to what's going on inside. The point of this exercise is not to force your mind to think of specific topics but to allow thoughts to come and go freely.

4. As you sit in silence, begin to **observe** your thoughts and feelings. Like meandering through an aviary to identify various birds and pay

attention to their different colors and songs, turn your vision inward and see what memories flutter by. Note the feelings that are attached to them. Listen to any thoughts that arise. Don't respond or react; just observe. Reflect on your behavior over recent days and recall how you interacted with others, performed your job, and related to your family members. Stay in this sanctuary until you feel you've perceived all there is to behold. Then, slowly open your eyes back up and return to the present moment.

5. The final step is to **write** down your insights. Writing is a powerful tool to gain clarity and understanding. What images popped into your mind during your reflection? Were there particular thoughts that stood out more than others? What tones or attitudes did you perceive? What insight did you gain? What did you learn about yourself? What areas of your life could you improve upon? Reflect on these questions as you write. This process is not just about recording what happened during your quiet time; it is about understanding yourself better.

How can you apply the knowledge you gained from this exercise to your conscious moments in daily life? Regularly practicing this internal assessment will help you understand your convictions, know why you respond to people and events in certain ways, and be aware of your triggers. From there, you can pinpoint the areas that need to be tweaked.

Regulating Your Nervous System

The autonomic nervous system controls your unconscious responses and determines whether your body should go on the defensive or just chill out. It consists of two distinct branches:

- The **sympathetic nervous system** handles sudden, stressful situations. It regulates the fight-or-flight response and signals the body to take protective and defensive action for survival. Cortisol and adrenaline are released to increase heart rate, blood pressure, and breathing to prepare the body to work if it needs to confront or escape someone or something—like if you need to run away from that bear by your hermit cottage.

- The **parasympathetic nervous system** handles recovery and relaxation. Activities like yoga, deep breathing, and meditation signal it to bring your heart rate back into a regular pattern and settle the body into a state of calm.

When your nervous system is out of whack, the sympathetic system remains on high alert, and the parasympathetic doesn't get the chance to help you unwind. Anxiety remains high, blood pressure stays elevated, and you feel overwhelmed and powerless even after a legitimate stressor is removed—like after the bear has returned to its den. When your nervous system is dysregulated, you continue to feel scared, uncomfortable, and on edge, and you experience physiological discomforts as well, like chronic pain and illness.

Dr. Linnea Passaler (2023), a surgeon and clinician with Heal Your Nervous System, says the nervous system "is the foundation of our lived experience, connecting our body and mind, regulating our emotional and mental state, immune system, and every other body system." It not only involves our whole being, but it also regulates how we interact with other beings, even allowing for spiritual connections.

According to Passaler, this interconnected system is built upon four pillars:

1. **Body:** This includes all the physiological aspects of your physical body, its operating systems, and cellular structure. The respiratory system enables you to breathe, allowing oxygen to enter your bloodstream. The circulatory system pumps this oxygen-rich blood throughout your body. Each part of your body has a role, and when you take care of your physical health, you enable these systems to work well.

2. **Mind:** The mind encompasses the thoughts and emotions that shape your daily life as well as all of your internal, non-tangible workings. This includes your feelings, how you reason, and your ability to make decisions. Self-awareness is a major component of your mental landscape that allows you to recognize your emotions and thoughts and respond appropriately to different situations. A healthy mind requires effective coping strategies. For example, journaling can help you understand your feelings better. When you write down your thoughts, you can reflect on them and gain clarity. Mindfulness and meditation promote mental wellness by encouraging you to focus on the present moment, thereby reducing stress and anxiety. Talking to someone about your feelings, whether a friend or a therapist, and verbalizing your thoughts can diffuse emotional turmoil and help you build strong mental resilience.

3. **Connection:** This refers to your relationships, how you relate to others, and how you participate in society and the general community. Humans are social beings, and your connections are important to your well-being. Healthy relationships provide support, love, and a sense of purpose. Spending time with those closest to you can strengthen emotional bonds and create a support network during tough

times, and participation in community activities gives you a sense of belonging. Simple gestures like a random phone call or quality time with loved ones can strengthen these connections. Effective communication skills like active listening, which involves fully concentrating on what someone else is saying before responding, shows respect and deepens the connection between you and your loved ones.

4. **Spirituality:** This alludes to your search for meaning and your need to connect with and be a part of something bigger than yourself. It can manifest in numerous ways, whether through organized religion, personal beliefs, or a connection to nature. Engaging in spiritual practices can offer comfort and insight into your life. For many, attending religious services creates a sense of community and belonging, encourages shared values, and fosters a supportive environment. On the other hand, individual practices like meditation or spending time in nature can enhance your spiritual experience and evoke feelings of wonder and gratitude. It is also helpful to explore your personal values and beliefs. Ask yourself what you stand for or what gives your life meaning. Engage in reflective practices to clarify these thoughts and take time to ponder life's big

questions to achieve personal growth and satisfaction.

Overall well-being is found in the balance of the body, mind, connection, and spirituality. Each aspect complements the others, creating a holistic approach to living a fulfilling life.

Healing the nervous system requires you to attend to all four of those aspects. You can't just treat the symptoms of one and expect them all to fall in order, and there is no quick fix. Regulating your nervous system in a healthy way is a lifelong journey. You need to maintain an awareness of your mental and physical states. The self-observation exercises we discussed in the last section are great for this! You also need to learn and practice healthy coping mechanisms and work to heal the negative effects of chronic dysregulation.

Here are some practical ways to calm your nervous system and restore it to a functional state:

- **Relive happy times.** This does not mean to ruminate or put the memory reels on repeat, but it does mean to visualize something that has brought you pleasure, like a serene day at the beach, a decadent dessert, or an exquisite art installment. Neuroscientist and mental health expert Caroline Leaf says, "When you visualize a happy cluster of memories, this generates a frequency in the brain that overrides the negative frequency the toxic stress caused and calms down the nervous system" (Estrada & Lucas, 2024).

- As Peter Pan advised, "**Think of a wonderful thought**, any merry little thought" (Fain & Cahn, 1953). Recall happy memories, joyful conversations, or silly childhood songs. Replace negative thoughts with positive ones, and if you struggle, try putting those negative ideas to the tune of an upbeat song to take the air right out of its sails.

- **Try some deep breathing exercises**. Slow, deep breaths let the brain know there's no need for urgency and help the body to calm down after a real or perceived threat. Ten rounds of box breathing is a quick and easy way to settle the nervous system. Simply breathe in for four counts, hold it for four counts, breathe out for four counts, and hold that for four counts.

- **Pause and apply the 30–90-second rule** to balance the brain and body before responding to any interaction. Take 3–5 slow, deep breaths, inhaling to fully expand the ribs and lungs and exhaling to empty them completely. Then, scream into a pillow to literally blow out your frustrations. And finally, do a physical action like a couple of yoga stretches or a few quick burpees.

- **Relax under a weighted blanket** to send proprioceptive input to the brain. This gentle pressure improves the awareness of your body's position in the space around you and effectively lowers the heart rate.

- **Eat.** Don't stress eat! Have a snack of healthy fats, like avocados, nuts, or fatty fish, to keep the myelin layer surrounding nerve cells healthy. Think of it as fluffing your nervous system's pillows.

Practice these techniques and do them often to restore balance and maintain a healthy nervous system that functions optimally no matter what's going on around you.

The Aim Is Not To Be Calm 24/7

You don't want to completely subdue it because the nervous system triggers the natural reflexes and activates bodily functions that preserve you from harm. You don't want it so relaxed that you have no qualms about giving that grizzly a bearhug, but you also don't want it on hyperdrive and being so on edge that you live life barricaded inside a safe room, inside a safe house, inside a safe compound, never setting foot out the door.

Equanimity is a psychological term that refers to the mind and body's ability to work together to remain steady and calm amid life's twists and turns. In contrast to neuroticism, someone in a state of equanimity maintains composure in uncomfortable situations instead of becoming overwhelmed by fear and anxiety. It requires nervous system regulation and borrows a bit of insight from stoicism in that it encourages detachment from adversity and acceptance of things beyond your control.

Epictetus (n.d.), the ancient Greek Stoic philosopher, observed, "We cannot choose our external circumstances, but we can always choose how we respond to them." Choosing not to respond to every stimulus is a sign of a healthy nervous system.

Below are several practical strategies to help you reach and maintain this state of holistic well-being:

- **Practice daily mindfulness meditations** to preserve a sense of calm in tense situations. You don't need specialized training to get started; simply find a quiet spot to sit comfortably. Breathe deeply a few times to settle in. Focus on your breath, noticing the way it feels as you inhale and exhale. If your mind starts to go off in a different direction, gently put your focus back on your breathing. You can start with just five minutes a day and gradually increase the time as you become more comfortable.

- **Set aside time for self-reflection** to assess your mental and emotional well-being. Maybe create a quiet space in your home that's just for you where you can think without distractions. You might want to set a specific time each week, perhaps on a Sunday evening, to sit down with your journal and write out your thoughts and feelings about the past week. Ask yourself questions like how you felt during different moments, what made you happy, and what challenges you faced.

- **Lead a healthy lifestyle** that consists of regular physical activity, nutritious eating, sufficient rest, and quality sleep. Aim to incorporate at least 30 minutes of exercise into your daily routine. This could be a brisk walk, cycling, or dancing in your living room. Eat a balanced diet that includes vegetables, fruits, lean proteins, and whole grains. Make sure you take time to unwind in the evening and limit screen time before bed to improve your sleep quality.

- **Express gratitude** for everything in your life, including the trying times that help you grow. You might start a gratitude journal in which you list three things you are thankful for each day. These could be big, like a supportive friend, or small, like a delicious meal. Focusing on what you appreciate shifts your mindset and helps you see the positive even in difficult situations.

- **Embrace challenges** as learning opportunities and not as threats to your success or contentment. When faced with a hurdle, take a moment to assess the situation. Ask yourself what you can learn from it and how it can help you grow. For instance, if you are learning a new skill and find it difficult, remind yourself that struggle is part of the learning process. By viewing challenges positively, you can build resilience and confidence.

- **Utilize Jin Shyin Jyutsu**, the ancient Japanese art of finger pressing, when you're in a stressful moment and cannot step away from it immediately. Simply wrap the thumb and fingers of one hand around the thumb and consecutive fingers of the other; hold each for a minute or two before progressing to the next digit; then repeat with the other hand.

- **Build meaningful connections** with friends, family, or coworkers. Start by reaching out to someone you haven't spoken to in a while. You could schedule a lunch or simply send a message to check in. Engage regularly with others to build trust and deepen relationships. You might also want to join clubs or groups that interest you, such as a book club or a sports team. The more support you have, the better you'll feel emotionally.

- **Go outside.** Take a walk in the park, relax on a porch swing, or sip a cup of tea on the balcony. Going outside is a wonderful way to clear your mind, refresh your spirit, and enjoy nature, and being in natural sunlight helps your body produce vitamin D, which is vital for overall health. Try to make it a habit to spend some time outside every day.

- **Soak up the sun.** Protect your skin from damaging rays, then spread out a blanket in your yard, at a local pool, or a nearby beach, and take in the sun's warmth. The cozy conditions will warm your mood, and the dose of vitamin D will do you good too!

- **Say *no* more often.** Lighten your load and give yourself free time. It's easy to feel overwhelmed by the many requests we receive from others. Recognize that you don't have to accept every invitation or task that comes your way. Start by assessing your current commitments and determining which ones are truly important. Practice politely declining requests that do not align with your priorities and gain back time for relaxation and personal projects.

- **Do things for *you*.** Participate in activities that promote creativity and leisure. Make time each week to do something you enjoy outside of work and responsibilities. Give yourself a break from daily pressures and allow yourself to relax and recharge. It's important to find something that brings you joy and fits into your lifestyle.

- **Listen to music** and sing along to lift your spirits and relax. Music has a powerful effect on emotions and can be a great way to express yourself. Create a playlist of your favorite tunes and set aside a few minutes each day to listen and sing, whether in the car, cooking, or just relaxing at home.

- **Play with your pet!** Research has proven that having a pet lowers stress and anxiety, reduces blood pressure, lessens depression, decreases loneliness, and makes you feel loved and happy (Marie, 2022). If you don't have one, get one! If you don't want that responsibility or are unable to own one, visit a friend who has a pet, stop by the pet store and ask to hold a hamster, or volunteer at a shelter.

Slow down and enjoy your life. Adopt an improvement mindset, include regular self-reflection, and adjust your strategies as often as necessary, and you will successfully balance your emotions and revitalize your overall well-being.

Chapter 7:

Cultivating Emotional

Intelligence

Emotional intelligence (EI)—also referred to emotional quotient (EQ)—is the set of skills you possess to recognize, name, and regulate your emotions and to identify and understand those of others. Having a strong EI helps you build compassionate relationships and make decisions that align with your personal goals and values.

Psychologist, journalist, and author Daniel Goleman did not establish the theory of EI; however, he did make it popular with the public with the release of his 1995 book that was simply titled *Emotional Intelligence*. His interpretations of EI quickly spread to administrative and executive business offices and revolutionized not only how the corporate world interacts with clients but also how they assess potential hires. Academic systems around the world have also incorporated EI curricula into their educational programs.

The concept of EI really took off in the 1990s as researchers became curious why people with high intelligence quotients (IQ) excelled in areas of knowledge but did not always find success in social, personal, or worldly pursuits. On this realization that people with "book smarts" don't always have "street smarts," psychologists John Mayer and Peter Salovey coined "emotional intelligence" to represent this underlying skill set, categorizing EI characteristics into four components:

- Being aware of your own emotions on a nonverbal level.

- Managing your emotions, controlling them, and being emotionally flexible in changing circumstances.

- Empathizing with others on an emotional level by identifying and understanding what they feel.

- Creating and maintaining relationships, developing social skills, cooperating in teamwork, and working through conflict.

Goleman added a fifth category: motivation. This is the influence emotional factors have over the choices you make, goals you pursue, and amount of perseverance you display in light of challenges.

Let's take a closer look, get a good *feel* for the subject, and learn ways to better manage your emotions.

Deconstructing Emotional Intelligence

Deconstruction is a trendy topic these days, especially in the food arena. Really! You can find recipes for anything from deconstructed eggrolls to deconstructed beef Wellington to deconstructed pecan pie and more online. I once saw a deconstructed peanut butter and jelly sandwich on a cafe menu, and I thought, *Do they just give you the jars and a bag of bread? Now they're just getting lazy!*

Well, let me assure you there's nothing lazy about deconstructing emotional intelligence. Not that it's exceptionally difficult to swallow in its entirety, but it does digest more easily when we take it one bite at a time.

Let's first understand the link between emotions and overthinking. In Chapter 5, we talked about how the unknown is a major stressor. Humans have an innate need to control what happens in their lives. But because so much of life is unpredictable, and because your command over any particular aspect is limited and dependent upon other people and variable circumstances, you might feel helpless sometimes. A perceived loss of control can lead to fear of the unknown, and fear of the unknown can lead to obsessive thought patterns that keep you desperately trying to put life in the *right* manageable order.

Fear might be the engineer, but traumatic events, childhood experiences, cognitive distortions, mental health disorders, and learned behaviors can all provide the locomotion that chugs this crazy train down the track to Distressville. By the way, to soothe your sorrows, you might want to pick up some deconstructed chocolate bars at the platform's food court—you know, a cup of hot cocoa!

Aside from the steamy mug, none of those experiences are positive, and most—if not all—can create a real emotional upheaval. You may feel sad, mad, scared, worried, hopeless, concerned, insecure, unsafe, overwhelmed, ungrateful, confused, and distraught, as well as any number of other shades of feeling depicted on Plutchik's wheel of emotions. Not only does overthinking perpetuate a cycle of futile contemplation, but it also plunges you into a pool of potentially unlimited unhealthy emotions, which then begin to negatively affect your physical health and cause you to dwell on sicknesses, treatments, and long-term prognoses, creating new worries and unknowns and fears and an overwhelming lack of control. Do you see where this is going? That's right, nowhere.

You can derail this train, though. You can deconstruct it! Remove the cars that cause you pain and get aboard a track to wellness.

Processing Emotions Thoughtfully

In Chapter 1, we talked about studies performed in the 1970s that sought to identify how many human emotions there are. Psychologist Paul Eckman determined there were only six basic ones that were common to all people around the globe, and he named them in three sets of opposing pairs: happiness and sadness, disgust and fear, and anger and surprise. You and I both know there are many more than that, right? What about nervous or hurt? Is eager an emotion? Or guilty?

Researchers at the University of California Berkeley Greater Good Science Center conducted a study to examine "the full palette of emotions that color our inner world" in 2017. They had 853 male and female volunteers view 2,185 video clips and report their emotional responses. A total of 27 distinct emotional categories were identified, ranging from nostalgic to grossed out, from contempt to triumph, and many more in between. They discovered numerous distinguishable emotions previously believed to be variants of the six basics, but they also noticed "smooth gradients of emotions" instead of the anticipated "finite clusters." This indicated an interconnection between the known emotions and how we experience them (Anwar, 2017).

More recent research finds the theory of basic emotions losing traction in favor of a potentially infinite number. Theo Tsaousides of *Psychology Today* (2023) suggests, "It all depends on how we conceptualize what an emotion is. The practical answer is that there are as many emotions as you can name." I don't know about you, but I get emotional just thinking about that possibility! And I'm not talking about one of the six. I feel a bit overwhelmed, astonished, and a little bit mortified.

How can I possibly manage an unlimited number of feelings, much less give each one a name? The thought alone is almost enough to send me on an overthinking roller coaster that could last for hours.

There's really no reason to be bothered, overcome, or exasperated, though. If you follow the helpful tips from Emma McAdam of Therapy in a Nutshell (2024), you'll feel relieved, optimistic, and hopeful to learn how emotion processing can further help in managing how you feel. Check out McAdam's O.W.E.C.A. method:

- **O: Observe** your feelings without automatically believing them or dismissing them.

- **W:** Be **willing** to recognize that feeling something doesn't necessarily make it an objective truth.

- **E: Explore** and actively seek alternative emotional responses and verify them with facts.

- **C: Choose** a path that aligns with your values and don't just react emotionally.

- **A:** Act on what truly matters to you without letting your immediate emotional state direct your response.

When feelings like bitterness surface, it's easy to believe your emotions and react harshly. Yet, if you step back to consider the emotions that are popping up, see how others may blend in, and consider how your personal history might influence your response, you can give rational thought a chance to provide clarity, and you will be able to navigate your inner emotional terrain more effectively.

Strategies to Manage and Express Emotions

Learning to recognize and work through emotions is only the first step to bolstering your EI. You also need to know what to do with them and how to express them appropriately. It's probably safe to assume that you are not an infant, toddler, or child if you are reading this book. That's good because it means you probably have a bit of experience in this area.

Eckman's six basics may expand exponentially throughout your life, but when you were a baby, those core emotions drove your survival. You were sad and angry if you were hungry or dirty, and you may have been fearful that sustenance and cleanliness wouldn't come your way. When it did, though, you were happy! And depending on what food you received, you may have also been surprised—or disgusted.

As you entered toddlerhood, you began to connect emotions to certain situations. Fear was probably dominant at this point because you had yet to realize that when Mom or Dad left your sight, they weren't gone for good. As you neared preschooler and early childhood age, you began to adopt strategies to handle tough feelings, like distancing yourself from the source of upset.

Moving into and through childhood, you developed secondary emotions. As each was validated—or invalidated—you learned to differentiate what was appropriate—and inappropriate—ways to handle these new feelings. Puberty did more to intensify emotions than to introduce new ones, and as you entered adulthood, you had a pretty good grasp on the subject.

That didn't mean you had mastered it, though. Many people continue to struggle with emotional conflicts throughout their lives—hence, overthinking exists. Some people have no buffers, while others seem hypertuned to one or two domineering feelings. Childhood experiences, life traumas, and your folks' parenting style also impact your management methods.

If you constantly struggle with being reactionary or even indecisive about how to respond appropriately to an emotional stimulus, below are some helpful steps you can take to improve your emotional management and expression:

- **Perform five acts of kindness weekly.** A 2016 study published in Psychosomatic Medicine proved the old adage that helping someone else helps you. Reduced stress-related activity, increased reward-related activity, and greater caregiver-related activity were revealed in participants' brain scans, showing giving someone else support does indeed benefit your own health (Inagaki et al., 2016). Here are some things you could do:

- **Help a neighbor with their groceries:** This act may seem small, but it can make a big difference in someone's day. If you see a neighbor struggling with bags, approach them and ask if they need assistance. It can be as easy as carrying a few packages to their door. You might also offer to pick some things up for them next time you are out and about.

- **Write a heartfelt note:** This can be a handwritten letter or a simple message to a friend to express your appreciation for their friendship and tell them what they mean to you. You might mention specific memories or times when they supported you. A few sentences acknowledging their kindness and warmth can really brighten their day—and yours.

- **Volunteer at a local shelter:** Volunteering is a fantastic way to give back to the community and get your focus off of yourself. Local shelters and food banks always appreciate extra hands. This kind of work might involve serving meals, sorting donations, or even organizing events. If you are unsure where to start, look online for volunteer opportunities in your area or ask around in your neighborhood. Many places have flexible hours, so you can find a time that works for you.

○ **Pay for a stranger's meal:** Paying for someone else's meal or buying them coffee can create a chain reaction of kindness. This simple gesture can surprise and delight them and encourage them to pass on the kindness to someone else. You don't have to have a lot of money; even a small gesture can have a big effect.

○ **Donate unused items:** Take some time to go through your belongings and select items you don't use anymore but are still in great condition. This could be clothing you've outgrown or household items just taking up space. Deliver them to local charities or shelters that accept donations or contact organizations that offer pick-up services.

- **Go outside every day,** even if it's just for 10–15 minutes. Sunshine provides vitamin D, and fresh air is cleansing for your lungs. Observe all the sights, sounds, and feels of the surrounding environment with each of your five senses, and feel your mind and spirit lift. Here are some simple things you can do outdoors:

  - **Take a hike:** Hiking is an excellent way to enjoy nature while also getting some exercise. You could walk trails at a local nature preserve or loop the sidewalk around your neighborhood park. Be sure whichever trail you choose suits your fitness level, and check out resources like trail maps and guidebooks if you're not familiar with the terrain. Some can help you identify the flora and fauna you'll see along the way. Wear comfortable shoes and dress in layers if you anticipate changing weather conditions, and remember to bring a water bottle and light snacks like granola bars or fruit to keep your energy up.

  - **Have a picnic:** A picnic in the park is a delightful way to enjoy good food and company. It can be a simple outing with minimal planning but maximum enjoyment. You can set up on picnic tables, in grassy areas, or near beautiful views. Sandwiches, fruits, and finger foods are popular choices. If you want something other than water, bring lemonade or iced tea. Don't forget to bring a blanket to sit on, napkins or wet wipes for messes, and garbage bags for cleaning up afterward. For more fun, toss a frisbee or play card games and create some lasting memories.

○ **Plant a tree or some flowers:** Planting a tree or flowers is a rewarding activity that benefits both you and the environment. So that they actually grow well, be sure to choose plants that are appropriate for your soil conditions and local climate. If you are new to gardening, ask an expert at your local gardening center to help you get started. Water your plants regularly. It's a good idea to research the plants you're interested in. Some need more water than others. Also, provide adequate sunlight.

○ **Play a sport:** Playing sports with friends is a fantastic way to stay active while having fun. Choose a sport everyone enjoys or pick something new you're interested in learning. Pickleball is pretty popular these days! Why not give it a try? Organize a time and place to meet, make sure everyone knows the basic rules of the game, bring the necessary equipment, and challenge each other to a competition. Even if you or your team loses, you're sure to laugh together, boost your health, and strengthen your bonds with your friends.

○ **Stargaze:** Stargazing at night requires little to no preparation and can be done nearly anywhere as long as you're away from the bright lights of the city. If your own backyard is in a bright part of town, find a location with minimal light pollution like a quiet park or field. Bring along a blanket to lie down on and dress warmly if it's a cool evening. Give yourself about 20 minutes to allow your eyes to adjust to the darkness—especially if you are the one who drove to the location and are still seeing spots from oncoming headlights—and then you'll be able to see more stars. You might also want to download a stargazing app on your phone to help you identify constellations and planets in the sky. Consider bringing snacks or drinks so you can linger awhile and relax under the peaceful night sky.

- **Get offline.** Disconnect from social media, turn off the TV, and don't read a news report. All of those things are full of potential triggers that can fray your nerves, cause you to ruminate and catastrophize, and jack up your anxiety. Get the updates you need to stay aware of current events, but don't doom scroll or interact with trolls. Here are some clever offline activities:

  ○ **Watch your favorite old movie:** Watching your favorite old movie can be nostalgic—but the good kind that entertains you and not the bad kind that leads you down rabbit holes. It allows you to revisit characters and stories that made you feel good. Pop some corn, plop down in a comfy spot on your couch, and veg out. Add some fun by inviting friends over for a themed movie night, dressing up as the characters from the film, and preparing snacks that suit the scene.

  ○ **Draw or paint:** Art can be a wonderful outlet for creativity. Trying your hand at painting or drawing doesn't require you to be a professional. Start with simple materials like pencils, colored pencils, or watercolors. You can find tutorials online or simply draw what you see around you. Take a moment to sketch your favorite mug or a tree in your backyard. If you feel bold, grab a canvas and some paint. Don't worry about making it perfect; focus on expressing yourself.

○ **Have a game night:** Game nights can create lasting memories with friends or family. Board games like Monopoly, Scrabble, or Life and card games like Uno, Skip-Bo, or Phase 10 can spark laughter and conversations. You could also play video games, but try to choose uplifting ones that give you more of an old arcade experience instead of online games that isolate you in headsets and dystopian worlds. Keep snacks and drinks handy and just have fun.

○ **Go to the library:** Libraries are treasure troves of knowledge and adventure. Walk through the aisles and see what catches your eye. Do you prefer fiction or non-fiction? history? fantasy? science fiction? If you want to learn something new, look for books on topics you've always been curious about. Don't hesitate to ask a librarian for recommendations on popular titles or hidden gems. Be sure to check out the calendar for events like book clubs, author readings, or special interest classes.

○ **Do a DIY or craft project:** DIY projects can be a fun way to express creativity and make something unique. If you love to craft, make a simple project like personalized greeting cards. You can use supplies you already have at home or visit a local craft store for more materials. Follow online tutorials for guidance or let your imagination lead you. If you enjoy home improvement, repaint a room or refurbish an old piece of furniture.

• **Replace negative emotions** with compassion. This is often easier said than done, but it provides lasting inner peace. Instead of dwelling on the anger and hurt someone caused you, work toward empathy and forgiveness. Instead of allowing upset to fester, you'll find yourself freed from emotional chains. Here are some positive thoughts you can tell yourself to combat negative emotions:

- **Overcoming challenges:** Life is full of challenges, and facing them can often seem daunting. However, it is essential to recognize that these challenges are opportunities for growth. When you encounter a difficult situation, take a moment to reflect on how you can overcome it. For example, if you struggle with a project at work, break it down into smaller tasks. This approach makes the challenge more manageable and allows you to build confidence as you complete each step.

- **Embracing new opportunities:** Each day brings a fresh start and is an opportunity to make choices that can lead to positive changes in your life. Set a good tone for your day with your morning routine. Maybe sit down and plan or assess your goals, practice gratitude, or engage in a brief exercise session.

- **Receiving support from loved ones:** Friends and family can provide encouragement during tough times and celebrate alongside you during victories. Make it a point to connect with loved ones regularly. Grab a bite to eat at your favorite restaurant, video chat for an hour, or plan to take a trip together. When faced with challenges, reach out to those you trust and share your feelings. Their support can offer a new perspective and remind you that you are not alone in your struggles.

○ **Defining your future:** Your personal history does not have to set the stage for your future. Everyone makes mistakes, and it is essential to learn from them rather than let them define who you are. Identify what knowledge you gained from those experiences and note how they can guide you toward success in the future. Set clear goals for yourself and remember that *you* have the power to shape your future with each decision and action you take.

○ **Prioritizing your well-being:** Make it job one to take care of yourself both physically and mentally. Allocate time for self-care activities like exercise, reading, mindfulness, or hobbies. Make a list of activities that bring you joy and schedule time to engage in them regularly. Don't neglect your emotional health. If something is bothering you, journal about your feelings or talk to someone you trust.

- **Laugh!** It's no joke; laughter really is good medicine. It improves your mood, relieves stress, brings oxygen into your lungs, and strengthens social bonds. It lowers the amount of stress hormones in the body, increases blood flow, and reduces your risk of heart attack. It's no laughing matter! Okay, maybe it is. Read some "dad jokes," watch a funny movie, or spend an evening at the comedy club. Laugh more; stress less. Here are some things that will tickle your funny bone:

  ○ **Silly animal videos:** Silly animal videos bring a smile to anyone's face. This is one of my personal go-tos! These videos usually show animals behaving in unexpected ways, and they're super entertaining. Some of them capture animals in absolutely absurd situations that somehow always seem to work out just fine. You can easily find clips on social media platforms, and longer versions are sometimes hosted on YouTube. You're likely to find yourself in a cycle of laughter instead of a cycle of overthinking!

- **Funny memes:** Funny memes have become a regular part of online culture. These amusing images or snippets of text often reflect everyday experiences like dealing with a Monday morning or the struggles of "adulting." If you don't find one that makes you giggle, create your own and spread joy to the internet! You don't have to be a graphic designer. Just choose an image that makes you laugh and add some witty text. Message them to your friends and see how they react. They'll probably send you one back.

- **Comedy TV shows or movies:** Watching comedic TV shows or movies is a fantastic way to unwind and escape from the everyday pressures of life. Sitcoms like *Friends* or *The Office* feature relatable characters and humorous situations that resonate with a lot of people, and old favorites like *Whose Line Is It Anyway?* are sure to trigger some belly laughs instead of triggering rumination tracks. You can set up a movie night of classic comedies and mix in some newer films. Watch alone or with your peeps and crank up the laugh factor.

o **Hilarious childhood memories:** Awkward moments from childhood might tempt you to overthink, rehash embarrassing times, and wish you could disappear from those moments, but some make for the best stories, and those are the ones that not only make your heart swell but also leave you laughing. Everyone has experienced a cringe-worthy feeling at some point, whether it's tripping over your own feet during a school play or saying something embarrassing in front of your crush. These moments remind us that we all make mistakes, and laughing about them can help us take life a bit less seriously. Think back to your childhood and try to recall a particularly entertaining experience. Maybe you had an embarrassing haircut or wore mismatched clothes to school. Share these stories with your friends and get them to share their own. You'll all find comfort in knowing that others have felt the same way, and it will diminish the feelings of devastation you get when you ruminate. This sharing experience can actually be therapeutic.

○ **Puns and wordplay:** Using clever language or double meanings to create humor often elicits groans and giggles simultaneously. A lot of them that make you roll your eyes are called dad jokes now, like this one: "I'm reading a book on anti-gravity; it's impossible to put down." Admit it—you snickered! Greet friends with a punny play on words or include them in casual conversations and brighten someone's day.

Give your nervous system a break. Apply the techniques suggested in this chapter each day and grow in your emotional health as you learn to develop your emotional intelligence.

Chapter 8:

Building Your Anti-

Overthinking Toolkit

So who was right, Dostoyevsky or Ray? Is overthinking a disease or just the result of an underused imagination? As we've seen, clinically speaking, overthinking is definitely not a disease, although it can lead to both mental and physical disorders. And while Ray was onto something by suggesting you don't use your creativity enough to get out of the rumination loop, I think the problem is exactly the opposite: You overthink because you come up with far too many imaginative possibilities. It's not a matter of having enough options but too many believable ones. Theoretically, if you didn't completely exhaust yourself, you could keep going and going and going like the Energizer Bunny because you might never arrive at the *right* solution or even one that is *good enough*.

Throughout this book, we've examined overthinking—being careful not to overthink it along the way—and no matter which angle we approach it from, one thing always rings true: This is a dangerous habit. You're likely familiar with what my friend calls "analysis paralysis"— running conversations, situations, memories, future possibilities (which are *probabilities* to your mindset), perceived failures, insults, choices, and, well, useless information through your mind for seemingly endless periods of time. Those moments can be triggered by the need to make a decision, regret over an argument, embarrassment from an incident, or simple things that have nothing to do with life at all, like *does thunder only happen when it's raining?*

Mental rumination is probably the most common expression of this habit, but overthinking can also manifest in other ways:

- **Reflecting:** You may spend excessive time thinking about the past and longing for days gone by.

- **Being agitated:** Your nerves are fried, you're not sleeping well, and you're very short-fused.

- **Reacting quickly and angrily:** You are on edge and jump at any words that are spoken in your general vicinity.

- **Brooding:** You focus on a negative thought so frequently that it weighs you down and keeps you in the sad, fearful, and maybe even angry and disgusted zones of the emotion wheel.

- **Depression disorders:** Long-term lingering in the depths of despair can result in persistent feelings of sadness and a loss of interest in life.

- **Anxiety disorders:** Like depression, prolonged feelings of heightened worry and angst can lead to an assortment of disorders, like social anxiety, agoraphobia, selective mutism, and panic disorder, just to name a few.

You may even find that your overthinking follows a particular motif. A 2022 study from the University College of London (UCL) studied a group of young adults aged 18–24 who ruminated in response to loneliness. They discovered five common themes in the participants' experiences (Yun et al., 2022):

- **Loneliness-related:** fearing being alone, having depressive thoughts, feeling unloved or that no one cares for or about you, feeling like you have no friend to guide or support you, thinking your family is not concerned about your well-being, believing that if you had friends you could always be around then you wouldn't have the chance to ruminate.

- **Others-related:** focusing on social relationships, obsessing over negative interactions you've had with others in the past, wondering if you are treating people correctly, wondering why people aren't treating you correctly, contemplating *Why doesn't anybody like me?*

- **Life- and death-related:** fearing death, stressing over the uncertainty of life, being unsure about an afterlife, feeling scared of how you'll die, worrying about the possible loss of a loved one, contemplating the meaning of life, wondering *Will my mom or dad still be here when I'm [a parent, retired, fill-in-the-blank]?*

- **Time-related:** focusing on periods of time like a certain event that happened in the past or a future event that you are "predicting," thinking about how you could have done or said something differently in a particular instance, thinking that you are a failure because you've "had all this time" to accomplish your goals but have nothing to show for it, promising yourself that you're going to work things out and do better.

- **Overthinking outcome-related:** having an awareness of your overthinking and stressing over how it's affecting you, knowing that your overthinking stops you from sleeping but feeling helpless because you have no off button, crying all night over a particular rumination cycle, worrying about how your habit is affecting those around you.

The majority of the participants involved in this study said that their most reliable method of handling their overthinking habit was distraction. It's actually something I applied to my own overthinking tendencies: Redirect your focus. Shift your mind from the trigger to something else. The study participants said they would go for a walk, call up their friends to hang out or participate in something that required focus and attention. We'll explore some of these ideas in the sections that follow.

The UCL research could potentially lead to targeted interventions and therapeutic treatments that could be more effective than the ones currently in use because they would hone in on precise stimuli. In this chapter, we're going to consider some strategies we haven't yet explored and help you design an approach and custom-tailor a plan that fits your specific needs.

Setting Realistic Goals, Measuring Progress, and Adjusting Strategies

I've always been a fly-by-the-seat-of-my-pants kind of girl. I only lock in dates and times for things that have to be on those dates at those times. I am not married to the clock or the calendar, and that can make goal-setting and goal-pursuing a bit tricky. In my journey to becoming a recovering overthinker, I discovered that one reason I was so successful at this habit was that it really caters to my impromptu mentality. Overthinking doesn't show up promptly for its 3:15 p.m. appointment every Tuesday and Thursday and leave when the timer dings. No, if overthinking wore pants, it would fly by the seat of them too. *Does overthinking wear pants? What would that look like? I'm picturing a speech bubble shaped like SpongeBob's friend Bubble Buddy, but instead of a top hat, he's sporting a pair of Calvins. You know? I love jeans, but they don't love me. They just don't fit me right. Even as a teen when I was tiny and lean, if I got some to fit my waist, I couldn't get them over my thick thighs, and if I got them loose enough for my legs, three of me could fit into the waist. Sweats, now they're the way to go! Easy to fly in too. Where was the last place I flew? Texas, I think...*

Oops! Right, yeah, goals. As I was saying, I've never been good with keeping structure *structured*. That is, until I had to. You know very well that overthinking can disrupt routine, barge into business meetings, and butt into private conversations. It can also crash parties, drift into your dreams, and dump buckets of ice on intimate moments. It doesn't usually inflict immediate injuries, but it definitely leaves long-lasting damage in its wake. It must be stopped, and you're going to need some discipline to make that happen.

Setting goals used to scare and intimidate me. They look really good on paper, but I'd had little success following through with them. That's not to say I failed at everything I attempted; I just didn't necessarily get from Point A to Point B in an ordered way. I always felt a sort of pride in that—I did things *my way*, baby. "They" said I had to do it their way, but guess what? My way worked just fine too. Took a little longer and had a few more dips and curves than theirs, but it still got me there. And I'm a bit more exhausted from the whole process than my friend, who followed the prescribed order, but it's okay. It's okay. I'm okay.

Let me make this easy for you: Give in now. Really. Why do things the hard way just to say you could? Let's talk about some simple ways to set goals and the most effective ways to reach them.

Reaching Your Goals Is Easier Than Reaching for the Stars

A goal is something you desire to accomplish. You probably set several basic goals every day: Get up, eat well, exercise, work, and sleep. Some people make a daily to-do list and then assess it in the evening to see how productive they were—or weren't. Even without a list, I bet if you were to look back over this day, you'd probably check off many things on that list, and you could probably write in a few more extras. So, if you think about it, setting and achieving goals isn't all that hard, and you already know how to do it!

The keys to goal success follow:

1. Take a deep breath in and out. Empty your mind. Shake out your limbs and roll your neck. Okay, now, take your right hand and reach it up to your left shoulder. Next, move that hand a little higher, lift it slightly in the air, and pat yourself on the back. Congratulate yourself for making the determination to take this first step toward breaking the overthinking habit and

committing to taking the necessary actions to reach success. Job well done!

2. Alright, the next step takes a little brain work, but it's not hard. Think. Stop! I forgot to tell you to focus on what you want to accomplish. Okay, go again: Think. Cue *Jeopardy!* music. Stop. Now that you know what you want, you can write it down on a piece of paper—in ink, so you can't erase it later and say it was never there.

3. Look at the goal you wrote down. Is it realistic? Is it achievable? Will it benefit you? Is it what you really want? *Yes* should be the answer to all of those questions, by the way.

4. Put a date on the calendar by which you'd like to reach this goal. Again, make sure it's realistic. Trying to stop ruminating within the next 48 hours will likely set you up for failure. You may be anxious to get on with things, but change takes time. Rushing yourself will only frustrate you more.

5. You've gotten ready, and you've committed to a goal. Now, write down every step you will need to take to get from where you are at this moment to that future destination. List as many or as few, as necessary. Break complicated ones into multiple smaller ones so you don't

overwhelm yourself with something difficult and give up because "it's too hard." Assign each milestone a [realistic] date on the calendar.

6. Each morning, look at your list. Consider what you can do to meet the next milestone. Each evening, cross the day off your calendar and reassess your game plan. If it's one of your target dates, and you met a milestone, celebrate! And when you eventually accomplish the overall goal, repeat step number one above. Give yourself a pat on the back, take a deep breath in and out, smile, and move ahead into the new you.

Set the right goals, allow yourself time to reach them, set the steps, mark the milestones, and follow through to greater happiness and fulfillment. Then, you can return to flying by the seat of your pants!

Creating Your Own Anti-Overthinking Toolkit

We've given you a lot of strategies to stop overthinking. Let's take a quick look back before we dive into some other ideas we haven't mentioned and figure out a personalized plan of action:

- Chapter 1:

    - Pause a moment to calm down so you can *respond* instead of *react* to stimuli.

    - Identify your emotional triggers and create a mental plan to deal with them appropriately when you encounter them again.

    - Do the opposite of what your emotions tell you to do.

    - Shift your perspective with cognitive defusion, acceptance and commitment therapy, or mindfulness practices.

    - Seek professional help.

    - Practice self-care.

    - Establish a routine.

    - Challenge negative thoughts.

    - Set realistic goals.

    - Limit stress.

- Chapter 2:

    - Get regular moderate to vigorous physical exercise.

- ○ Have a mental health screening.

- ○ Eat a nutritious diet.

- ○ Allow yourself only a certain amount of time to overthink.

- ○ Practice grounding techniques.

- ○ Do breathing exercises.

- ○ Practice yoga.

- ○ Walk with mindful intention.

- Chapter 3:

  - ○ Practice mindfulness techniques like those below:

    - ■ Body scan

    - ■ Mindful walking

    - ■ Mindful meditation

    - ■ Alternate nostril breathing

    - ■ 5-senses scan

    - ■ Mindfulness-based stress reduction

- - Meditate.

  - Keep a journal.

- Chapter 4:

  - Identify the character of your inner voice.

  - Journal about your inner dialog.

  - Attend cognitive behavioral therapy and practice cognitive restructuring.

  - Don't sabotage yourself.

  - Practice visualization.

  - Make gratitude a habit.

- Chapter 5:

  - Put the past in the past.

  - Focus on the present moment with these mindfulness techniques:

    - Body focus

    - View ASMR videos.

    - Feel your heartbeat.

- ■ Write down each day's accomplishments.

  - ○ Embrace uncertainty.

  - ○ Set goals.

- ● Chapter 6:

  - ○ Practice self-observation.

  - ○ Restore and regulate your nervous system.

  - ○ Embrace challenges as learning opportunities.

  - ○ Utilize Jin Shyin Jyutsu finger pressing to relieve stress.

  - ○ Build personal connections.

  - ○ Spend time outdoors.

  - ○ Say *no* more often and avoid overcommitting yourself.

  - ○ Listen to music.

  - ○ Play with your pet.

- Chapter 7:

    - Cultivate your emotional intelligence.

    - Process emotions thoughtfully.

    - Do acts of kindness.

    - Get offline and disconnect from your devices.

    - Replace negative emotions with compassion.

    - Laugh.

It doesn't seem like there's much left, but we've saved some of the more creative ones till the last. Which of these appeal to you?

- **Ecstatic dance:** This might be good for you fly-by-the-seat-of-your-pants people because it doesn't stick to rigid structures. It's all about dancing freely and expressing your emotions through uninhibited movement.

- **Self-massage:** Can't afford a day at the spa? That's okay! You can loosen up your muscles, relieve aches and pains, and reduce the stress in your body yourself. Just position yourself in a comfortable, quiet place. Maybe light candles or put on soothing music to help you relax. Close your eyes if you want to. Then start by rubbing the soles of your feet. Move through the arches and heels, and then work upward along the calves, all the way to your shoulders and neck. Release the tension wherever you can reach.

- **The 3–2–8 TikTok workout:** There are two popular variations of this viral exercise plan. The first requires you to do strength training 3 days a week, Pilates and barre each 2 times a week, and walk 8,000 steps every day. The other option is to do Pilates and barre 3 days a week, strength training 2 days, and still walk 8,000 steps a day.

- **Ground yourself with nature:** Kick off your socks and shoes and barefoot it through the grass and dirt. Use your toes to grip the grass. Feel its coolness and the softness of the earth. Shake your hands to release any negative energy you've built up.

- **Repeat positive affirmations:** Make a list of positive statements about yourself and your life. They will help you combat fears with truths and give you courage and confidence to face the day. Try statements like

    ○ I let go of past hurts and face the future without fear.

○ I release my desire to control all aspects of my life.

○ I am present in this moment.

○ I am learning every day.

- **Celebrate others:** Take your focus off of yourself and your own achievements or perceived failures and look at those around you. Rejoice in your sister's engagement, cheer your spouse across the marathon finish line, or raise a toast to your best friend's job promotion.

- **Throw away your worries, literally:** Take out a piece of paper and grab a pen. Set the timer for 10 minutes, and sit down in a quiet place. List every worry, obsession, rumination, fear, or concern that's been weighing on your mind. When time's up, read over the list and pay attention to how each item makes you feel. Then, wad the paper into a ball and slam-dunk it into the nearest trash can. This physical act doesn't actually make your problems go away, but it takes away their pressure.

Personalized Action Plan

Did you know that you process an average of 6,000 thoughts per day? Overthinking rarely introduces new thoughts but recycles ones you've already considered. According to Jeff Stone of *Psychology Today* (2024), if you slow down, step back from your "noisy inner experiences," and learn from them, you can "quiet your motormouth mind."

We've provided a lot of tools to help you do just that. It's time now for you to figure out a plan that will work for you—not your best friend, not your boss, not your dog, but you specifically. Here are some things to consider that will help you sort that out:

- Remove yourself to a quiet place that is free from distraction.

- Open your journal, pick up a pen, and list aspects of your personality.

- Draw a line under that list and create a new list of all the hobbies you enjoy. Include all areas that appeal to you, like playing sports, traveling, or bicycling.

- The next list should show places you like to go that make you feel safe, secure, and unstressed.

- Next, name the people in your life who make you feel supported, encourage and uplift you, and celebrate your victories.

- Then, write down a statement that will serve as your motivation throughout the overthinking habit-breaking process. What do you want to achieve? Why do you need to do this? What changes do you hope to see in yourself?

Once you have recorded your "about you" information, revisit the various methods we've discussed throughout this book and consider which ones are a good match for the you that you described in your journal. What activities do you think you would actually do? Which ones do you think you'd stick with long enough to make a difference? Which ones would be the most effective for you personally?

Go back to Chapter 3 and look at the sample mindfulness schedule. Then, grab your calendar and pencil in a plan. Try that for one week, and then reassess the situation. Do you need to substitute any of the practices for something different? Mix things up and go again for another week. At that point, lock things in—schedule them into your calendar in ink and commit to a routine. Keep your goals and milestones in mind as you plot out your weeks, and soon, you will stop your stinking overthinking.

Tips for Friends and Family Who Are Dealing With an Overthinker, aka YOU

One of the five overthinking themes revealed by the UCL study was outcome-oriented. An example of this type of rumination is worrying about how your overthinking is affecting other people. Is your all-night tossing and turning disrupting your spouse's sleep? Is your own resulting exhaustion stopping you from participating in family activities and making your kids feel neglected? Is your frequent contemplation distracting you from your job and compromising team projects? Is your dog staring at you with drooly jowls and pleading puppy eyes because you ruminated right through its dinnertime?

While you know the heavy tolls overthinking can take on you, you also need to be aware of the harm you may be causing to those you love and who care about you. Overthinking can ruin relationships. You may be wondering how thoughts that are concealed in the privacy of your head can bother anyone else. Well, even though no one can hear your internal conversations, your speech, attitude, and behavior toward those around you can all be influenced by what you're thinking, how often you are ruminating, and the duration of time you spend in that cycle of contemplation. Let's talk about it below:

- Overthinking can lead you down the wrong path and cause you to develop faulty beliefs. This may result in your making false accusations based on what you *think* is going on when the truth of the matter is way different. My friend's ex-husband used to do this. He would get so worked up in his mind that he would convince himself a situation had occurred in a very different way than it actually had. Then he'd pick a fight with her over something that never really happened—though in his head of overthought, it had.

- Your internal overanalysis can destroy trust. If your partner is unusually quiet over dinner and insists nothing's wrong, but you run it through a few loops of your overthinking roller coaster, you may arrive at a wrong conclusion. You might think they want to break up or they don't love you anymore and then behave coldly toward them or say hurtful things. This can lead to a mutual breach of trust when, in fact, neither partner actually *did* anything wrong.

- If your overthinking habit impacts your job performance, you could face a demotion, pay cut, or worse, loss of employment, and that can have a harsh fallout on how you provide for and contribute financially to your family. Your coworkers may also lose faith in you and not trust you to perform your duties satisfactorily. Similarly, if your work requires you to interact with customers, they may perceive your lack of focus, seek assistance from other representatives, and possibly alert your supervisor.

- When you are not fully present with your partner or your children, they can feel unloved and undervalued and believe you don't think they're worthy of your time. It can inflict lasting emotional wounds and create huge rifts in the relationships that matter the most to you.

People can easily perceive when your mind is in other places, and sometimes, irreparable damage is done. Hurt feelings and broken trust could litter your life and leave you with yet another tangent to ponder, worry about, contemplate, consider, twist, turn, and chase down rabbit holes.

Until you learn to master the techniques provided in this book, break that overthinking habit, and snap out of your analysis paralysis, the people nearest and dearest to you could use some help putting up with you—I mean, patiently and lovingly supporting you.

Here are some simple strategies your friends and family members can practice to help themselves through your overthinking (Rebecca, 2023):

- **Be patient:** Yep, it's that easy! Ha! Patience may be a virtue, but it's often developed by suffering through undesirable situations, isn't it? Someone who supports an overthinker needs to remain calm and understand that this habit annoys the one who's doing it as much as it bothers them. And, although, both of you would like it to stop, that's much easier said than done. Have you ever heard of the polar bear experiment? The late social psychologist and Harvard University professor Daniel

Wegner broke ground with his revelation "that trying to suppress unpleasant thoughts actually *increases* their recurrence long-term" (Myler, 2024). In his experiment, Wegner asked participants to talk for five minutes about the thoughts that were running through their minds at the present moment *without thinking about a polar bear*. He found that they ended up verbalizing thoughts about a white bear about one time during each of the five minutes. So A) you can't just not think about something because someone tells you not to think about it, and B) thought suppression doesn't work. This leads to our next point.

- **Let you talk:** If something's on your mind enough that you start running in circles with it, maybe you should let it out—or, as Wegner suggested, free the bears. But there's a catch. Your supportive friend should encourage you to verbalize your thoughts, but only for a limited time—like around 10–15 minutes. This forces you to be concise and efficient with your words, focus on the point of your pondering, and communicate it in an effective way. It lets them in on an intimate piece of you and demonstrates to you that they genuinely care about your well-being and want to help you if you'll let them— and not just ruminate about your misinterpretations of their dinnertime introspection.

- **Listen without judging:** Your supportive friend or partner should allow you to express what's muddling through your mind without getting annoyed with you for thinking so much about that *stupid* thing or criticizing you for hanging on to something for so long because, after all, *the past is in the past*. They shouldn't think less of you for having developed this habit but should be proud of you for taking steps to address it.

- **Give honest support:** They should listen without making any judgment calls, but—and this is a big *BUT*—they should not lightly dismiss it either. They should be honest—but not hurtful—when they give you feedback, and they should communicate clear boundaries to you that they cannot just drop what they're doing and come to your rescue every time you feel pulled down the overthinking path.

- **Challenge the beliefs you're holding on to:** They should question the things you express that don't match up to what they know about your values and convictions. As we've mentioned, overthinking can result in faulty beliefs—like dwelling on your spouse's quietude during dinner to the conclusion that they hate you. They can also encourage you to think positively about yourself and prompt you to boost your self-esteem by reminding you of your good qualities, your amazing talents, and the joy you bring to them and others. They should challenge you to list the evidence to back up any flawed foibles and help you counter false concepts with truthful ones.

- **Help you focus on the positive:** Much overthinking is spent on negative ideas like doom-dreaming, predicting failure, and catastrophizing. You might spend your time ruminating about how you caught the Thanksgiving turkey on fire last year, running through each moment of that dreadful day and rolling your eyes at all the teasing and tormenting people threw at you. Your support team, though, could help you change your perspective on that memory: "Hey, we all learned that whole chickens cook up pretty well in the pressure cooker—and in much less time—and they taste just as heavenly as turkey when stuffed with dressing and smothered in gravy." And they could encourage you not to let that one bad experience undermine your future holiday feasts and festivity.

- **Encourage a creative release:** Perhaps you need an outlet for the buildup of rumination frustration. A cooking class might be a good idea, uh-hum! Maybe painting, dancing, singing, or gardening suits your passions better. Remember, Amit Ray suggested that overthinkers were being undercreative with their imaginations, so sign up to learn something new or start practicing a hobby you already know. Your friend and you can do these things together and support each other in a fun way. They could also help you find healthy coping mechanisms—like mindfulness practices, journaling, or yoga— and encourage you to do them daily.

- **They should not try to change you:** You are who you are, and your loved ones love you for *you*. They want to help you change this habit, not make you into someone else, so they need to be sure to focus on the overthinking problem without trying to compromise your convictions or coax you into becoming something or someone that you're not.

- **Help you find professional assistance if necessary:** Some emotional issues run too deep for you to process on your own, but therapists are specially trained to bring those to light and help you heal. Some forms of treatment encourage spousal or partner participation, so it's something you might be able to attend together or work on as a couple. Whichever method you choose, their encouragement will be your support as you learn to overcome your difficulties.

Breaking the overthinking habit and restoring a healthy emotional state can take time. It's important for those who are close to you to remain calm when you are struggling, extend empathy to you and what you're experiencing, and be compassionate as you learn to work through your challenges and manage your thoughts. They want you to be the best version of you, and they can demonstrate that desire through their steadfast, loving, and loyal presence.

Conclusion

Overthinking can be described as passive, futile, critical, vague, wasteful, pointless, consuming, destructive, and addictive. And I think we've seen in this book how true every one of those descriptors is! Even on the odd occasion that overthinking is entertaining, it's still a harmful habit with innumerable consequences.

As we've learned, though not a disease *or* an underuse of imagination, overthinking can lead to emotional distress, psychological disorders, and faulty thought patterns. If you allow it to continue, it can consume your mind and separate you from the important things—and people—in your life. Persistent rumination, analysis paralysis, continual contemplation, or whatever you want to call it, can leave you unbalanced and unwell, both mentally and physiologically. It can impact job performance, disrupt relationships, and leave you dealing with not only your overthinking habit but all the resulting fallout, which, by the way, is likely to make you overthink even more.

But there is hope! And we've revealed it in the pages of this book. We've helped you understand why you overthink and how to change your brain physically by practicing healing techniques. We've examined several routes you can take on this journey, and we've explored a plethora of tools to help you *stop your stinking overthinking*!

In *Stop Your Stinking Overthinking: Strategies for Quieting the Busy Mind, Letting Go, and Staying Present*, you've been given

- tips for managing, reducing, *and stopping* overthinking.

- practices that will enhance your overall well-being.

- ways to regulate your nervous system.

- tips for setting, working toward, and achieving your anti-overthinking goals.

- strategies to retrain your mind and grow empowering habits.

- tips for limiting stress and eliminating overthinking triggers.

- ways to tailor an action plan to your personal needs.

Remember that overthinking is not built into your being. It's a habit—a nasty one like picking your nose! And that means you have a choice to keep on keeping on in this burden of excessive thought or to break free, regain your freedom, and throw that boogery tissue away!

You picked up this book. That was your first step toward health and healing.

I wish you great success in your journey, and I'd love to hear about how this book has benefited you. If you feel so inclined, please leave a review on Amazon and share your experience. And if you know of anyone who might benefit from the advice in these pages, consider gifting them a copy so they, too, can *stop* their *stinking overthinking*!

THE STINKING
VERTHINKING TRAP

BREAK FREE TO FIND YOUR BALANCE, VITALITY, AND INNER CALM

BARBARA HEAVENS

The Stinking Overthinking Trap

Break Free to Find Your Balance,
Vitality, and Inner Calm

Barbara Heavens

Introduction

We've all been there—tossing around at 2 a.m. with our brains on full blast, mentally rehearsing that awkward conversation with our boss for the 47th time. Or standing in the shower, replaying that stupid thing we said at a party *three years ago*. (Just me? No? Phew.) I call this the "stinking overthinking trap," when your mind gets caught in an endless game of mental pinball and the flippers just. won't. stop.

My personal overthinking low point? Probably that time, I spent two weeks agonizing over whether I should text "Thanks!" or "Thank you!" to my neighbor who watered my sad-looking houseplants while I was away. *Two weeks*, people. I even made a pros and cons list. (For the record, I went with "Thanks so much!"—the coward's compromise.)

Overthinking used to run my life. My brain was like that friend who texts you at midnight with "You up?" and then proceeds to analyze every interaction they had that day. Except it was *my own brain* doing this *to me*. The mental gymnastics were exhausting—I'd second-guess every decision, from "Should I change careers?" down to "Is this the right brand of toilet paper?"

The impact was real. Sleep? Ha! Good luck with that when your mind is staging Olympic-level worry competitions at 3 a.m. Focus? About as effective as trying to read a book while someone blasts an air horn in your ear. And don't get me started on my poor husband, who once had to sit through my 45-minute analysis of whether our waitress was subtly insulting my drink order. (Spoiler: She wasn't. She literally did not care about my mojito.)

If you're sitting there nodding so hard you're risking whiplash, you're not alone. We're living in the golden age of overthinking. Our phones ping with new things to worry about every 2.7 seconds. The news cycle makes sure we're constantly updated on fresh disasters to obsess over. And social media is basically an all-you-can-eat buffet for comparison anxiety.

I finally hit my breaking point after a particularly spectacular overthinking spiral about—I kid you not—whether my email sign-off sounded "too aggressive." (It was "Best regards." The horror!) I realized I was spending more time in my head analyzing life than actually, you know, *living* it.

So, I made changes. Not overnight, and definitely not perfectly. There were setbacks like that time I tried meditation and spent the entire 20 minutes mentally redecorating my living room and planning my grocery list. But gradually, I found what worked. The mental noise quieted down. I started sleeping better. I could watch a movie without pausing it six times to worry about whether I'd left the garage door open.

This book isn't some magical cure-all written by a perfectly enlightened guru who has transcended all human worries. Hell no. I still overthink sometimes! Just last week, I spent an hour wondering if my neighbor thinks I'm weird because I awkwardly waved at her with a mouth full of bagel. But these episodes are now the exception, not the rule of my life.

I want to share what's worked for me and for clients in my coaching practice—real, practical stuff based on science that actually helps in the real world. We'll cover:

- The different flavors of overthinking—from replaying embarrassing moments on mental repeat to creating disaster scenarios about things that haven't even happened (and probably never will). I call this last one "disaster porn," and it's my personal specialty!

- The anxiety-overthinking loop from hell. It's like a toxic relationship between two terrible roommates in your brain, each making the other worse.

- Why overthinking can be as addictive as scrolling through social media at 1 a.m. when you have an important meeting the next day. Your brain gets hooked on the "solving" sensation even when there's nothing to solve.

- How our poor, overtaxed brains are drowning in information overflow. No wonder we're all walking around like mental zombies half the time!

- Simple mindfulness practices that don't require you to become a monk or sit cross-legged for hours. (Though if that's your thing, rock on!)

- How to call BS on your own thoughts. This was HUGE for me—learning to say, "Thanks for sharing, brain, but that's actually ridiculous" when my mind tried to convince me everyone at the party was judging my laugh.

- Real talk about sleep, food, and exercise—because it's hard to have a chill mind when your body is running on energy drinks and panic.

- Practical strategies for when you feel yourself sliding back into overthink mode. Like that time I created a "worry appointment" for myself—scheduled worry time so my anxiety knew it would get its turn and could shut up until then. (Sounds crazy, worked amazingly well!)

I'll share plenty of my own embarrassing stories throughout—like when I almost canceled a trip to Italy because I convinced myself the Airbnb host secretly hated me based on their use of a period instead of an exclamation point. Or the time I rehearsed asking for a raise so many times that when the actual meeting came, I started with "As I've been practicing saying..." Smooth.

Look, I'm not some fancy expert with a wall of degrees. I'm just someone who got sick of living in my own head and found ways to break free. No big words, no complicated theories—just stuff that works in real life when you're freaking out about whether that text message your friend sent seemed "kind of short."

If you're exhausted from mental spin cycles, if you've ever found yourself googling "how to know if you're overthinking about overthinking," or if you just want to enjoy a movie without pausing it to analyze the subtle subtext of the main character's coffee order, this book is for you.

The version of you that isn't mentally exhausted all the time still exists. The you that can make a decision without creating seventeen contingency plans is in there somewhere. Let's go find that person together!

So, grab a drink (maybe not a mojito if you're like me and still slightly traumatized), get comfortable, and let's talk about how to tell your overactive brain to chill the hell out. Your future, well-rested, less-stressed self is going to be so grateful.

Turn the page. Your mind deserves a break!

Part 1:

Understanding Overthinking

Chapter 1:

What Is Overthinking?

Overthinking is when your thoughts get stuck on an endless hamster wheel, spinning round and round without getting anywhere useful. It's like having a hyperactive detective in your brain who refuses to close any case, ever. That work email you sent? Better analyze the tone for the seventeenth time! That weird look your friend gave you? Time to launch a full investigation into whether they secretly hate you!

Define Overthinking

So, what exactly is this mind monster I call overthinking? Let me paint you a picture.

It's Tuesday night, 2:17 a.m. You're wide awake, staring at the ceiling, mentally replaying that comment you made during the team meeting. "I should have phrased it differently," you think. "Everyone probably thought I was an idiot." Your brain helpfully supplies fourteen alternative versions of what you could have said instead. None of this will change what happened, but your mind doesn't care—it's committed to this late-night feature film of regret.

That, my friend, is overthinking in its natural habitat.

Overthinking comes in several delicious flavors, each with its own special way of making you miserable:

- **Rumination**: This is when your brain gets stuck replaying past events like a movie critic who watched the same bad film fifty times. My personal rumination record? Two weeks obsessing over calling my boss by the wrong name. (For the record, she didn't care and had forgotten by lunchtime.)

- **Excessive planning**: This is overthinking disguised as productivity. It's when you create seventeen contingency plans for a simple dinner party, including detailed scenarios for what you'll do if someone spills wine, brings an unexpected guest, or aliens invade during dessert.

- **Self-criticism**: This charming form of overthinking is when your inner voice turns into that mean girl from high school. Everything becomes evidence of your flaws. Forgot to buy milk? Obviously, you're a failure at basic adulting. Someone didn't text back immediately? Clearly, you're fundamentally unlikable.

- **Analysis paralysis**: When you've gathered so much information and considered so many angles that you've completely short-circuited your decision-making ability. This is how I ended up with 47 open browser tabs researching vacuum cleaners for six months while continuing to use a broken one that made sounds like a dying whale.

These forms often overlap and feed each other in what I call the "Mental Merry-Go-Round From Hell."

You start by ruminating about a mistake, which triggers self-criticism, which leads to excessive planning to "never let that happen again," which causes analysis paralysis because now you're overwhelmed, which gives you something new to ruminate about... and round we go!

The effects of this mental circus extend far beyond just feeling anxious.

Overthinking seeps into every corner of your life:

- **Personal effects**: The most immediate casualty is your peace of mind. Your brain never fully relaxes because it's always chewing on something. Sleep becomes elusive as your mind decides 3 a.m. is the perfect time to replay every embarrassing moment from your life. Your self-confidence takes a beating too—it's hard to feel self-assured when your brain is constantly second-guessing everything you do.

- **Career impact**: Overthinking can absolutely tank your professional life. Decisions take forever because you're considering every possible outcome (including ones that have a 0.0001% chance of happening). Emails sit in your drafts folder for days because you're rewriting them to eliminate any possible misinterpretation. Creative thinking suffers because your brain is too busy with unnecessary analysis to make new connections.

- **Effects on others**: Here's the part we often don't recognize—overthinking doesn't just torture us; it affects everyone around us. Your partner gets dragged into hour-long discussions about whether your friend's tone of voice meant she's secretly mad at you. Your kids learn that making decisions is a long, stressful process, rather than something that is sometimes simple and intuitive. Friends start introducing topics with "Don't overthink this, but..."

The good news? Recognizing these patterns is the first step to breaking free from them. And unlike some self-help books that make you feel like you need a personality transplant, the strategies we'll explore are designed for real humans with real, messy brains.

Psychological and Physiological Effects

I convinced myself I had a brain tumor because I had a headache for two days straight. I googled symptoms at 3 a.m. (rookie mistake), diagnosed myself with approximately seventeen fatal conditions, and drafted a mental will dividing my precious collection of mismatched coffee mugs among my loved ones. I even practiced my "brave face" in the mirror for when I'd break the news to my family.

The actual diagnosis when I finally dragged myself to the doctor? Dehydration and tension from—wait for it—stress and overthinking. The irony wasn't lost on me: I'd literally worried myself sick about being sick.

The Mental Mess

Overthinking creates a psychological tornado that tears through your emotional landscape:

- **Stress and anxiety**: These are overthinking's BFFs. Your body can't tell the difference between imagining a disaster and actually experiencing one. So, when you spend hours picturing worst-case scenarios, your body helpfully floods with stress hormones as if those scenarios were really happening.

- **Depression**: Overthinking and depression feed each other like two terrible roommates sharing bad habits. Ruminating on negative thoughts creates the perfect breeding ground for depression, which then gives you even more negative stuff to overthink.

- **Agitation and erratic behavior**: Ever snapped at someone because you were stuck in your head about something completely unrelated? *Raises hand sheepishly.* Overthinking puts your nervous system on high alert, making you jumpy, irritable, and about as pleasant to be around as a caffeinated raccoon.

- **Tanking self-esteem**: Overthinking is like having a full-time critic living in your head, pointing out every flaw and mistake with gleeful enthusiasm. After a while, you start believing the nasty reviews.

- **Decision paralysis**: When you overthink, even tiny choices become overwhelming. The mental cost-benefit analysis never ends, and you're left frozen like a deer in headlights.

The Body Battleground

While all this mental chaos is happening, your body is taking a beating too:

- **Brain changes**: Chronic overthinking actually rewires your brain, strengthening neural pathways that focus on threats and problems. It's like building a superhighway for negative thoughts while the positive thinking roads become overgrown with weeds.

- **Sleep disruption**: Ever tried to sleep while your brain is hosting the Overthinking Olympics? It's like trying to nap in the middle of a rock concert. Sleep disruption then leads to even more overthinking because your tired brain can't regulate emotions properly.

- **Immune system impacts**: Your immune system takes a serious hit when you're constantly overthinking. Those stress hormones I mentioned earlier? They suppress immune function when they stick around too long.

- **Digestion disasters**: The brain-gut connection is real. When your mind is in overdrive, your digestive system often goes haywire. Stomachaches, nausea, appetite changes—it's like your gut is staging a protest against your overthinking.

- **Muscle tension and pain**: All that mental stress gets stored in your body, creating tension that leads to headaches, back pain, and general achiness. My shoulders used to live somewhere up around my ears from holding so much tension. My massage therapist once asked if I was training to become a professional statue.

- **Heart health hazards**: The constant activation of your stress response isn't great for your heart. Increased blood pressure, elevated heart rate—it's like putting your cardiovascular system on a roller coaster it never asked to ride.

These effects aren't permanent. Your brain and body are remarkably resilient and can bounce back when you start breaking the overthinking cycle. I'm living proof—my blood pressure normalized, my sleep improved, and my immune system strengthened once I got my overthinking under control.

Common Myths about Overthinking

The other day, I saw this meme of a woman staring into space with the caption, "Me overthinking whether I locked the door even though I checked three times." Everyone in the comments was like, "OMG, so me!" and "I'm in this photo, and I don't like it!" Here's the thing, though—that's not overthinking. That's just having a normal brain fart.

Actual overthinking would be, "I think I locked the door, but what if I didn't? A burglar could break in. All our stuff would be stolen. We'd lose irreplaceable photos. Insurance might not cover everything. We'd have to move because I'd never feel safe again. My partner would resent me forever for ruining our lives with one careless mistake. This is proof I can't handle basic adult responsibilities..." And on and on until you're mentally rehearsing your divorce proceedings over a door you probably locked anyway.

See the difference?

Let's bust some common myths about overthinking that might be keeping you stuck in that mental hamster wheel:

Myth #1: Overthinking is just being forgetful or absentminded. Nope! Those moments when you can't remember where you put your phone (while talking on it) or walk into a room and forget why you're there are just normal brain glitches we all experience. They're usually caused by your attention being divided, not by overthinking. True overthinking is an active process of excessive, often repetitive thought that goes far beyond momentary confusion.

Myth #2: Overthinking is the same as careful planning. Oh, how I wish this were true! I've often justified my overthinking spirals as "just being thorough." But there's a massive difference between thoughtful preparation and overthinking.

Careful planning means considering relevant factors and making decisions based on the information available. Overthinking means getting stuck in analysis paralysis, considering increasingly unlikely scenarios, and never reaching a conclusion.

Myth #3: Smart people overthink more. This myth is particularly dangerous because it makes overthinking feel like a badge of honor. "I overthink because my brain is just so powerful and complex!"

While intelligence and overthinking can coexist, they're not the same thing. Some brilliant people make decisions quickly and confidently, while some average thinkers can get trapped in overthinking cycles.

Overthinking isn't using your intelligence—it's misusing it. It's like having a Ferrari but only driving it in tight circles in a parking lot. All that horsepower, going nowhere.

Myth #4: Overthinking helps prevent problems. This was my personal favorite myth for years. "If I think through every possible scenario, nothing can go wrong!"

The painful truth I had to accept? Overthinking often creates more problems than it solves. It increases anxiety, clouds judgment, and wastes mental energy on unlikely outcomes while potentially missing obvious solutions.

Myth #5: Overthinking and worrying are the same thing. While these two troublemakers often hang out together, they're not identical. Worrying is focused on specific concerns about the future, while overthinking can involve the past, present, or future and often includes excessive analysis rather than just anxiety.

All squares are rectangles, but not all rectangles are squares. Similarly, all worrying involves some overthinking, but not all overthinking is worry. When I spent three days analyzing exactly how my voice sounded during a presentation

I'd already given, that wasn't worry—it was pure, unproductive overthinking about something I couldn't change.

Myth #6: You can think your way out of overthinking. This is like trying to put out a fire by throwing more fire on it. You can't use the same overthinking patterns to solve your overthinking problem. That's just... more overthinking!

Trust me, I've tried. I once read a book about overthinking and then spent two weeks overthinking whether I was implementing the strategies correctly. The irony was completely lost on me at the time.

The truth is, breaking free from overthinking often requires stepping outside your usual thought patterns—something we'll explore in the coming chapters.

Chapter 2:

Why We Overthink

So there I was, standing in my kitchen at midnight, staring into my open refrigerator for the fourth time in an hour. I wasn't hungry. I wasn't even looking for anything specific.

I was just trying to distract myself from the endless loop playing in my head about whether I'd offended my friend earlier that day with an offhand comment about her new haircut.

"Did she seem quiet afterward? Was her laugh a little forced? Should I text her to apologize? But what if she didn't notice anything, and my text makes it weird? Maybe I should wait until tomorrow. But then what if she's been upset all night?"

As I finally closed the fridge door (sorry, electric bill), I had to ask myself, "Why do I *do* this to myself?"

The Perfect Storm: How Anxiety, Perfectionism, and Fear Keep the Overthinking Engine Running

I once spent three hours drafting a two-sentence email to decline a dinner invitation. THREE HOURS. I wrote version after version, analyzing each word choice, second-guessing the tone, and imagining how the recipient might interpret every possible variation.

"Sorry, I can't make it Friday" (too blunt?). "Unfortunately, I'm unable to attend" (too formal?). "I'd love to, but I'm already committed elsewhere" (but what if they ask where?).

By hour three, I was so mentally exhausted that I nearly canceled all my plans for the month just to avoid sending the damn email.

This is what happens when anxiety, perfectionism, and fear of failure throw a party in your brain.

Anxiety: The Overeager Security Guard

Anxiety is like having an overzealous security guard patrolling your mind. This guard means well—they're trying to protect you from threats—but they see danger *everywhere*.

"What's that? Someone didn't immediately respond to your text? Emergency! They must hate you now! Analyze every interaction you've had with them for the past year to figure out what you did wrong!"

The problem is that anxiety doesn't just warn you about legitimate threats; it treats everything as potentially dangerous. A slightly awkward conversation becomes a social catastrophe. A minor mistake at work becomes career suicide. That weird pain in your side? Definitely a rare tropical disease you read about once (never mind that you've never left your time zone).

When anxiety is running the show, your thoughts become a search party looking for problems—even when there aren't any to find. And because anxiety is never satisfied with simple answers, the search never ends. That's why you can spend hours trying to "solve" a problem that doesn't actually exist.

Perfectionism: The Impossible Dream

Ah, perfectionism. It sounds so positive, doesn't it? Who doesn't want to do things perfectly?

But perfectionism isn't about doing your best—it's about setting standards so impossibly high that you're guaranteed to fall short. It's like trying to drive to the moon in your Honda Civic. You're not going to make it, pal, no matter how determined you are.

Perfectionism fuels overthinking because it keeps moving the goalposts. Just when you think you've figured something out or made a decision, your inner perfectionist chimes in: "But is it the *best* decision? Is there a *better* way? Have you considered *every* possible angle?"

And so the mental hamster wheel keeps spinning. You keep searching for the perfect solution, the perfect response, the perfect plan—not realizing that "perfect" doesn't exist in the messy reality of human life.

Fear of Failure: The Dream Crusher

Fear of failure is the voice that whispers, "What if you mess this up? What if everyone sees you're not as competent as they thought? What if this is the mistake that finally exposes you as a fraud?"

This fear keeps you stuck in overthinking loops because it makes the stakes feel impossibly high for even minor decisions. When you're terrified of making the wrong choice, you'll analyze options until your brain turns to mush rather than risk being wrong.

Fear of the Unknown: The Uncertainty Allergy

Humans hate uncertainty. We'd rather know something bad is definitely going to happen than not know what's coming at all. This is why people will stay in unhappy situations rather than risk change—at least the current misery is familiar! When faced with uncertainty, your brain tries to create certainty through overthinking. If you can just think about all possible outcomes, maybe you can prepare for anything! (Spoiler alert: You can't.)

This is why you might lie awake the night before a job interview, mentally rehearsing answers to questions that will never be asked. Or why you might obsess over whether your new relationship will work out, creating elaborate scenarios of potential problems before you've even had your third date.

The Shadows That Follow Us: How Our Past Shapes Our Overthinking

Remember that time as a kid when someone laughed at your drawing, and now, twenty years later, you still feel that twist in your stomach when sharing your creative work? Or how about when your dad's constant criticism left you second-guessing every decision? These aren't just memories—they're active forces shaping how your brain processes information today.

Our minds don't develop in a vacuum. By the time we're adults, we've been molded by countless experiences, some so subtle we barely noticed them happening. Yet these experiences create the mental pathways we use every single day.

When Yesterday Crowds Out Today

Jake grew up with a mom who constantly worried about money. "Don't touch that, we can't afford to replace it!" was her daily refrain. Now, at 35, despite his comfortable salary, Jake agonizes over every purchase, running through worst-case scenarios for hours before buying even necessities.

His childhood programming runs deep, whispering, *Danger lurks in every financial decision.*

This is how the past hijacks the present. Those early lessons weren't just heard—they were absorbed into the very structure of Jake's thinking patterns.

Trauma Doesn't Just Go Away

"Just get over it" might be the least helpful advice ever given. Trauma isn't something we simply walk away from. Whether it's a single devastating event or years of subtle undermining, trauma rewires our brains.

Sarah survived a car accident at sixteen. Fifteen years later, she still maps out alternative routes to avoid the intersection where it happened. More significantly, she overthinks every travel plan, imagining disaster scenarios that keep her awake at night. Her brain is doing exactly what it was designed to do: Protect her from experiencing that pain again, even if the protection itself causes suffering.

The Cultural Blueprint

We don't just inherit genes from our families—we inherit ways of seeing the world. If you grew up in a household or culture where expressing emotions was considered weak, you might now overthink every feeling, analyzing whether it's "appropriate" to feel hurt, angry, or sad rather than simply experiencing the emotion.

Cultural influences extend beyond family, too. Growing up in a community that valued academic achievement above all else might leave you overthinking every professional choice through the narrow lens of status and credentials, missing opportunities that could bring genuine fulfillment.

Breaking Free Without Denying Your Story

Here's the tricky part: acknowledging these influences doesn't mean blaming your past for everything or feeling helpless about changing. It means understanding the source code that's running your mental programs.

Next time you catch yourself in an overthinking spiral, try asking, "Whose voice is this really? Mine today, or something echoing from my past?"

Sometimes, simply recognizing "This fear isn't about my current reality—it's my eight-year-old self's reaction" creates enough distance to loosen overthinking's grip.

Brain Traffic Jams: When Your Thoughts Can't Find the Exit

Have you ever driven through a roundabout several times because you missed your exit? Your thoughts do the exact same thing when you're overthinking.

Your Brain's Superhighways and Dirt Roads

Picture your brain as a big landscape crossed with countless roads. Some are eight-lane superhighways you've traveled a million times—like your route to work or your morning routine. Others are barely visible dirt paths you rarely use— like trying to remember high school calculus.

When you think a thought repeatedly, something remarkable happens: Your brain physically changes. The neural pathways—those roads your thoughts travel on—actually get wider and more efficient. It's like upgrading from a bumpy dirt road to a smooth highway.

This explains why it is so difficult to break free from overthinking. You've paved premium highways for your worry thoughts!

The Physical Reality of Mental Loops

"But it's just thinking," I hear you say. "How can thoughts physically change anything?"

The truth is, your thoughts aren't just abstract concepts floating in some mysterious mind-space. They're actual electrical signals traveling along physical cells called neurons. These neurons connect to each other through junctions called synapses (think of them as the intersections in our road analogy).

When you repeatedly worry about that embarrassing thing you said at last week's meeting, you're sending electrical traffic down the same neural route over and over. Your helpful brain, trying to be efficient, responds by strengthening that route.

This strengthening involves physical changes:

- Neurons grow more branches to connect with others.

- Synapses become more efficient at transmitting signals.

- Supporting cells multiply to maintain these busy highways.

- In scientific language, we call this "neuroplasticity," but I prefer "mental road construction."

Stuck in the Loop: The Brain's Default Mode

Ever notice how your mind wanders to the same worries during quiet moments? That's your brain's default mode network (DMN) at work. I just call it your "worry wanderer." This network activates when you're not focused on anything specific.

For overthinkers, the DMN often defaults to well-traveled worry highways. It's like your mental GPS is broken and keeps rerouting you through "Anxiety Avenue and Rumination Road."

Breaking the Loop: Creating New Roads

Here's the good news: You can build new mental highways. Better yet, those old worry roads will actually start to fade when unused, like paths in the woods growing over with weeds.

When you consciously direct your thoughts differently, you're literally carving new physical paths through your brain tissue. At first, it feels bumpy and requires effort—like driving on a rough trail instead of the familiar highway. But with repetition, these new constructive thought patterns become your brain's preferred routes.

The Science of Changing Your Mind

Let me share a little secret from neuroscience that changed my life: Neurons that fire together, wire together. This means whatever you practice strengthens in your brain.

Practice worrying? You get better at worrying. Practice calm responses. You get better at responding calmly.

It's that simple—and that difficult.

Your Brain's Incredible Power to Change

The most amazing thing about your brain is not its tendency to get stuck; it's its remarkable ability to unstick itself when given the right tools.

Every time you interrupt an overthinking loop, you're physically weakening that neural pathway. Every time you choose a different response, you're building a new, healthier route.

Your brain is always changing. The question is, are you directing that change, or are you overthinking on autopilot? Those thought loops aren't just habits; they're actual physical structures in your brain. And anything physical can be changed with the right approach and a bit of persistence.

Mind Traffic Jam: How Modern Life Overwhelms Your Mental Highway

Remember when you had to wait for the evening news to find out what happened in the world? When work emails couldn't reach you at the dinner table? When "following" someone meant physically walking behind them rather than getting updates about their breakfast choices?

Those days are gone, my friend. And while I'm not suggesting we return to carrier pigeons and typewriters, our brains are paying a steep price for our always-connected modern existence.

Your Poor Brain: Designed for Lions, Dealing With Notifications

Our brains evolved during simpler times when the main concerns were "Is that a lion?" and "Where can I find food?" Today, that same ancient hardware is processing an estimated 34GB of information daily, equivalent to about 174 newspapers' worth of content. Every. Single. Day.

No wonder you're overthinking! Your mental processing center is working overtime without hazard pay.

The Bottomless Scroll: Social Media's Mind Trap

Each time you scroll through social media, your brain gets tiny hits of dopamine—the feel-good chemical that keeps you coming back for more.

But along with those little pleasure zaps comes a barrage of information your brain feels compelled to process:

- Your cousin's political rants.

- Your colleague's perfect vacation photos (that make your last staycation look like solitary confinement).

- Breaking news alerts about disasters halfway around the world.

- Targeted ads reminding you of products you don't need but suddenly want.

- And all this happens while a little voice whispers, "Everyone else has their life together. Why don't you?"

That's why heavy social media users experience more rumination and overthinking. Your brain never gets the signal that it's caught up on processing all the input.

The Work-Life Blur: When Your Brain Can't Clock Out

Remember offices? Those buildings we used to leave at the end of the workday? Now our homes have become our offices, our phones keep us tethered to work 24-7, and the average employee checks work emails 74 times a day (Evans, 2014). Yes, you read that correctly—74 times!

When your brain can't distinguish between work time and rest time, it remains in problem-solving mode constantly. That spreadsheet issue follows you to the dinner table. That client email haunts your shower thoughts. Your brain never fully disengages from work puzzles, creating perfect conditions for overthinking.

News Cycle Nausea: When Information Becomes Toxic

In the past, news cycles moved at human speed. Today, they operate at algorithm speed.

The constant stream of (mostly negative) news triggers our threat-detection systems repeatedly. Your brain, being the helpful worrier it is, thinks, "Danger! I must keep thinking about this problem until it's solved!"

But here's the kicker: Most news stories highlight problems you personally cannot solve. So, your brain keeps spinning its wheels, analyzing threats it can't address, creating the perfect overthinking storm.

Digital Amnesia: When Google Becomes Your Memory

Why remember anything when you can Google it? While convenient, our outsourced memory has consequences.

Knowing information is readily available online makes us less likely to commit it to memory.

The downside? Your brain gets less practice at information processing and retrieval, making it more likely to get stuck in overthinking loops when faced with problems.

Understanding how modern life overwhelms your brain is the first step toward relief. Your overthinking isn't a personal failure; it's a natural response to an unnatural information environment.

Chapter 3:

The Consequences of Overthinking

You've probably heard that classic joke about the overthinking mind: "My brain has too many tabs open, and I don't know which one is playing music." We laugh because it's true, but what happens when those tabs never close? When does the mental music ever stop?

The Emotional Hangover: When Your Mind Drinks Too Much Worry

Remember the last time you woke up after too many glasses of wine? That foggy head, the sensitivity to everything, the general feeling that the world is a bit too much today? Welcome to the emotional hangover of overthinking—except this one doesn't clear up after a greasy breakfast and two aspirin.

The Anxiety Spiral

Overthinking and anxiety are like toxic best friends who bring out the worst in each other. Your overthinking mind says, "Hey, let's consider every possible thing that could go wrong!" Then anxiety chimes in: "Great idea! And let's feel all of those disasters happening right now!"

Before you know it, you're sitting perfectly safe in your living room while experiencing the emotional equivalent of falling from an airplane without a parachute.

What's actually happening is that your body can't tell the difference between real threats and imagined ones. Each worry thought triggers the same stress response as if you were facing actual danger. No wonder you feel exhausted, you're emotionally running from tigers all day long while physically sitting at your desk.

The Confidence Thief

Nothing steals self-esteem quite like overthinking. It's like having a hypercritical roommate who follows you everywhere:

- "Should you really wear that?"

- "Remember that slightly awkward thing you said three years ago? Everyone else does."

- "They're probably just being nice to you because they pity you."

This constant self-questioning erodes your confidence until making even small decisions feels overwhelming. I once spent forty-five minutes deciding whether to order the chicken or fish at a restaurant. By the time I ordered, I wasn't even hungry anymore. The waiter probably thought I was writing a doctoral thesis on menu options.

The Short Fuse Phenomenon

Ever notice how the more you overthink, the shorter your temper gets? There's a reason for that. Overthinking burns through your mental resources like a teenager burns through data when the Wi-Fi goes down.

When your mental energy is depleted from hours of circular thinking, you have less capacity to handle normal frustrations. The person who cuts you off in traffic isn't just inconsiderate; they become the physical manifestation of everything wrong with humanity.

Your partner leaving dishes in the sink isn't a minor annoyance; it's clear evidence that they don't value your feelings or respect your home. At least, that's how it feels when your emotional reserves are drained from overthinking.

The Desperation Decision-Making

Perhaps most dangerous is how overthinking can lead to poor choices made from a place of desperation. When you've analyzed a problem from every possible angle, your mind craves resolution—any resolution.

This explains why overthinkers sometimes make impulsive decisions that seem completely out of character. After weeks of deliberating whether to stay in a job, you might suddenly quit without any backup plan. After months of analyzing relationship problems, you might make a major relationship decision based on a minor disagreement.

It's like being lost in a maze for hours and then deciding to just smash through the nearest wall. At least it's doing something.

The Prison of Your Own Making

The cruelest irony? Overthinking convinces you that more thinking is the solution, trapping you in an endless loop. You feel stuck inside your own head, watching life happen from behind glass while you try to figure it all out first.

The good news? This prison has a door, and you already have the key. In the coming chapters, we'll explore practical ways to step out of the overthinking trap and back into your life, not because you've solved all your problems, but because you've learned how to carry them differently. Your thoughts may feel like facts, but they're really just mental weather—constantly changing, sometimes stormy, but always passing through if you don't try to hold on to them.

When Your Body Pays the Bill: The Physical Cost of Mental Loops

Ever noticed how your shoulders creep up toward your ears during a particularly intense overthinking session? Or how does your jaw feel like you've been secretly moonlighting as a nutcracker? Your body keeps the score of your thought patterns, and unfortunately, it doesn't offer forgiveness for mental overdrafts.

The Stress Response That Never Clocks Out

Your body's stress response was designed for short bursts of action, like running from a predator or fighting off a threat. It was never meant to stay activated for the eight consecutive hours you spend worrying about that comment your boss made last Tuesday.

When overthinking keeps your stress response permanently switched on, your body pumps out cortisol and adrenaline like they're going out of style. These hormones are great for helping you escape a burning building, not so great when they're flooding your system while you're just sitting at your desk replaying conversations in your head.

The Exhaustion That Sleep Can't Fix

"But I got eight hours of sleep last night!" you protest to your reflection as dark circles stubbornly remain under your eyes. The problem? Overthinking creates a quality of sleep that's about as restful as napping on a roller coaster. Your body might be in bed, but your mind is running the Boston Marathon.

You fall asleep rehearsing tomorrow's presentation, wake up at 3 a.m. wondering if you offended someone five years ago, and then spend the pre-alarm hour mentally redecorating your living room.

No wonder you're tired. Your brain hasn't had a break since 2017.

From Headaches to Heart Disease: The Longer-Term Fallout

Those tension headaches that have become your faithful afternoon companions? They're the tip of the iceberg. Chronic overthinking contributes to serious health issues that take years to develop but minutes to diagnose:

- **Heart disease**: Turns out, your heart doesn't appreciate being kept on high alert 24-7.

- **High blood pressure**: Your blood vessels can only take so much stress-induced constriction.

- **Diabetes**: Stress hormones mess with blood sugar regulation like a toddler messes with your organized drawers.

- **Compromised immune function**: Your body's defense system gets too tired fighting imaginary tigers to deal with actual viruses.

I'm not sharing this to scare you—well, maybe a little healthy fear is good—but to connect dots you might not have connected yourself. That chronic health issue you've been trying to solve with diet changes and medication?

Your overthinking habit might be the silent saboteur.

The Cognitive Catch

Here's a cruel irony: Overthinking actually makes you worse at thinking. It's like revving your car engine in park until you run out of gas.

When your brain is overwhelmed by circular thoughts, your working memory suffers, your attention scatters, and your decision-making abilities would make a Magic 8-Ball look reliable. "Ask again later" becomes your default response to even the simplest questions.

The Lifestyle Spiral

Then there's the domino effect on your daily habits. When you're mentally exhausted from overthinking:

- **Exercise feels impossible:** Who has the energy to run when they've been mentally running all day?.

- **Healthy eating requires too many decisions:** Frozen pizza requires zero thought, which feels like blessed relief.

- **Screen time increases**: Scrolling doesn't require mental energy from your already depleted reserves.

Before you know it, you've gained fifteen pounds, your muscles have forgotten what movement feels like, and your relationship with your couch has become more committed than most marriages.

Breaking the Body-Mind Feedback Loop

The good news? This physical toll isn't a one-way street. Just as your thoughts affect your body, your body can influence your thoughts. Sometimes the fastest way to break an overthinking spiral is through physical intervention—a brisk walk, deep breathing, or even just standing up and stretching. We'll explore these bodily escape hatches from overthinking in later chapters.

For now, simply noticing how your body responds to your thought patterns can be illuminating. That tension headache might actually be your body's way of waving a red flag: "Hello? Overthinking alert! Anyone listening down there?"

Love and Overthink: When Your Head Gets in the Way of Your Heart

Remember that time you sent a text message and got a simple "ok" in response? If you're an overthinker, that two-letter word probably launched a feature-length movie in your mind starring you as the villain who somehow ruined everything. Meanwhile, the sender was probably just busy or driving.

The Romantic Relationship Tax

In romantic relationships, overthinking acts like an unwelcome third wheel—one that shows up uninvited and hogs all the attention.

Take Sofia and Mikelson. When Mikelson said he needed space after an argument, Sofia's overthinking transformed "I need thirty minutes to cool down" into "He's planning his escape, probably consulting divorce lawyers, and I'll die alone with seventeen cats."

By the time Mikelson returned, ready to talk calmly, Sofia had already rehearsed twenty different breakup scenarios and was emotionally exhausted. Overthinkers often create problems that don't exist, then solve those imaginary problems with real emotions. The result? Partners who feel they can't win: "If I say something, it gets overthought. If I say nothing, my silence gets overthought."

The cruel paradox is that while overthinking stems from caring deeply, it can make you seem emotionally unavailable. Your body is present, but your mind is busy analyzing the relationship rather than experiencing it.

Parent-Child Complications

If you're a parent who overthinks, you might find yourself stuck in planning mode instead of playing mode. Your child asks to go to the park, and while you're calculating sun exposure risks and evaluating the likelihood of playground injuries, childhood is happening without you.

Or perhaps you're the adult child of an overthinker. You call with exciting news, only to have your parent immediately jump to all the potential downsides of your opportunity. Their anxiety masquerades as concern, but it lands as a lack of faith in your abilities.

I once spent so long researching the "perfect" birthday gift for my nephew that I missed the ordering deadline entirely. Nothing says "happy birthday" like a belated present and an aunt who can tell you the pros and cons of every toy on the market!

Friendship Friction

Friendships should be our safe harbors, but overthinking can turn them into anxiety-producing territories. Consider these common scenarios:

- You analyze a friend's tone in a group chat until you're convinced they're mad at you, leading to awkward interactions based on a problem that doesn't exist.

- You decline invitations because you're overthinking what to wear, what to say, or how you'll be perceived.

- You hesitate to reach out because "they probably don't want to hear from me," creating actual distance from imagined rejection.

Before you know it, friendship becomes another source of stress rather than support.

Extended Family Dynamics

Extended family relationships—with their historical baggage and intermittent contact—create perfect overthinking conditions. After the annual holiday gathering, you might spend weeks dissecting Aunt Martha's comment about your career choice or Uncle Bob's question about your love life.

These overthinking spirals are particularly frustrating because you might only see these family members once or twice a year, yet they can occupy mental real estate for months.

Breaking the Cycle

The common thread across all these relationships? Overthinking keeps you in your head when connection requires presence. While you're busy analyzing the relationship, you're missing opportunities to actually experience it.

Small changes can make big differences:

- Ask for clarification instead of assuming meaning.

- Share your overthinking tendencies with loved ones so they understand your process.

- Set a time limit on how long you'll mull over interactions.

Remember: most people don't analyze your words and actions with the intensity you apply to theirs. That "ok" text probably just means "ok"—nothing more, nothing less.

The Career Quicksand: When Overthinking Sinks Your Professional Life

Remember the last time you spent forty-five minutes crafting a two-sentence email? Or when you had three different browser tabs open researching the "perfect" approach to a simple task that should have taken fifteen minutes? Welcome to the professional consequences of overthinking—where careers move at the speed of second-guessing.

The Paradox of Paralysis

Here's the great irony of overthinking at work: It masquerades as thoroughness while actually tanking your productivity. You think you're being diligent by considering every angle of that proposal, but meanwhile, your colleague, who thinks at a normal human speed, has already submitted their work, gotten feedback, made improvements, and is now happily scrolling through vacation rentals while you're still perfecting paragraph three.

I once spent so long deliberating over the font for a presentation that I missed the actual deadline for submitting the content. True story. My boss was not impressed with my extensive knowledge of serif versus sans-serif typography.

The "I Don't Wanna" Syndrome

Overthinking creates a particularly nasty form of procrastination—one where you're mentally exhausted before you even begin. When every task feels like it requires Olympic-level mental gymnastics, suddenly organizing your sock drawer seems like a compelling alternative to starting that report.

This "I don't want to" syndrome isn't laziness; it's your brain's reasonable rebellion against the unnecessarily complicated approach you've taken to work. It's like your mind is saying, "If we're going to make this simple task into a doctoral dissertation, I'd rather check out entirely."

Decision Fatigue: The Silent Career Killer

Every decision you make drains a little mental energy. Overthinkers burn through their daily decision allowance before lunch, leaving them in a state of mental fog precisely when critical thinking is most needed.

By 3 p.m., simple questions like "Should I respond to this email now or later?" feel as complicated as solving advanced calculus. This decision fatigue leads to one of two problematic outcomes: either avoiding decisions entirely (creating bottlenecks) or making hasty, poor choices just to be done with the matter (creating mistakes).

Neither impresses your boss.

The Burnout Expressway

While your coworkers take the normal road to their career destinations, overthinking puts you on an express lane to burnout. Every project becomes an endurance test, every email an exercise in anxiety, and every meeting a potential minefield of saying the wrong thing. No wonder you're exhausted by Wednesday afternoon. You're not just doing your job; you're doing your job plus running a continuous mental simulation of everything that could possibly go wrong.

The Real-World Consequences

Overthinking at work isn't just annoying; it can derail your career in tangible ways:

- **Missed deadlines:** Because perfect is the enemy of done.

- **Strained work relationships:** As colleagues get frustrated waiting for your input.

- **Poor performance reviews:** When your output doesn't match your capabilities.

- **Passed-over promotions:** As decisive colleagues advance while you deliberate.

- **Disciplinary actions:** When procrastination finally catches up with you.

I had a friend who was brilliant at her job but nearly got fired because her overthinking led to consistent delays in project completion. Her boss interpreted her perfectionism as a lack of commitment rather than what it really was—analysis paralysis.

Part 2:

Breaking Free from the Overthinking Trap

Chapter 4:

Awareness Is the First Step

If you've made it this far, congratulations! You've already done something many overthinkers never do—acknowledge that those endless mental loops aren't actually helping you. That's huge. Seriously. Give yourself a moment to appreciate that first step.

Now comes the part where we get personal, where we turn the spotlight from overthinking in general to overthinking in your life specifically. Don't worry; this isn't where I ask you to lie on a couch and talk about your childhood (though if that helps, go ahead and get comfortable). This is about becoming a detective in your own life, investigating the specific ways overthinking shows up for you.

Getting to Know Your Overthinking Habits

You can't fix what you don't understand. Think about it like this: If your car starts making a weird noise, you need to figure out what's causing it before you can repair it. Your overthinking works the same way.

Self-awareness is your flashlight in the dark room of your thoughts. Without it, you're just bumping into furniture and stubbing your mental "toes." When you shine that light on your thinking patterns, suddenly you can see what's actually there instead of what your anxious mind imagines.

Remember those first three chapters? Now's the time to put them to work. Grab a notebook (yes, an actual one—your phone has too many distractions), find a quiet spot, and let's play detective with your own mind.

Start by asking yourself, *How often do I actually overthink throughout the day?* Be honest—no judging yourself here. Is it five times? Twenty? Are we talking constant background noise or occasional thought spirals?

I used to overthink so much that my partner once asked if I was rehearsing for a debate while I was brushing my teeth. Turns out, I was mentally arguing with my boss about something that hadn't even happened yet. Talk about productive use of toothbrush time!

Next, track how long these thinking loops last. Five minutes? An hour? Do they follow you to bed and become uninvited guests in your dreams? Understanding the duration helps you recognize just how much of your life these thought loops are stealing.

What themes keep popping up? Work stress? Relationship worries? That embarrassing thing you said at a party in 2017? Our brains have favorite grooves they like to get stuck in—identify yours.

The gold mine of this exercise is spotting your triggers. Does checking social media send you into comparison spirals? Do certain people activate your insecurity button? Maybe Sunday evenings trigger Monday dread? Knowing your triggers is like having an early warning system.

My friend, Jamie, discovered that every time her phone rang unexpectedly, she'd spiral into catastrophic thinking. Once she recognized this trigger, she could prepare a quick mental response: "It's just a phone call, not an emergency."

This detective work isn't always comfortable. You might discover thought patterns you've been running from. That's okay. Actually, it's great because now you can see the cage you've built around yourself, and you can't escape a cage you don't know exists.

Try this: Carry a small notebook for a week. When you catch yourself overthinking, jot down the time, the topic, how long it lasted, and what might have triggered it. Don't try to stop it yet—just observe like you're watching someone else's mind. This distance alone can be revolutionary.

Self-awareness isn't about judging yourself harshly. It's about becoming curious about your mind's habits. Think of yourself as a scientist studying an interesting specimen, which happens to be your own brain.

Breaking the overthinking cycle starts with this honest look in the mirror. You can't change what you don't acknowledge. Simply noticing your patterns has already started weakening their hold on you. Awareness itself is the first crack in the overthinking prison walls.

Overthinking Bootcamp: Your Personal Toolkit for Mental Clarity

Imagine your brain is like a hyperactive puppy. It needs training, patience, and sometimes a gentle redirect. These exercises aren't about silencing your thoughts; they're about becoming the confident dog trainer of your own mind.

Journaling

Grab a notebook that makes you smile. Seriously, if cute unicorns or sleek leather binding motivate you to write, go for it. The goal? Dump your thoughts onto paper like you're cleaning out an overstuffed closet.

Try this: Every morning or evening, write for 10 minutes without stopping. No editing, no judging. Just pure, unfiltered brain vomit. You'll be surprised what patterns emerge.

I once discovered I was overthinking work presentations three weeks before they even happened. Talk about unnecessary stress!

Mindfulness

Mindfulness sounds fancy, but it's really just paying attention to the present moment. Close your eyes right now. Take a deep breath. Notice how your body feels. Hear the sounds around you. When a thought tries to hijack your attention, gently—and I mean gently—guide it back.

Pro tip: Start with five-minute sessions. Your mind will wander. That's normal. It's like trying to teach a toddler to sit still—frustrating but possible with practice.

Timed Overthinking

This might sound counterintuitive, but hear me out. Schedule specific "overthinking time." Give yourself 15 minutes a day to worry, analyze, and spiral. When the timer goes off, you're done. It's like putting your anxious thoughts in a timeout.

One of my support group members called this her "worry appointment." She'd literally put it in her calendar: 4:30 p.m. Overthinking Session. After that? Thoughts, you're dismissed!

Setting Boundaries

Boundaries aren't just for relationships; they're for your brain too. Learn to say no to conversations, situations, and even your own thoughts that drain your energy. It's okay to tell your brain, "Not now, we've got better things to do."

Opening Up

Talking about your overthinking with trusted friends or a counselor is like releasing pressure from a steam valve. You don't need to solve everything; sometimes, just speaking your fears out loud makes them shrink.

Goal-Setting

Break big worries into tiny, manageable steps. Instead of "I'm a total failure," try "I'll send one job application this week." Small wins build confidence faster than you can say "self-doubt."

These exercises aren't about perfection. Some days, you'll nail them. Other days, your brain will feel like a chaotic mess. That's completely okay. Progress isn't linear; it's more like a drunk person trying to walk a straight line.

Your Journaling Roadmap

Forget everything you know about "perfect" journaling. This isn't about writing a Pulitzer Prize-winning novel. This is about getting brutally honest with yourself—messy handwriting, random tangents, and all.

The Thought Detective Prompts

Grab a notebook that makes you happy.

1. **The worry excavation:** Write down your current top three worries. Then ask yourself:

   o   How likely is this worry to actually happen?

   o   What's the worst-case scenario?

o   What's the best-case scenario?

o   What's most likely to happen?

2. **Thought pattern safari:** Track your thoughts like you're a wildlife researcher:

o   What triggered this thought?

o   How does this thought make my body feel?

o   How long have I been carrying this thought?

o   Is this thought helpful or harmful?

3. **The emotional weather report:** Describe your emotional state like a meteorologist:

o   What's the current emotional temperature?

o   Are there any storm warnings (big emotions)?

o   What's causing this emotional climate?

Reflection Techniques That Actually Work

The 5-Minute Brain Dump

Set a timer for five minutes. Write everything that comes to mind without stopping or editing. No judgment, no filter.

It's like giving your brain a good shake and seeing what falls out.

The Conversation Replay

After a challenging interaction, write out

- what actually happened.

- what you're telling yourself happened.

- the difference between these two stories.

The Gratitude Hack

Every day, write three things you're grateful for. But here's the twist: They have to be specific. Not "I'm grateful for my family," but "I'm grateful my sister made me laugh so hard at dinner I snorted soda out of my nose."

Pro Overthinker Tips

- Some days, you'll write novels. On other days, you'll manage a single sentence. Both are victories.

- Your journal is your judgment-free zone. No one else needs to read this.

- If writing feels hard, try voice notes or typing on your phone.

- Consistency matters more than perfection.

Your brain is not your enemy. It's just trying to protect you, sometimes a bit too enthusiastically. Journaling is your way of saying, "Thanks for looking out for me, but I've got this."

Ready to start your thought treasure hunt?

Chapter 5:

Challenging the Thoughts

Remember when you were a kid and believed there was a monster under your bed? No matter how many times your parents checked, you just knew it was there, waiting for them to leave.

Then one day, you finally worked up the courage to look for yourself and found nothing but dust bunnies and a missing sock.

Your overthinking works exactly like that childhood monster. It's scary, it seems real, and it keeps you up at night. But when you shine a light on it and really look? It's mostly just dusty old fears wearing a scary mask.

Here's the thing about our brains: They're fantastic storytellers. They spin tales about who we are, what others think of us, and what we're capable of achieving. The problem? Many of these stories are complete fiction.

- "I'm not smart enough for this job."

- "Everyone at the party will think I'm awkward."

- "I always mess up important things."

- "They're only being nice because they feel sorry for me."

Sound familiar? These thoughts aren't facts; they're interpretations. Often, they're deeply flawed interpretations based on fears, past experiences, or things others have told us during vulnerable moments.

Identifying Cognitive Distortions

Your brain is like that friend who's always got some wild gossip to share. The problem is, half the time they've got their facts completely wrong.

Those irrational thoughts buzzing around your head have a fancy name in psychology circles—cognitive distortions. But let's call them what they really are: mind tricks. Your brain is playing pranks on you. The good news? Once you can spot these tricks, they lose a lot of their power.

The Most Wanted List of Mind Tricks

All-or-Nothing Thinking

This is black-and-white thinking with no gray area. Either you're a complete success or a total failure.

"I made one mistake in my presentation, so the whole thing was a disaster."

Reality check: Life happens in shades of gray. One mistake doesn't erase everything else you did well.

Fortune Telling

When you predict the future, somehow it's always terrible.

"If I ask her out, she'll definitely say no and probably laugh about it with her friends."

Reality check: Unless you've developed psychic powers (in which case, we need to talk about lottery numbers), you don't know what will happen.

Mind Reading

You're convinced you know what others are thinking, usually about you, and usually bad.

"My boss didn't smile at me this morning. She must be planning to fire me."

Reality check: People have their own stuff going on that has nothing to do with you. Maybe she just had a fight with her teenager or spilled coffee on her favorite shirt.

Catastrophizing

Taking a small problem and turning it into a five-alarm disaster.

"I forgot to respond to that email. My career is over."

Reality check: Most problems are fixable speed bumps, not life-ending sinkholes.

Emotional Reasoning

Believing that if you feel something, it must be true.

"I feel like an impostor, so I must be one."

Reality check: Feelings aren't facts. They're just your brain's interpretation of what's happening.

How to Catch Yourself in the Act

The tricky part about these mind games? They happen so automatically that they feel completely normal and true.

Here's how to become a thought detective:

1. **Get curious, not furious:** When you notice anxiety or stress rising, pause and ask, "What am I telling myself right now?" Be curious about your thoughts rather than immediately believing them.

2. **Write it down:** There's something powerful about seeing your thoughts on paper. Often, they look different and less convincing when they're outside your head.

3. **The evidence test:** Ask yourself, "What actual evidence do I have that this thought is true? What evidence do I have that it's not true?" Like a good detective, gather facts from both sides.

4. **The friend test:** Would you say this thought to a friend in your situation? If not, why are you saying it to yourself?

5. **The so-what game:** Follow your thought to its logical conclusion. "So, what if this happens? Then what? And then what?" Often, you'll find that even if your fear comes true, you'll handle it.

I caught myself in a classic mind trick last week. After a typo in an important email, I spiraled into "I'm so careless, they'll think I'm unprofessional, I'll lose credibility forever." When I wrote it down, I had to laugh. One typo = career death? Even for an overthinker like me, that was a stretch.

Your thoughts are not facts—they're just thoughts. Sometimes they're helpful, sometimes they're wildly off-base.

Your job isn't to stop having these thoughts (impossible) but to get better at recognizing when your brain is playing tricks on you.

So, ready to start catching your brain in the act?

Reframing Overthinking

Ever watched someone skilled in martial arts use an opponent's momentum against them? That's exactly what we're going to learn to do with your overthinking. Instead of fighting those thoughts head-on (and getting exhausted in the process), you'll learn to redirect their energy.

The Question Everything Approach

Remember how annoying four-year-olds are with their endless "why" questions? Channel that energy! When a negative thought pops up, hit it with questions:

- "Where's the actual evidence for this?"

- "Am I confusing feelings with facts?"

- "What would I tell my best friend if they had this thought?"

- "Is this thought helpful or just making me feel worse?"

- "What's another way to look at this situation?"

I once spent three days convinced a friend was mad at me because she didn't reply to my text. My brain constructed an elaborate story about how I'd offended her.

When I finally questioned this belief, I remembered she was on a camping trip with spotty cell service. Overthinking: 0, Reality: 1.

The Courtroom Method

Pretend you're a lawyer presenting evidence in a case. Your negative thought is the prosecution's claim. Your job? Be the defense attorney.

Prosecution: "Everyone at work thinks I'm incompetent."

Defense: "Your Honor, the evidence shows three colleagues specifically thanked me last week. My boss gave me positive feedback on my last project. One mistake doesn't define my entire professional reputation."

The key is being fair, not dismissing all negative thoughts, but not accepting them without evidence either.

Thought Experiments That Work

The Time-Travel Test

Ask yourself, "Will this matter in a week? A month? A year?" Most overthinking focuses on things that won't even register on your radar in the near future.

The Compassion Flip

When your inner critic goes wild, imagine it's speaking to someone you love. Would you let anyone talk to your friend that way? Probably not. So, why accept it for yourself?

The Percentage Game

Instead of all-or-nothing thinking ("This will definitely fail"), assign realistic percentages: "There's maybe a 20% chance this goes badly, which means there's an 80% chance it goes fine or even great."

A Quick Word on CBT and Friends

Cognitive behavioral therapy might sound fancy, but it's basically what we're doing here: examining the connection between thoughts and feelings, then changing the thoughts to improve the feelings. We'll deeply discuss CBT techniques in the next chapter, along with mindfulness practices and emotional reasoning strategies.

For now, remember this: Your thoughts are just thoughts. They're like weather: sometimes sunny, sometimes stormy, but always changing. You don't have to believe every thought that pops into your head.

My Favorite Reframing Tool

When I catch myself in an overthinking spiral, I use what I call the "So What" method. I follow my fear to its conclusion.

"What if I bomb this presentation?"

- "So, what? People might think I'm nervous."

- "So, what? They'll probably forget about it by tomorrow."

- "So, what? Even if they remember, one bad presentation doesn't define my career."

Each "so what" takes the power away from the fear until it shrinks to its actual size, usually much smaller than it first appeared. Remember, getting good at reframing takes practice. Your brain has been running these thought patterns for years. Be patient with yourself as you learn these new mental moves. We'll build on these foundations in the next chapter with more advanced techniques.

Developing Healthier Inner Dialogue

Imagine sharing your living space with someone who follows you everywhere, commenting on everything you do:

- "That outfit makes you look terrible."

- "Why did you say that? Everyone thinks you're an idiot now."

- "You'll never get this right. Why even try?"

You'd probably kick this roommate out, right? Yet most of us let this voice—our inner critic—live rent-free in our heads 24-7.

Meet Your Inner Critics and Cheerleaders

We all have multiple voices in our heads. No, I'm not suggesting you need psychiatric help! These voices are simply different parts of our thinking patterns:

- **The drill sergeant:** Harsh, demanding, never satisfied. "That's not good enough! Do it again!"

- **The catastrophizer:** Always predicting doom. "If this meeting goes badly, your career is over!"

- **The perfectionist:** Nothing is ever quite right. "99% is basically failing."

- **The compassionate friend:** Kind, understanding, and encouraging. "You're doing your best with what you have."

- **The wise observer:** Sees the bigger picture. "This is hard right now, but it's just one moment in a much larger story."

The problem isn't having these voices; it's which ones we let dominate.

Self-Criticism vs. Self-Compassion: The Ultimate Showdown

Let's clear up a big misconception: Self-compassion is not self-indulgence. It's not about giving yourself a pass to do whatever you want without consequences. Self-criticism says, "You're so lazy! What's wrong with you?" Self-compassion says, "This is difficult, and you're struggling right now. What do you need to take the next small step?"

Self-criticism says, "Everyone else can handle this. You're just weak." Self-compassion says, "Many people find this challenging. Being human means sometimes finding things hard."

Here's the plot twist: Research consistently shows that self-compassion motivates us more effectively than self-criticism (Godkin, 2020). Think about it, who would you work harder for? A boss who berates and insults you or one who believes in you while holding you to high standards?

Your Inner Voice Makeover

Ready to renovate that inner dialogue? Here's your toolkit:

Notice the Voice

You can't change what you don't notice. Start by simply observing your inner chatter without judgment. "Ah, there's my inner critic again."

Name the Voice

When you catch harsh self-talk, label it, "That's not me; that's my perfectionist talking." This creates instant distance and perspective.

Talk Back (Respectfully)

When your inner critic says, "You always mess things up," respond with, "Actually, that's not true. Remember when I handled that situation last month?"

Speak in the Third Person

Instead of "I'm so stupid," try "Sally, you're feeling frustrated right now." This simple shift reduces emotional reactivity.

The Golden Question

When you're struggling, ask yourself, "What would I say to a friend in this situation?" Then offer yourself the same kindness.

I used to have an inner voice that sounded suspiciously like my seventh-grade math teacher: critical, impatient, and convinced I'd never "get it." When I started noticing this voice, I realized how much unnecessary suffering it caused me. Now, when it appears, I thank it for trying to protect me (because that's often what the critical voice thinks it's doing), and then I choose a more helpful perspective.

Remember, the goal isn't to eliminate negative thoughts. It's to build a healthier relationship with all your thoughts. Some days, your inner critic will be louder than others. That's okay. With practice, your compassionate voice will get stronger and more automatic.

Your mind is like a neighborhood. You can't control who moves in, but you can choose who you invite over for coffee.

Chapter 6:

The Power of Presence

By now, you've discovered how your thoughts can hijack your life, dragging you backward into regrets or catapulting you forward into worst-case scenarios. Meanwhile, life itself happens right now, in this moment, often without you noticing.

The frantic pace of modern living doesn't help. Between pinging notifications, packed schedules, and the pressure to always be "on," we rarely settle fully into the now. Instead, we operate on autopilot—physically present but mentally elsewhere, rehearsing tomorrow's presentation or replaying last week's argument while stirring dinner.

But here's the thing about overthinking: It can only thrive when we abandon the present. Think about it—have you ever overthought something while being completely absorbed in the moment? Probably not.

Snap Back to Now: Mindfulness Techniques That Actually Work

Let's be honest—when was the last time your mind was actually where your body was? This morning, while brushing your teeth, were you mentally rehearsing your presentation? Or during lunch, did you replay that awkward conversation from yesterday?

So, how do we train our wandering minds to stay put? Enter mindfulness: your personal teleportation device back to reality.

The 5-4-3-2-1 Grounding Technique

When your thoughts are spiraling, try naming:

- 5 things you can see right now.

- 4 things you can touch.

- 3 things you can hear.

- 2 things you can smell (or like to smell).

- 1 thing you can taste.

I tried this during a particularly brutal overthinking episode before a job interview.

By the time I reached "taste," I had completely broken the thought loop and remembered I was just a person sitting in a car, not a collection of imagined failures.

The "Name That Thought" Practice

When a thought pops up, simply label it: "Planning thought." "Worry thought." "Memory thought." Then watch it float away.

This one makes me laugh because I've caught myself with some ridiculous categories: "Catastrophic thought where somehow I end up living in a cardboard box because I forgot to reply to that email."

Once named, these thoughts immediately lose some power.

The Three-Minute Breathing Space

This one's perfect for busy days:

1. **Minute one:** Notice what's happening in your mind and body right now. No judging, just noticing.

2. **Minute two:** Focus completely on the sensation of breathing.

3. **Minute three:** Expand awareness to your whole body.

I've done this while waiting for coffee, sitting on trains, and even in bathroom stalls during stressful meetings (hey, we do what we must).

The "What's Not Wrong Right Now?" Practice

Our brains are wired to scan for problems. Counter this by asking, "What's actually okay right now?"

Maybe your feet are comfortable. The air is breathable. Your heart is beating without your supervision (thanks, heart!). This isn't toxic positivity, it's reality checking.

The "Feel Your Feet" Reset

Whenever you catch yourself overthinking, immediately shift attention to the sensation of your feet against the floor. Feel the pressure, temperature, and texture. This instantly pulls you back to your body in the present moment.

I keep a sticky note on my laptop that says "FEET!" As strange as it looks to visitors, it's saved me from countless overthinking spirals. Remember, the goal isn't to empty your mind or never think about the past or future.

That's impossible (and sometimes unhelpful). The goal is to recognize when you're no longer present and have a toolkit to bring yourself back.

With practice, you'll start catching yourself earlier in the overthinking cycle. That pause—that moment of noticing—is your growing power of presence. It's the difference between being dragged around by your thoughts and remembering that you're the one who's supposed to be driving this thing.

Mind-Quieting Magic: Simple Practices for Chaotic Brains

You don't need to be a Zen master to find some mental quiet. Let's explore some down-to-earth practices that can help tame that mental circus.

Breathing: Your Built-in Chill Button

Remember when someone told you to "just breathe" during a stressful moment, and you wanted to scream? Turns out, they weren't entirely wrong, just really bad at explaining why.

Try this: Breathe in for a count of four, hold for two, and exhale for six. When we extend our exhale longer than our inhale, we actually trigger our parasympathetic nervous system—the body's "rest and digest" mode.

I've used this during panic-inducing work presentations and while trying to assemble furniture with instructions clearly written by sadists.

The 4-7-8 breath works wonders too: Inhale for 4, hold for 7, and exhale for 8. Just three rounds can noticeably calm an overthinking storm.

The first time I tried this before bed, I was genuinely annoyed at how well it worked; I'd spent years battling insomnia with far more complicated methods.

Mother Nature: The Original Therapist

Forest bathing sounds like something involving outdoor tubs and mosquitoes, but it's actually just mindfully spending time among trees. There's science behind why a walk in natural settings calms us, something about fractal patterns and negative ions that our ancestors evolved with.

You don't need actual forests either. A neighborhood park, a tree-lined street, and even watching leaves move outside your window count. The key is to really notice the different shades of green, the patterns of light, and the sounds of birds or rustling leaves.

My personal overthinking kryptonite is water: oceans, lakes, even streams in city parks. Something about moving water seems to wash away mental noise. One particularly anxious day, I sat by a fountain for twenty minutes and left feeling like I'd had a brain massage.

Body Scan: The Ultimate Reality Check

When thoughts won't stop spinning, try this: Starting at your toes and working upward, mentally scan each part of your body. Notice sensations without judgment: pressure, temperature, tension, and relaxation.

This practice works because you cannot simultaneously focus on physical sensations and spin overthinking narratives. It's like trying to watch two movies at once; the brain simply can't do it. I once caught myself catastrophizing about a minor work issue while doing a body scan.

By the time I reached my shoulders, I realized they were practically touching my ears from tension, over an email! This awareness alone helped me laugh and let go.

Guided Meditations: Mental Training Wheels

If sitting in silence makes your thoughts louder, try guided meditations. Having someone's voice direct your attention gives your thinking mind a job; just follow the instructions. Apps, YouTube, and many libraries offer free options.

Start with just five minutes. I began with three minutes because even five seemed impossible for my squirrel brain.

Now, I can do fifteen without mentally redecorating my house or planning dinner.

The Three-Step Emergency De-Frazzle

When overthinking hits hard:

1. Name five things you can see.

2. Take three deliberate breaths.

3. Press your feet firmly into the floor.

This simple sequence interrupts the thought spiral by forcing your attention into your senses. I call it my "panic pivot" and have used it everywhere from job interviews to first dates.

Remember, these practices aren't about achieving perfect mental silence (does anyone actually get that?). They're about creating space between you and your thoughts—just enough room to remember that you are not your thoughts, and not every thought deserves your full attention.

Reality Check: Finding Peace in What Actually Is

Let's talk about that voice in your head—you know the one. The commentator who's never satisfied, the one who replays embarrassing moments from 2015 at 3 a.m., or spins elaborate disaster scenarios about next week's presentation. If that voice had its own reality show, it would be called "Overanalyzing Everything."

Here's the truth: That voice isn't you. It's just a noisy roommate you never asked for.

Mindfulness offers something radical: the chance to step back and observe that voice without believing everything it says. And in that space between you and your thoughts lies freedom from the overthinking trap.

The Art of Mental Decluttering

Think of your mind like your living space. When it's cluttered with old regrets, future worries, and unnecessary "what-ifs," there's hardly room to exist in the present moment.

I realized this one morning while making coffee. I was physically standing in my kitchen, but mentally I was rehearsing an argument with my boss that hadn't happened (and never did). I had completely missed the smell of the coffee, the warmth of the mug, the morning light—actual, real things happening right then.

Mental decluttering starts with a simple question: "Is this thought about something real and happening right now?" If not, you can acknowledge it and gently set it aside, not forever, just for this moment.

It's like having a messy junk drawer. You don't need to throw everything away; you just need to stop rummaging through it when you're trying to cook dinner.

The Self-Acceptance Paradox

One of mindfulness's greatest gifts is the realization that you don't need to fix yourself to find peace. In fact, the constant fixing attempts—the endless self-improvement projects—often fuel overthinking.

Try this weird paradox: What if you're actually okay exactly as you are right now?

I know, I know. My inner critic screamed when I first encountered this idea. But there's freedom in temporarily putting down the self-improvement project and simply being with yourself as you are.

Next time you catch yourself overthinking, try saying, "Even with these thoughts, I'm okay." Not perfect, not finished growing, just basically okay in this moment.

From Imagination to Reality

Overthinking loves to pull us into elaborate stories. "If I say this, then they'll think that, which will make them do this, and eventually lead to disaster." Sound familiar?

The mindful approach asks, What do I actually know right now? Not what I'm imagining, remembering, or forecasting—what's real?

Last year, I spent three weeks worrying about a medical test result. My mind created vivid scenarios of treatments, telling people how life would change, complete with emotional soundtracks!

When I finally got the (normal) results, I realized I'd lived through an entire illness that never existed. Mindfulness trains us to distinguish between actual facts and the stories we build around them. It's the difference between "My friend hasn't texted back" (fact) and "My friend is mad at me forever because I'm a terrible person" (story).

The Present Moment Scavenger Hunt

Try this game: Throughout your day, collect moments of simple awareness. The taste of your lunch. The feeling of a breeze. The sound of laughter.

These small moments of presence add up, gradually training your mind to stay more often in what's real rather than what's imagined. They're like little weights strengthening your present-moment muscles.

Mindfulness isn't about having an empty mind; it's about having a mind that knows the difference between what's happening and what's being imagined. And in that difference lies freedom from the overthinking trap.

Chapter 7:

Letting Go of Perfection

I once spent three hours writing an email. Not a book chapter, not a business proposal, but a simple email to a colleague. I rewrote the opening line seventeen times. I agonized over word choices as if lives depended on them. I even changed fonts twice, despite knowing the recipient would see it in whatever default email font they used.

Perfectionism might be the most exhausting form of overthinking. It masquerades as high standards and attention to detail, but in reality, it's a relentless inner critic that whispers, "Not good enough yet," when everyone else is saying, "This is great!"

The Never-Ending Search: When Perfect Becomes the Enemy of Done

I once spent two weeks choosing a coffee table. Not because I couldn't find one; I found dozens. But what if the round one looked better than the rectangular one? What if the wooden one scratched easily? What if the glass one would show fingerprints? What if there was a *perfect* coffee table just one more website away?

Meanwhile, my living room remained table-less, with guests balancing drinks on their knees.

The Perfectionist Brain: Always On the Hunt

Perfectionists don't just want good solutions; they want THE solution. The flawless, unimpeachable, everyone-will-be-impressed solution. And therein lies the problem.

While most people can say, "This option looks good enough; let's go with it," the perfectionist thinks, "But what if there's something better I haven't considered yet?" It's like being stuck in a mental revolving door, spinning through the same options again and again, unable to exit.

My friend Lisa, a graphic designer, once confessed she had 37 versions of a client's logo saved on her computer. When I asked which one she submitted, she laughed nervously and said, "I'm still working on it." The deadline was three days earlier.

The Fear Factory: Making Mountains of Molehills

Behind perfectionism lurks something most of us don't want to admit: fear. Fear of criticism. Fear of failure. Fear of not measuring up.

When we believe that making mistakes equals being a failure, we'll do mental gymnastics to avoid any possible error. Every decision becomes not just a choice but a reflection of our worth.

Perfectionism turns molehills into mountains and mountains into Mount Everests. No wonder we overthink; we're trying to climb Everest in flip-flops.

The Impossible Math of Perfection

Here's the math problem perfectionists set for themselves:

- Consider all possible options (infinite).

- Predict all possible outcomes (also infinite).

- Choose the one perfect solution with zero downsides.

No wonder our brains get stuck in loops! We've assigned ourselves a literally impossible task.

Breaking the Loop: First Steps

Understanding this connection is your first step toward freedom. When you catch yourself in an overthinking spiral, ask:

- *Am I searching for perfect, or would good enough actually work here?*

- *What's the real cost of delaying this decision while seeking perfection?*

- *If a friend were in my position, what would I advise them?*

Sometimes, I set a "decision timer" for less important choices. Ten minutes to pick a restaurant. Thirty minutes to choose a gift. When the timer goes off, I go with the best option I've found so far. The world hasn't ended yet.

Loosening the Grip: How to Stop Micromanaging Your Life

My friend Jake once missed his flight because he insisted on reorganizing his entire suitcase at the check-in counter. Everything had to be perfectly folded, categorized, and arranged by color. Meanwhile, the final boarding call echoed through the terminal. When I asked why he didn't just fix it later, he looked genuinely confused. "But it wouldn't be right," he said.

The need to control is perfectionism's bossy older sibling. It's not just about doing things flawlessly; it's about making sure everything and everyone around us meets our exacting standards, too. Let's look at some practical ways to loosen that white-knuckle grip on life without feeling like we're free-falling into chaos.

Practice the Art of Strategic Sloppiness

Yes, you read that right. Try deliberately doing something slightly imperfectly. Leave one dish unwashed. Send an email with a typo. Let your partner load the dishwasher their way.

The first time I tried this, I left a small pile of laundry unfolded overnight. I actually checked on it twice to make sure it wasn't somehow multiplying or causing household disasters. By morning, I had to admit something shocking: absolutely nothing bad happened.

Start with low-stakes situations and work your way up. Think of it as exposure therapy for your inner control freak.

Embrace "Good Enough" as a Legitimate Destination

For control enthusiasts, "good enough" sounds like settling for mediocrity. But here's a perspective shift: Good enough is often the optimal balance between effort and outcome.

Try the 80/20 rule: Recognize that you'll get about 80% of the value from the first 20% of the effort. Those final perfectionist touches? They're usually invisible to everyone but you.

Delegate Without Hovering

The hardest part of delegation isn't assigning tasks—it's resisting the urge to peek over shoulders every thirty seconds. Next time you delegate, try this: Set clear expectations, then physically remove yourself from the situation. Go for a walk. Work in another room. Turn off your phone if you have to. I once asked my partner to plan our weekend trip. For three days, I bit my tongue to avoid asking questions or making suggestions. The result? A fantastic trip I never would have planned, with surprises I couldn't have anticipated. Plus, he felt trusted and appreciated.

Break Down the Mountain

Control issues often flare up when we face complex tasks. Everything feels important when you're staring at one massive challenge.

Try breaking things down into smaller chunks, then ask, "If I had to pick just three essential elements to focus on, what would they be?"

For a presentation, maybe it's the main message, one compelling visual, and answering the obvious questions. For a dinner party, perhaps it's good food, comfortable seating, and a welcoming atmosphere. The rest is just bonus material.

Reality-Check Your Catastrophizing

When the thought of relinquishing control makes you panicky, challenge those thoughts:

- What's the worst that could realistically happen?

- How would I handle that outcome if it did occur?

- What's the cost of maintaining this level of control?

I once refused to let anyone help with Thanksgiving dinner. By the time guests arrived, I was sweaty, cranky, and too exhausted to enjoy the company.

The following year, I let people bring dishes and help with setup. Was everything exactly as I would have done it? No. Was it still a lovely meal with much better company? Absolutely.

Treat Yourself Like a Friend

Notice your self-talk when things aren't perfect. Would you speak to a friend that way? Probably not. Next time you catch yourself saying, "I can't believe I messed that up. I'm so incompetent," try switching to, "Well, that didn't go as planned, but I'll figure it out."

Remember, the goal isn't to abandon all standards. It's to create space for being human—imperfect, sometimes messy, and ultimately much happier when we're not trying to control every molecule in our path.

Thriving in Disaster: Finding Freedom in Flaws

My bathroom wall has a small dent where I once tried to hang a towel rack. I missed the stud, the rack pulled out, and I was left with damaged drywall and wounded pride. For months, that dent bothered me every time I saw it—a glaring reminder of my imperfection.

Then one day, my five-year-old niece pointed at it and asked what happened. After I explained my DIY disaster, she shrugged and said, "Everyone messes up sometimes. My teacher says that's how we get smarter."

Out of the mouths of babes, as they say. Most of us weren't born perfectionists; we learned it somewhere along the way. Which means we can unlearn it, too.

Redefining Mistakes as Plot Twists

What if we viewed mistakes not as failures but as unexpected plot developments in our life story?

When I accidentally added salt instead of sugar to a cake recipe (yes, really), I discovered that salt actually enhances chocolate flavor in small amounts. My "mistake" led me to experiment with salted desserts long before they became trendy.

Next time something goes wrong, try asking, "What does this make possible now?" instead of "How did I mess up?"

This simple shift can transform a dead end into a detour that might lead somewhere interesting.

Building Your Resilience Muscles

Think of making "imperfect" decisions as strength training for your resilience muscles. Each time you survive a less-than-ideal outcome, you prove to yourself that you can handle it.

Start with low-stakes decisions where the consequences don't matter much. Order something unusual at a restaurant. Take a different route home. Wear that bold outfit you're not sure about.

I once showed up to a meeting with mismatched shoes (black and navy in similar styles). Instead of dying from embarrassment, I pointed it out with a laugh.

Not only did everyone forget about it by the next day, but it actually broke the ice in what had been a tense project.

The "Worst-Case Reality Check"

When perfectionism paralyzes you, try this technique:

1. Ask yourself, "What's the absolute worst realistic outcome of this decision?"

2. Then ask, "Could I handle that if it happened?"

3. Finally: "What resources or support would help me handle it?"

I use this when public speaking, which terrifies me. Worst case? I mess up badly and feel embarrassed. Could I handle that? Yes, though it would be uncomfortable. Resources?

Breathing techniques, supportive friends, and the knowledge that everyone forgets about these things quickly.

Suddenly, the fear loses some of its power.

The 70% Rule

Waiting until you're 100% certain is a recipe for paralysis. Instead, try the 70% rule: If you're about 70% confident in a decision, that's usually enough to proceed.

This rule acknowledges that perfect certainty is rare. Even experts make educated guesses. The difference is that they don't let uncertainty stop them from moving forward.

When I was torn between two job offers, I realized I'd never be 100% sure which was best. But I was about 75% confident in one direction, so I made the leap.

Six years later, it remains one of the best decisions I've made.

Building a Mistake-Friendly Environment

Surround yourself with people who don't expect perfection. Share your fears and mishaps with trusted friends. Laugh at yourself when appropriate. Celebrate others who take risks, even when they don't pan out perfectly.

In my house, we now have a monthly "failure dinner" where everyone shares something that didn't go as planned and what they learned. It's become a surprisingly fun tradition that has slowly rewired how we all view mistakes.

The Freedom in "Oh Well"

Perhaps the most powerful phrase in the imperfection toolkit is simply "Oh well."

Sent an email with a typo? Oh well. Said something awkward in a meeting? Oh well. Made the wrong choice at a restaurant? Oh well.

This isn't about not caring or lowering standards. It's about the appropriate emotional response. Not everything deserves the weight we give it.

Remember, embracing imperfection isn't about celebrating mediocrity. It's about freeing yourself from the paralysis of perfectionism so you can actually accomplish more, experience more, and yes, even excel more in the things that truly matter.

Part 3:

Cultivating Balance and Vitality

Chapter 8:

The Art of Decision-Making

Standing in the cereal aisle, I watched a woman hold two boxes of oatmeal for what seemed like twenty minutes. She'd pick up one, read the label, put it back, grab the other, compare prices, check ingredients again, and then start the whole process over. I actually finished my entire grocery shopping, and she was still there when I passed by on my way out.

I recognized that look, the paralyzed expression of someone trapped in decision limbo. I'd worn it myself countless times, from choosing restaurants to picking career paths. It's the face of an overthinker who knows that somewhere out there exists the "perfect choice," and settling for anything less feels like giving up.

From Chaos to Choice: Breaking Down Decisions Into Bite-Sized Pieces

I once stood in front of my closet for thirty minutes trying to decide what to wear to a casual dinner. Thirty minutes! Meanwhile, my friend Tania could plan an entire vacation in the same time. What was her secret? She had learned something I hadn't: good decision-making isn't about being smarter; it's about having a process.

Most of us approach decisions like we're trying to solve a jigsaw puzzle in the dark while someone shouts random instructions. No wonder we get overwhelmed. But when you break decision-making into manageable steps, even complex choices become surprisingly straightforward.

Step 1: Narrow Down the Real Question

Before going into options, get crystal clear on what you're actually deciding. This sounds obvious, but overthinkers often expand simple choices into philosophical dilemmas.

"Should I change jobs?" becomes "What's my life purpose, and how do I achieve career fulfillment while maintaining work-life balance?" when the real question might be "Am I happy enough here to stay another year?"

My neighbor spent months agonizing over whether to renovate her kitchen until she realized she was really asking, "Do I want to live in this house long-term?" Once she answered that (yes), the renovation decision became much simpler.

Step 2: Understand What Really Matters

Not all factors in a decision carry equal weight. Smart decision-makers identify their top three priorities and focus on them.

When I was choosing between apartments, I initially considered seventeen different factors: from ceiling height to proximity to my favorite coffee shop. But when I narrowed it down to my actual priorities (price, commute time, and having enough space for guests), the choice became obvious.

Ask yourself, "If I could only consider three things about this decision, what would they be?"

Step 3: Take It in Small Bites

Complex decisions don't have to be made all at once. Break them into smaller, manageable pieces and tackle them one at a time.

Choosing a career path? Start by exploring what type of work environment you prefer. Deciding where to live? First, narrow down the geographic region, then the neighborhood, then specific properties.

My friend Lisa wanted to start a business but felt overwhelmed by all the decisions involved. We broke it down: first, she'd validate the business idea by talking to potential customers. Only after getting positive feedback would she move to step two: creating a basic business plan. This approach turned a paralyzing choice into a series of small, doable steps.

Step 4: Set Your Research Limits

Here's where overthinkers get stuck: endless information gathering. Productive decision-makers set boundaries on their research phase.

Try the "three sources rule"; for most decisions, three good sources of information are enough. More than that and you're probably procrastinating rather than researching.

When buying my car, I gave myself one week to research and two dealerships to visit. Without those limits, I would have researched until the car industry evolved to flying vehicles.

Step 5: Listen to Input (But Don't Crowdsource)

Good decision-makers seek relevant input without turning every choice into a democracy. Ask one or two people whose judgment you trust, not your entire social network.

I learned this the hard way when I asked everyone for restaurant recommendations for a first date. I received fourteen different suggestions and spent so much time weighing options that I was twenty minutes late to dinner.

Step 6: Recognize "Good Enough" When You See It

Perfect decisions are rare. Good ones are everywhere. When you find an option that meets your main criteria and doesn't have any deal-breaking flaws, that's often your answer.

The apartment that checks your three priority boxes? Take it. The job that offers growth in your field and reasonable pay? Say yes. The restaurant with good reviews and a convenient location? Make the reservation.

The Magic of Time Limits

Perhaps the most important skill is setting decision deadlines. Without them, choices expand to fill infinite time.

For small decisions (what to order, which movie to watch), give yourself two minutes. Medium decisions (which phone to buy, vacation destination) get a day or two.

Big decisions (job changes, major purchases) might deserve a week or a month, but not more.

The goal isn't to make perfect decisions; it's to make good decisions and move forward with confidence. The best choice is often the one that gets you unstuck and moving toward your goals, even if it's not theoretically optimal.

Decision-making is a skill, and like any skill, it improves with practice. Start with small, low-stakes choices and work your way up.

Before long, you'll find yourself spending less time agonizing and more time living.

Your Decision-Making Toolkit: Fast and Confident Choices

My uncle Jim can walk into any restaurant and order within thirty seconds. I used to think he was just indecisive or didn't care about food quality. Turns out, he had a system: scan the menu for three things that sound good, pick the first one that fits his budget, done. While I spent fifteen minutes agonizing over every option, he was already enjoying his meal.

That's when I realized successful decision-makers aren't necessarily smarter; they just have better tools.

The 80/20 Rule: Your New Best Friend

This rule states that 80% of your results come from 20% of your efforts. In decision-making terms, you'll get 80% of the benefit from the first 20% of information you gather.

When I was house-hunting, I initially planned to research every neighborhood, school district, and future development plan in the city. My realtor (a wise woman) suggested I focus on three neighborhoods that met my basic needs. Within those areas, I found my perfect home in two weeks instead of the six months I'd planned.

The lesson? Get enough information to make a good decision, then stop researching and start deciding.

Smart Education vs. Information Overload

There's a difference between educating yourself and drowning in data. Smart education means understanding the basics well enough to spot good options and avoid obvious mistakes.

For most decisions, you need to know:

- What are the main factors that matter?

- What's a reasonable price range or timeline?

- What are the major red flags to avoid?

When I bought my first car, I spent one evening learning about reliability ratings, typical price ranges, and what to look for during a test drive. That basic knowledge was enough to make a good choice without becoming an automotive expert.

Trusting Your Gut (Yes, Really)

Your intuition isn't mystical; it's your brain processing patterns and information faster than your conscious mind can track. That "gut feeling" often contains valuable data.

Try this: after gathering basic information about a decision, sit quietly for a moment and notice your first instinct. Not the voice analyzing pros and cons, but the immediate feeling of "yes" or "no" in your body.

I used to dismiss gut feelings as unscientific until I started tracking them. Turns out, my initial instincts were right about 80% of the time. The times I ignored them and chose the "logical" option often led to regret.

Understanding Probability (Without Math Nightmares)

You don't need to be a statistician, but understanding basic probability helps prevent overthinking worst-case scenarios. Ask yourself, "What's the realistic likelihood of this bad outcome?" Often, we treat low-probability events like certainties. Yes, the restaurant might give you food poisoning, but millions of people eat out safely every day. My friend Shasha avoided flying for years because of crash statistics she'd googled. When we looked at actual probability (you're more likely to be struck by lightning), she realized her fear was based on possibility, not probability.

Setting Quick Decision Boundaries

Boundaries prevent endless deliberation. Before you start researching any decision, set limits:

- How much time will I spend on this?

- How much information is enough?

- What's my budget or other hard constraints?

For minor decisions, I use the "two-minute rule": If it won't matter in two years, spend at most two minutes deciding. For bigger choices, I might allocate a weekend or a week, but never more.

The "Good Enough" Filter

Most decisions don't require optimization; they require action. Train yourself to recognize when an option meets your main criteria and has no deal-breaking flaws.

That apartment with a good location and reasonable rent? Take it, even if the kitchen isn't your dream setup. The job that offers growth and decent pay? Accept it, even if the office coffee is terrible.

Perfect is the enemy of good, and good is usually good enough to move your life forward. Most "wrong" decisions teach us something valuable and can be corrected along the way.

You're Better at This Than You Think: Building Trust in Your Own Judgment

My friend Rachel once called me at midnight, panicked about a job decision she'd been weighing for weeks. She'd researched the company, talked to current employees, and created a detailed pros-and-cons list. Yet she was terrified of making the wrong choice.

"What does your gut say?" I asked.

"That it's a good opportunity," she admitted. "But what if I'm wrong?"

"What if you're right?" I countered.

That simple question changed everything. Rachel had done her homework. She had good instincts. But somewhere along the way, she'd forgotten to trust herself.

Your Hidden Track Record

Stop for a moment and think about all the decisions you've made that worked out well. You chose friends who enriched your life. You learned skills that served you. You navigated challenges and came out stronger.

Sure, you've made some choices you'd do differently. We all have. But overthinking often makes us forget our successes while magnifying our mistakes.

I keep a "wins journal" where I write down good decisions I've made, big and small. Choosing to learn a new software program helped my career. Deciding to attend that networking event, where I met great friends. Even small wins, like picking the perfect restaurant for a special dinner.

Reading through it reminds me that my judgment is actually pretty solid most of the time.

The Preparation-Confidence Connection

Here's the secret successful decision-makers know: Confidence comes from preparation, not perfection.

When you've done reasonable research, considered your priorities, and thought through the basics, you're equipped to make a good choice. Not a perfect choice, but a good one.

Before my last job interview, I spent an evening researching the company, practicing common questions, and thinking about how my experience aligned with their needs. Walking into that interview, I felt prepared and confident. Did I answer every question perfectly? No. But I trusted that my preparation was enough.

Your Instincts Are Smarter Than You Think

That gut feeling isn't random; it's your brain processing information rapidly based on patterns and experiences you might not consciously remember.

When something feels "off" about a situation, that's often your subconscious picking up on subtle cues. When something feels "right," that's your brain recognizing positive patterns from your past experience.

I learned to trust this during apartment hunting. On paper, one place checked all my boxes. But something felt wrong during the visit. I couldn't pinpoint why, so I almost ignored it. Fortunately, I trusted the feeling and kept looking. Later, I discovered the neighborhood had serious parking issues that weren't immediately obvious, exactly the kind of detail my subconscious had somehow detected.

The Mistake: Fear Reality Check

Fear of making mistakes often stems from catastrophic thinking. We imagine that one wrong choice will derail our entire life. But think about it: How many of your past "mistakes" actually led to disaster?

Most poor decisions are reversible or teachable. The job that didn't work out led to better opportunities. The relationship that ended taught valuable lessons. The purchase you regretted became a funny story.

Very few decisions are truly irreversible. Most can be adjusted, learned from, or completely changed if needed.

Building Your Confidence Muscle

Like any skill, trusting your judgment gets stronger with practice. Start with small, low-stakes decisions and work your way up.

Choose a restaurant without reading every review. Pick a movie based on your initial interest. Buy the shirt you like without asking three friends for opinions. Each time you make a decision and survive the outcome (good or bad), you prove to yourself that you can handle the consequences of your choices.

The Permission to Be Human

Perhaps most importantly, give yourself permission to make imperfect decisions. You're not a computer calculating optimal outcomes; you're a human being navigating a complex world with incomplete information. Remember Rachel? She took that job. Six months later, she told me it was one of the best decisions she'd ever made.

Not because it was perfect, but because she'd trusted herself enough to try. You have good instincts. You've proven it before. Trust them again.

Chapter 9:

The Power of Boundaries

Picture this: You're at a party, and there's that one person who just won't stop talking. They corner you by the snack table and launch into a forty-five-minute monologue about their cousin's pet iguana. You smile politely and nod at the right moments, but inside you're screaming. You know you should excuse yourself, but somehow you just... don't.

Now, imagine your brain doing the exact same thing to you every single day.

When we hear about setting boundaries, we usually think about other people. We learn to say no to extra work projects, to pushy relatives, or to friends who always need a favor. And yes, that stuff matters. But here's what catches most of us off guard: It's also necessary to set boundaries with yourself.

When Your Brain Needs a Vacation (But You Can't Give It One)

Ever feel like your head is stuffed with cotton balls and your emotions are doing the cha-cha? Welcome to mental and emotional overload—that special kind of exhaustion where even deciding what to have for lunch feels like solving calculus.

Here's the thing: Boundaries reduce mental and emotional overload, whether you establish them between yourself and others or limit yourself in certain thoughts or behaviors. Think of boundaries as your personal air traffic controller, deciding what gets to land in your mental airport and what needs to circle around until further notice. Let's start with the obvious stuff—boundaries with other people. You know that friend who texts you their entire life story at 11 p.m.? Or your coworker who dumps their stress on you every Monday morning like you're their personal therapist? Without boundaries, you're basically running a 24-hour emotional support hotline. And frankly, most of us didn't sign up for that job.

When you don't have these boundaries, your brain becomes a dumping ground for everyone else's problems on top of your own. It's like trying to juggle flaming torches while someone keeps tossing you more. Eventually, something's going to get burned, and it's probably going to be you.

But here's where it gets tricky. The boundaries you need most are often the ones with yourself. Your mind loves to replay conversations from three years ago or create detailed disaster movies about things that will probably never happen. Without internal boundaries, you're letting your brain run wild like a toddler with a sugar rush in a toy store.

I used to think that entertaining every worried thought made me "thorough" or "prepared." Turns out, I was just wearing myself out. It's like doing mental jumping jacks all day—you get tired, but you don't actually get anywhere.

When you set boundaries with your thoughts, you're not ignoring problems or being irresponsible. You're choosing which thoughts deserve your time and energy. Some thoughts are worth your attention, like remembering to pay bills or planning your weekend. Others are just mental junk mail that somehow got past your spam filter.

The magic happens when you start treating your mental space like your physical space. You wouldn't let strangers walk into your house and rearrange your furniture, so why let random thoughts waltz into your head and redecorate your mood? Boundaries aren't walls—they're more like smart filters that help you focus on what actually matters.

Your Personal Boundary Blueprint

Setting boundaries sounds great in theory, but where do you actually put them? It's not like you can just buy a "Boundary Kit" on Amazon (though honestly, wouldn't that make life easier?). The truth is, you need boundaries in two main areas: outside your head and inside it.

The External Stuff (AKA Other People's Drama)

Let's start with the obvious culprits. Your relationships need boundaries; yes, even the good ones. That friend who calls during your favorite show, expecting a two-hour therapy session? Boundary needed. Your coworker who thinks "urgent" means "I just thought of this?"

Another boundary candidate.

Work boundaries are huge. If you're answering emails at midnight or taking calls during dinner, you've basically invited your job to move in rent-free. Your boss might not love it at first, but even they don't want a burned-out zombie on their team.

Then there's family: The people who knew you when you had braces and still think they can tell you how to live. Whether it's your spouse expecting you to read their mind or your mom still treating you like you're twelve, family boundaries can feel scary, but they're often the most important ones. Don't forget self-care boundaries either. Yes, saying no to that third commitment this week counts as self-care.

So does not checking your phone first thing in the morning or actually taking your lunch break instead of eating a sad sandwich at your desk.

The Internal Battlefield (AKA Your Own Personal Soap Opera)

Here's where things get interesting. You also need boundaries with your own thoughts and memories. Past experiences love to crash your present-day party uninvited. That embarrassing thing from high school? It doesn't get to ruin your Tuesday afternoon twenty years later.

Trauma has a way of barging into random moments, and family dysfunction can echo in your head long after you've moved out. These need boundaries too; not because you're ignoring what happened, but because you're choosing when and how to deal with it.

Poor self-image and negative self-talk are like having a mean roommate in your brain who never pays rent but always has opinions. You wouldn't let someone else talk to you the way you sometimes talk to yourself, so why give your inner critic a free pass?

And overthinking? That's the big one. Your brain will happily chew on problems all day if you let it. Sometimes you need to tell your thoughts, "Thanks for sharing, but we're closed for business right now."

The Art of No: A Masterclass in Not Being Everyone's Yes-Person

Let's talk about the hardest two-letter word in the English language: no. It's shorter than "hi" and simpler than "um," yet somehow saying it feels harder than explaining quantum physics to a goldfish.

The External No: Why You're Not a Human Vending Machine

Here's the thing about saying no without guilt: You have to stop treating yourself like you're a 24-hour convenience store. You know, always open, always stocked, and somehow expected to have exactly what everyone needs at any hour.

The guilt hits because we've been conditioned to think that saying no makes us selfish. But here's a reality check: If you say yes to everything, you're essentially saying no to yourself. And last time I checked, you matter too.

Start small. That PTA meeting you don't have time for? "Sorry, I can't make it." That extra project when you're already drowning? "I'm at capacity right now." Notice how you don't need a dissertation-length explanation. "No" is a complete sentence, even if it feels weird at first.

The secret sauce is prioritizing what truly matters. Make a list of your top three priorities right now. Got it? Good. Now, when someone asks you to do something, check if it fits those three things. If it doesn't, you have your answer.

Don't overburden yourself by accepting every offer or opportunity that comes your way. I used to think every opportunity was a gift I couldn't refuse.

Turns out, some gifts are just really pretty boxes full of stress and sleepless nights. Not every door you could walk through is worth walking through.

The Internal No: Setting Boundaries With Your Own Brain

Now, here's where it gets interesting: You also need to say no to yourself. Your brain is like that friend who means well but gives terrible advice at 2 a.m. Sometimes you just have to cut the conversation short.

As a step toward stopping the overthinking habit, only allow yourself to ruminate for a limited amount of time. Set a timer if you have to. "Okay, brain, you get fifteen minutes to worry about this thing, and then we're moving on." It sounds ridiculous, but it works better than letting your thoughts run marathons in your head all day.

Some wounds need professional help. If you're carrying around emotional baggage that's affecting your daily life, seek counseling. There's no shame in getting a professional to help you sort through the mess. Think of it like calling a plumber when your sink won't stop leaking; some problems need expert hands.

Here's a weird thought: treat yourself like you would a good friend. If your friend was constantly putting themselves down, you'd tell them to knock it off, right? Do the same with your internal self-talk. Don't accept certain attitudes or harsh words from your inner voice that you wouldn't accept from anyone else.

Practice gratitude to combat overthinking. When your brain starts its doom-and-gloom playlist, interrupt it with three things you're grateful for. It's like changing the radio station from heavy metal to something that doesn't give you a headache. Pay attention to what situations you place yourself in and what people you allow into your life. Some people are overthinking triggers while walking around in human form. You know the type; they turn "beautiful day" into "But what if it rains tomorrow and ruins everything?" If you can't avoid them completely, at least limit your exposure.

Dealing With Other People's Overthinking

Speaking of overthinking triggers, let's talk about dealing with others who are overthinkers. You can't fix them (trust me, I've tried), but you can set boundaries. When they start spiraling, you can say, "I can see you're really worried about this. Have you thought about talking to someone who can actually help?" Then redirect the conversation or excuse yourself.

You're not their therapist, and you're not required to get sucked into their mental whirlpool just because they're drowning in it.

Making Peace With Your Past

Establish boundaries with your past, too. You can't change what's already happened; I know, shocking revelation. It's futile to continue dwelling on things you can't fix. Your past already happened, and no amount of mental replay is going to change the ending.

This doesn't mean pretending bad things didn't happen. It means saying, "That was then, this is now, and I'm not going to let yesterday hijack today." Give your past a time limit, too. "I'll think about this for ten minutes, learn what I can from it, and then I'm focusing on what I can actually control."

Setting boundaries isn't about becoming mean or selfish. It's about becoming the person who gets to decide how their time and energy get spent. And honestly? That person deserves to be you.

Chapter 10:

Building Resilience Against Stress

Here's some good news that might surprise you: Overthinking is not a disease, and it's not a mental disorder. It's a habit, and as such, it can be stopped. You can learn from the experience and build up your resilience to strengthen your character as you move ahead.

I know what you're thinking: "If it's just a habit, why does it feel so impossible to break?" Fair question. But think about it this way: Biting your nails is also just a habit, yet plenty of people struggle with it for years.

The difference between overthinking and nail-biting is that overthinking happens inside your head, where nobody can see it, so it feels more mysterious and permanent than it actually is.

The truth is, you've probably already broken dozens of habits in your lifetime without even thinking about it. Remember when you used to check Facebook every five minutes? Or when you couldn't go to sleep without watching TV? Most habits fade away so gradually that we don't even notice we've stopped doing them.

Overthinking feels different because it seems to serve a purpose. Your brain tricks you into believing that all that mental spinning is actually productive, like you're problem-solving or preparing for the worst. But here's the reality check:

There's a huge difference between thinking something through and thinking something to death.

Your Anti-Overthinking Toolkit (Some Assembly Required)

Think of stress management techniques like having a good toolbox. You don't need every tool ever invented, but you want a few reliable ones that actually work when your mental pipes start leaking or your emotional circuit breaker trips.

The Greatest Hits (AKA What We've Already Covered)

Let's do a quick recap of some tools we've already put in your toolkit. Mindfulness is still your MVP—that simple practice of noticing what's happening right now instead of spiraling into what-if land. It's like having a mental anchor that keeps you from drifting into overthinking territory.

CBT techniques are your logic squad. When your brain starts creating disaster movies, CBT helps you fact-check the script. "Is this thought helpful? Is it even true? What would I tell a friend dealing with this?" Sometimes your brain needs a good reality check, and CBT is great at providing one.

Moving Your Body (Because Your Brain Lives There Too)

Here's something that took me way too long to figure out: Your body and mind aren't separate entities having a polite conversation. They're more like roommates who share everything, including stress. When your mind is spinning, your body feels it. When your body is tense, your mind gets the memo.

Exercise is like hitting the reset button on your stress levels. It doesn't have to be some intense gym session where you look like you're training for the Olympics. A twenty-minute walk works wonders. Dancing in your living room counts too, and yes, I'm talking about the kind where you pretend you're in a music video when nobody's watching.

The beauty of movement is that it gives your overthinking brain something else to focus on. Try having an elaborate worry session while you're concentrating on not tripping over your own feet in a dance class. It's surprisingly difficult.

Calming Your Nervous System (The Technical Stuff Made Simple)

Your nervous system is like your body's alarm system, and overthinking keeps hitting the panic button. Nervous system regulation sounds fancy, but it's really just teaching your body how to chill out.

Yoga and Pilates are fantastic for this. They combine movement with breathing, which is like giving your nervous system a nice cup of chamomile tea. Plus, it's hard to catastrophize about tomorrow's meeting when you're trying to figure out how to balance on one foot without falling over.

Deep breathing exercises work too. I know, I know—"just breathe" sounds like the most useless advice ever when you're stressed. But there's actual science behind it. Slow, deep breaths tell your nervous system, "Hey, we're not being chased by a bear right now. We can relax."

The Fun Stuff (Because Life Shouldn't Be All Work)

Music is pure magic for an overthinking brain. It's like giving your mind permission to focus on something beautiful instead of something stressful. Whether you're listening to it, playing it, or singing off-key in your car, music shifts your mental channel from the worry station to something more pleasant. Hobbies are your secret weapon against overthinking. When you're totally absorbed in gardening, cooking, or building model airplanes, your brain can't multitask its way into a worry spiral. You're present, focused, and giving your overthinking mind a well-deserved break.

The key is finding what works for you. Maybe yoga makes you feel zen, or maybe it makes you feel like a pretzel. That's fine; try dancing instead. Maybe meditation feels impossible, but painting helps you focus. Go with what feels good, not what you think you should do.

The goal isn't to become stress-proof—that's not realistic. The goal is to have reliable ways to dial down the stress when it shows up so it doesn't turn into a full-blown overthinking marathon.

The Body-Brain Connection: Why Your Mental Health Starts with Your Physical Health

Here's something that sounds obvious but somehow gets ignored all the time: Your brain lives in your body. I know, groundbreaking stuff, right? But seriously, we treat our minds like they're floating around in some separate dimension, completely disconnected from whether we've slept, eaten, or moved our bodies in the last 24 hours.

The truth is, how the techniques we've talked about work together with physical activity, nutrition, and sleep contributes to healthy mental energy management and reduces the likelihood of overthinking. Think of it like this: your brain is basically a really demanding houseguest who needs the right environment to behave properly.

Moving Your Body to Quiet Your Mind

Physical activity is like a magic reset button for mental energy. When you're stuck in an overthinking loop, your brain is essentially running in circles like a hamster on a wheel. Exercise gives all that spinning energy somewhere useful to go.

I used to think I was too busy to work out, especially when my mind was racing about deadlines and problems. Turns out, that's exactly when I needed to move the most. A good workout doesn't just tire out your body; it literally changes your brain chemistry. Those feel-good chemicals that get released? They're like nature's chill pills.

You don't need to become a gym rat or train for a marathon. Even a fifteen-minute walk can shift your mental state from "everything is terrible" to "okay, maybe I can handle this." The key is doing something that gets your heart pumping and gives your mind a break from its favorite hobby of worrying about stuff.

Feeding Your Brain (Not Just Your Cravings)

Let's talk about nutrition, and no, I'm not about to tell you to survive on kale smoothies and quinoa. But here's the thing—what you eat directly affects how well your brain works. When you're running on sugar crashes and caffeine spikes, your mental energy is all over the place.

Ever notice how you're more likely to overthink when you're hungry? Or how that 3 p.m. sugar crash makes everything seem more dramatic than it actually is? Your brain needs steady fuel to stay focused and calm. When your blood sugar is doing the roller coaster thing, your thoughts follow right along for the ride. I'm not saying you need to eat perfectly all the time; I still stress-eat cookies when life gets overwhelming. But having some basic protein and eating regular meals instead of surviving on snacks and caffeine makes a huge difference in how much mental energy you have for actual thinking versus spinning your wheels.

Sleep: Your Brain's Maintenance Mode

And then there's sleep: The thing we all know we need more of but somehow always sacrifice first when life gets busy.

Here's what happens when you don't get enough sleep: Your brain basically becomes that friend who's had too much coffee and not enough food. Everything seems like a bigger deal than it is.

Sleep is when your brain does its housekeeping, sorting through the day's information, filing away what's important, and taking out the mental trash. When you're sleep-deprived, all that mental clutter just piles up, making it way easier to get stuck in overthinking mode.

Good sleep doesn't just happen by accident, especially if you're prone to overthinking. Your racing mind loves to throw you a replay of every awkward conversation from the last decade right when your head hits the pillow. Having a wind-down routine, whether it's reading, stretching, or just putting your phone in another room, helps signal to your brain that it's time to stop processing and start resting.

Magic Happens When It All Works Together

The real magic happens when you get all three working together. Regular movement, decent nutrition, and enough sleep create the foundation for mental clarity. When your physical needs are met, your brain has the energy to focus on what actually matters instead of getting hijacked by every random worry that pops up.

It's not about being perfect; it's about giving your brain the basic support it needs to function well.

The Boring Stuff That Actually Works (Sorry, It's Not All Face Masks and Wine)

Let's clear something up right away: When I talk about self-care, I'm not talking about the Instagram version with bubble baths and shopping sprees. Real self-care is way more boring than that, and honestly, that's why it actually works. It's the daily stuff that keeps your mental foundation solid so you don't crumble every time life gets stressful.

Self-Care That Actually Matters

Real self-care starts with the basics, and I mean the really basic stuff. Good hygiene isn't just about not offending people; it's about feeling human. When you're in an overthinking spiral, sometimes a hot shower is the reset button you didn't know you needed. It's hard to catastrophize about tomorrow's presentation when you're focused on how good the hot water feels.

Taking time to do things you enjoy sounds simple, but most overthinkers are terrible at this. We feel guilty for "wasting time" on hobbies or activities that don't have some obvious productivity payoff. But here's the thing: Doing stuff you actually enjoy isn't selfish; it's maintenance. It's like changing the oil in your car. Skip it too long, and eventually something important breaks down.

Dedicating time each day or week to spending time alone isn't about becoming a hermit. It's about giving your brain some quiet space to just be, without having to perform or respond to other people's needs. Even fifteen minutes of sitting with your coffee before everyone else wakes up counts. Your mind needs downtime the same way your phone needs to charge.

The Healthy Habits Nobody Talks About

A balanced diet doesn't mean you have to eat like a fitness influencer. It just means not living off energy drinks and whatever's left in your fridge at midnight. When your blood sugar is stable, your mood is more stable. When your mood is stable, your thoughts are less likely to go off the rails.

I learned this the hard way after spending way too many afternoons convinced everything was falling apart, only to realize I'd forgotten to eat lunch. Turns out, half my "life crises" were actually just low blood sugar tantrums. Who knew?

Getting sunshine and fresh air sounds like advice from your grandmother, but she was onto something. Natural light helps regulate your sleep cycle, and fresh air gives your brain oxygen to think clearly. Plus, being outside for even a few minutes can interrupt a mental spiral just by changing your environment.

The Medical Stuff We Love to Ignore

Here's where it gets really unglamorous: regular medical checkups and staying on top of necessary treatments. I know, I know. Nobody likes going to the doctor or dealing with health stuff when they're busy worrying about everything else. But physical health problems have a sneaky way of making mental health problems worse.

That untreated thyroid issue? It could be making your anxiety worse. Those headaches you keep ignoring? They might be affecting your ability to think clearly. That prescription you stopped taking because you felt better?

Yeah, you probably felt better because the prescription was working. Taking care of your physical health isn't separate from taking care of your mental health; they're the same thing, wearing different outfits.

Why This Boring Stuff Builds Resilience

When you tend to these basic needs consistently, you're building a foundation that can handle stress without cracking. Think of it like this: If your basic needs are met and your body is functioning well, you have way more mental energy available for dealing with actual problems instead of being constantly drained by the basics.

Resilience isn't about being tough enough to handle anything. It's about having enough resources—physical, mental, and emotional—to bounce back when things get hard. And those resources come from the daily, boring habits that nobody posts about on social media.

The beauty of focusing on these fundamentals is that they work even when you don't feel like they're working. You might not notice the difference day to day, but over time, you'll realize you're handling stress better, sleeping more soundly, and spending less time trapped in overthinking loops.

It's not sexy, but it works. And sometimes that's exactly what you need.

Chapter 11:

Cultivating Calm and Inner Peace

Ten chapters into this book, you've probably gotten better at catching yourself when you start spinning out. Maybe you've tried some of the techniques to interrupt those thought loops. That's awesome. But there's still a gap between "not actively freaking out" and actually feeling peaceful, right?

I'm always fascinated by those rare humans who genuinely don't overthink things. They just... exist? Without second-guessing every email they send? Without replaying conversations from 2017? How?

Look, inner peace isn't reserved for meditation gurus or that irritatingly calm friend who does hot yoga and says things like "everything happens for a reason." Even your overthinking brain deserves some quiet time.

The Overthinking Toolkit: Real-World Calm for Your Chaotic Brain

Let's be real—the phrase "practice mindfulness" can trigger an eye-roll so hard you might pull a muscle. Especially when your brain is busy calculating 37 different ways your presentation could go wrong tomorrow while simultaneously replaying that awkward thing you said to your neighbor in 2018.

But here's the thing about finding calm when you're an overthinker: It's less about achieving some mystical state of enlightenment and more about giving your poor, overworked brain something else to do for five freaking minutes.

So, let's talk about what actually works in the real world when your thoughts are bouncing around like a toddler who found the Halloween candy stash.

Get Outside, for Crying Out Loud!

My therapist once told me to "try a nature walk" when I was mid-anxiety spiral. I wanted to throw something at her. But annoyingly, she was right. There's something about feeling grass under your feet or watching leaves do their leaf thing that pulls you out of your head. Even a quick lap around your office building can reset your brain. The overthinking part of your brain hates being reminded that an entire world exists outside your problems.

The Breath Thing Actually Works (I Was Skeptical, Too)

You know how people are always saying "just breathe"?

And you're thinking, "I AM breathing, Karen; that's not the issue here!" But there's a difference between the shallow chest-breathing we do while stress-scrolling Twitter and actual, intentional breathing. Try this: Breathe in for four counts, hold for seven, and exhale for eight. Do it three times when you're spiraling. I was shocked at how quickly it can interrupt a thought tornado.

Yoga: Not Just for Instagram Influencers

I avoided yoga for years because I'm about as flexible as a brick. But it turns out yoga isn't actually about touching your toes or looking cute in expensive leggings. It's about connecting your busy mind to your neglected body. Even five minutes of stretching while focusing on how your muscles feel can snap you out of an overthinking episode. YouTube has tons of "yoga for beginners who can't touch their toes and don't own crystals" videos. Trust me on this one.

Visualization (That Doesn't Require Artistic Talent)

When someone first told me to "visualize my happy place," I genuinely couldn't think of anything except my bed with Netflix and snacks. Which, valid! But visualization can be as simple as imagining your thoughts as leaves floating down a stream; you see them, but you don't jump in after them.

Or picturing your anxiety as a pushy salesperson that you can politely but firmly say "no thanks" to.

The Comfort Stuff That Isn't Meditation

Not everyone finds peace in silence. Sometimes the best way to calm an overthinking brain is to give it just enough distraction:

- Turn on music that matches the mood you want, not the mood you have.

- Surround yourself with soft colors and textures (I literally keep a piece of velvet in my desk drawer to touch when I'm stressed—weird but effective).

- Eat something that reminds you of feeling safe (my go-to overthinking snack is cinnamon toast; it's like a hug for your mouth).

- Pet an animal if you have one (my cat has unwittingly provided thousands of dollars' worth of therapy).

- Rock in a chair or swing in a hammock (the rhythmic motion tells your nervous system, "We're safe now.")

The "I'm Still Overthinking, But at Least I'm Doing Something Else, Too" Activities

Sometimes you can't stop the thoughts, but you can put them in the passenger seat instead of letting them drive.

- Journal it out (even if you just write "this sucks" fifty times).

- Call that friend who gets it (you know the one).

- Sleep with a stuffed animal (no judgment; my stuffed sloth Pablo sees all my 3 a.m. crises).

- Get a fidget toy (they're not just for kids; my spinner has survived many work meetings).

You don't have to be good at any of these things. You just have to try them when your brain is being a jerk. The goal isn't perfect peace; it's just to turn down the volume on your thoughts from "heavy metal concert" to "loud café." And sometimes, that's enough.

Boring Is Beautiful: Why Predictable Routines Save Your Sanity

The word "routine" has a PR problem. It sounds dull, restrictive, and vaguely adult, like fiber supplements or organizing your tax receipts. But for those of us with brains that treat every minor decision as a life-altering crisis, routines aren't boring; they're freaking lifesavers.

Here's something nobody tells you about overthinking: It feeds on uncertainty like a teenager feeds on pizza rolls. Every unstructured moment is an invitation for your brain to helpfully generate 47 different scenarios about what might happen next. Gee, thanks, brain! This is where daily routines come in, not as rigid prison schedules, but as little islands of certainty in your day where your brain can actually take a break from being... well, your brain.

Morning Routines: The Original Reset Button

I'm not going to sit here and tell you to wake up at 5 a.m. to journal and do sun salutations while drinking green juice. If that's your thing, awesome. But for the rest of us mere mortals, a morning routine can be much simpler.

The magic isn't in WHAT you do, but in the blessed predictability of doing it. When you wake up at roughly the same time and follow the same few steps, whether that's "bathroom, coffee, shower, breakfast, teeth" or some other sequence, your brain starts to recognize the pattern. And patterns don't require decisions. And fewer decisions mean less material for your overthinking machine to work with.

My own morning routine isn't Instagram-worthy. It's literally alarm, stare at the ceiling contemplating existence for exactly two minutes, bathroom, coffee (while checking phone despite knowing better), shower, clothes, and breakfast if there's time. But it's my routine, and my anxiety knows the choreography by heart.

Evening Wind-Down: Teaching Your Brain to Shut Up

Your brain is like a toddler at bedtime; it will use ANY excuse to stay up and keep the party going. "But wait! Have we thought about that work email from three weeks ago?

What if it was secretly passive-aggressive? Let's analyze it word by word at 11:43 p.m.!" A consistent bedtime routine is like a lullaby for your overactive mind. It signals, "We're done thinking for today. Thanks for your service. Please clock out now."

The sleep expert I know recommends turning off screens 30 minutes before bed, which always makes me laugh because what am I supposed to do with myself for 30 minutes? Just sit there with my thoughts? The very thoughts I'm trying to escape? Hard pass.

But I've found my own version that works: I still use my phone, but I switch to reading an extremely boring novel instead of scrolling through rage-inducing news. Then, I do the bathroom stuff, put on the same sleep shirt I've had since college (judge away), and make chamomile tea that I'll forget to drink until it's cold.

Is it perfect? No. Does my brain know this sequence means "shut up soon?" Mostly yes.

The Secret Sauce: Consistency, Not Perfection

Here's the thing about routines: They work because you do them most of the time, not because you do them perfectly every time. Your brain doesn't need military precision; it just needs enough familiarity to feel safe.

Some days you'll oversleep. Some nights you'll fall asleep on the couch watching videos of people cleaning their dishwashers (just me?). That's fine. The goal isn't perfection; it's reducing the total number of decisions your poor, overtaxed brain needs to make. Start small. Pick one part of your day that usually feels chaotic, and create even a three-step routine around it. Morning, evening, lunchtime, whatever.

Your overthinking brain will fight it at first, "But what if we need flexibility?" it'll argue, always looking for escape hatches to worry through.

Remind it gently that routines aren't cages; they're hammocks. They hold you when you're too tired to hold yourself. And for overthinkers, that's not boring, it's beautiful.

Mental Jiu-Jitsu: Throwing Your Thoughts Without Getting Thrown

Remember when we were kids and thought quicksand would be a much bigger problem in adult life? Turns out the real quicksand is our own thinking. One negative thought leads to another, and suddenly you're neck-deep in "everyone hates me, and I'll die alone with seventeen cats who will eat my face when I'm gone."

The good news? You can learn to spot the quicksand before you're in too deep. The better news? Even when life truly is a Category 5 hurricane of chaos, you can find that weird calm spot in the middle, like those freaky storm chasers who drive into tornadoes for fun, except without the near-death experience and with more pajamas.

Spotting the Thought Traps (Again)

If you've been skipping around in this book (no judgment, I do the same thing), you might want to flip back to Chapter 4, where we dove deep into thought patterns. But here's the CliffsNotes version for my fellow impatient readers:

Your brain is constantly narrating your life, but it's not exactly Morgan Freeman quality. It's more like that drunk guy at a sports bar who's never actually played the game but has *very* strong opinions about how everyone else is doing it wrong. The first step is simply noticing when this obnoxious announcer starts spouting nonsense. "Oh, there goes my brain again, telling me

I'm going to get fired because my boss didn't use an exclamation point in their email." Just labeling it as a thought, not a fact, creates some breathing room.

The RAIN Method (Not a Weather Forecast)

When you're really stuck in mental quicksand, try this four-step process that some smart people at Forbes came up with (and I've personally tested during countless 3 a.m. panic sessions):

- **R = Recognize:** "Well, hello there, intrusive thought about how everyone at the party secretly hated me! Fancy seeing you again!"

- **A = Accept:** This doesn't mean agreeing with the thought. It just means not fighting it or shoving it down with a mental pillow while it kicks and screams. "Yep, that's definitely a thought I'm having right now. It exists."

- **I = Investigate:** Get curious instead of furious. "Hmm, why might my brain be serving up this particular flavor of anxiety today? Am I tired? Hungry? Did someone tag me in a weird Facebook memory from 2012?"

- **N = Non-identify:** This is the magic part. "This thought is happening, but it's not ME. It's just a thought my brain produced, like how my nose produces snot sometimes. Gross but temporary."

I once used this while convinced a typo in a work email had ended my entire career. By the time I got to the "N" step, I was able to laugh at how my brain had constructed an elaborate firing scenario based on accidentally typing "pubic" instead of "public." (True story, unfortunately.)

Finding Your Inner Storm Chaser

Life gets chaotic. Your kid gets sick the same day as your big presentation, your basement floods during a family visit, and your car makes that expensive-sounding noise on the highway. These things happen whether you overthink them or not. The difference is whether you get swept away or find the calm in the center.

Here's how real humans (not Instagram yogis) stay centered when everything's falling apart:

- **Visualization that doesn't require artistic talent:** Picture yourself as a mountain. Weather happens around you—storms, sunshine, whatever—but the mountain remains. Cheesy? Yes. Effective when you're losing your mind? Also, yes.

- **Faith without the lecture:** If you've got a spiritual practice, lean on it. If you don't, that's cool too. The point is connecting to something bigger than your immediate problems, whether that's God, the universe, or just the realization that humans have been surviving chaos for thousands of years.

- **Thought renovation:** This is just a fancy way of saying "challenge your dramatic assumptions." When your brain screams, "This is the worst thing ever!" ask it for evidence. Has anything actually been "the worst thing ever" before? How did that turn out? Usually, we survive.

- **The positivity sandwich:** Between two slices of chaos, find one good thing happening. Your presentation bombed, but your hair looked amazing, and you didn't pass out from anxiety. Take the win where you can.

- **Control is mostly an illusion anyway:** Ever notice how the things we stress most about controlling are usually things we can't actually control? Other people's opinions, traffic, the weather, and whether your teenager makes good choices. Recognizing what's outside your control isn't giving up; it's focusing your energy where it actually matters.

- **Uncertainty is the only certainty:** The human brain hates not knowing. It would rather believe something terrible and certain than something unknown. But learning to sit with "I don't know what happens next" is like a superpower for overthinkers.

I remember when I tried to control my son's college application process and ended up with hives. I finally had to accept that checking the application portal seventeen times a day wouldn't change the outcome. The hives cleared up within a week of surrendering to the uncertainty.

Detaching from thoughts and staying centered aren't one-time achievements; they're practices. Some days you'll nail it, feeling all zen while chaos swirls. Other days you'll get sucked right into the tornado. That's not failure; it's being human. The goal isn't perfection; it's bouncing back faster each time. And sometimes, the most centered thing you can do is admit, "I'm not feeling very centered right now, and that's okay."

Part 4:

Living the New You—Moving Forward With Confidence

Chapter 12:

Creating a Life That Supports Balance

So, you've made it this far—congratulations! You've learned to recognize your thought spirals, interrupt them mid-spin, and even find moments of calm in the chaos. That's huge. But let's be honest: You're still living in the same life that created your overthinking habit in the first place.

It's like trying to quit sugar while working in a donut shop. Technically possible, but damn near impossible in practice.

I learned this lesson the hard way when I tried to reduce my anxiety while still maintaining five group chats that pinged 24-7, working for a boss who sent emails at 3 a.m., and living with a roommate who started political debates over breakfast. My therapist finally said, "You know, sometimes the problem isn't you; it's the water you're swimming in."

Your environment shapes your thinking more than any mindfulness app ever could. The people you spend time with, the physical spaces you inhabit, and the routines that structure your day—all of these things are either feeding your overthinking habit or starving it.

Designing Your Life: The Peaceful Mind Blueprint

Have you ever noticed how some spaces just feel right? You walk in and immediately breathe easier. Or how certain friends leave you energized while others drain every ounce of your mental battery? That's not random; it's the invisible architecture of your life at work.

You can actually design your life to quiet that overthinking mind of yours. I'm not talking about some complicated system that requires a PhD to implement. This is about simple, everyday choices that add up to major mental peace.

Start with your physical spaces. Look around your home or workspace right now. Does it make you feel calm or chaotic? Clutter isn't just visually distracting; it's mentally exhausting.

Your brain registers each item as something to potentially think about. That pile of unread mail? Your overthinking mind sees it as twenty different decisions waiting to be made.

You don't need to become a minimalist overnight (unless that's your thing). Just experiment with clearing one surface that you see daily. That nightstand drowning in random stuff? Clear it off, keep only what brings you peace, and watch how your bedtime overthinking might just ease up a bit.

Now, for the people part. We all have that friend who somehow turns every coffee date into a stress session. You know the one; they highlight every possible thing that could go wrong in any situation. While they might be lovely people, they're overthinking enablers.

Take a moment to mentally sort your relationships into three categories: energizers, neutrals, and drainers. The energizers leave you feeling lighter, more capable. The neutrals are fine either way. The drainers? They're the ones who send your thought spiral into overdrive.

I'm not suggesting you dramatically cut people off (though sometimes that's necessary). Instead, be intentional about exposure. Maybe that anxiety-inducing colleague doesn't need to be your lunch buddy five days a week. Perhaps your catastrophizing cousin is better in small doses. Surround yourself with people who help your mind settle rather than stir it up. Digital relationships count, too. That news site that leaves you convinced the world is ending? The social media account that makes you question every life choice? They're relationships, too, ones you can modify or end. I used to start every morning with twenty minutes of news scrolling.

No wonder my days began with worry! Now, I check headlines once, later in the day, and my mornings feel spacious instead of suffocating.

Then there's the magic of routine. Overthinking loves uncertainty; it's prime territory for your mind to explore every conceivable scenario. Creating gentle structures in your day reduces the mental load of constant decision-making.

This isn't about scheduling every minute. It's about creating predictable rhythms that your brain can relax into. Maybe it's a morning ritual of three deep breaths before checking your phone. Or a consistent bedtime that signals to your body it's time to power down.

I struggled with Sunday night insomnia for years, my mind racing with work worries. Creating a simple evening routine (shower, tea, ten minutes of reading something light) gave my brain the signal that it was time to transition.

The overthinking didn't disappear instantly, but it quieted considerably.

Your environment, relationships, and routines aren't just background features in your life; they're active ingredients in your mental well-being recipe. The beauty is that you get to be the chef. Mix, adjust, and taste-test until you find the combination that helps your mind find that sweet spot of clarity and peace.

Breaking Free: Nurturing Your Positive Mindset

You know that moment when you're doing great, feeling confident, and then—whoosh—you're right back where you started, overthinking everything again? Yeah, we've all been there.

Building Your Positive Mindset Toolkit

Your mindset is kind of like a garden. You can't just yank out the weeds (those negative thoughts) and walk away.

You've got to plant something good in their place, or those weeds come back faster than you can blink.

- **Start with your strengths:** We're weirdly good at cataloging everything we mess up, but terrible at remembering what we do well. Write down three things you're genuinely good at. Not world-changing stuff; maybe you make excellent coffee, remember people's birthdays, or can parallel park like a boss. These count.

- **Practice gratitude without the cheese:** I'm not talking about forced sunshine-and-rainbows gratitude. Find three real things each day that didn't completely suck. Your morning shower was hot. The traffic light turned green right when you got there. Your coworker didn't microwave fish in the break room again. Small wins matter.

- **Be your own best friend:** When you mess up, what do you tell yourself? If it's meaner than what you'd say to a friend in the same situation, you need to adjust your inner voice. Self-compassion isn't about lowering standards; it's about being reasonable with yourself.

- **Take care of the basics:** You can't think clearly when you're running on fumes. Sleep, food, movement, water. I know, I know—groundbreaking advice. But seriously, when did you last go to bed at a decent time without scrolling your phone until 2 a.m.?

- **Use positive affirmations that don't make you cringe:** Forget "I am a magnificent butterfly of success." Try something you actually believe: "I can handle whatever comes up today" or "I'm learning to trust myself more."

- **Stay in today:** Your brain loves time travel, replaying yesterday's awkward conversation or fast-forwarding to next month's presentation disaster. When you catch yourself drifting, bring your attention back to right now. What do you see, hear, and smell?

- **Redirect the negative spiral:** Notice when your thoughts start spiraling, then ask, "Is this helping me solve anything, or am I just rehearsing problems?" If it's the latter, do something else. Call someone, take a walk, organize your junk drawer, or whatever breaks the cycle.

- **Laugh at yourself (nicely):** Humor deflates anxiety better than almost anything. When I catch myself catastrophizing about sending a typo-filled email, I remind myself that no one's getting fired over "teh" instead of "the."

- **Choose your crowd carefully:** You know those friends who could find something wrong with winning the lottery? You love them, but maybe don't call them when you need a pep talk. Stick close to people who see what's possible, not just what could go wrong.

Staying on Track (Without Falling Into Old Traps)

Here's the thing about breaking habits: your brain doesn't like empty spaces.

If you just try to stop overthinking without replacing it with something else, you're basically creating a vacuum that your old patterns will rush to fill.

- **Replace, don't just erase:** When you feel the urge to spiral, have a replacement ready. Instead of mentally rehearsing every possible disaster, write down what you know for sure right now. Instead of analyzing that text message for the fifteenth time, text someone else about something completely different.

- **Redefine what success looks like:** Success isn't never having anxious thoughts; it's catching them sooner and bouncing back faster. Some days, success is only spiraling for ten minutes instead of two hours. That's progress.

- **Know your triggers and have an escape plan:** Maybe it's certain topics, times of day, or even particular rooms where you tend to overthink. You don't have to avoid everything forever, but knowing your weak spots helps you prepare.

- **Use your crew:** That support group you've been putting together? Actually lean on them. Not just when everything's falling apart, but for regular reality checks. Sometimes just saying out loud, "I'm going down the rabbit hole about work again," is enough to snap you out of it.

Change isn't a straight line; it's more like a drunk person trying to walk home. Sometimes you make progress, sometimes you bump into things, but you usually get there eventually.

Goals That Don't Make You Want to Hide Under a Blanket

Let's talk about goals for a minute. Not the kind you set on New Year's Eve after three glasses of champagne, where you decide you're going to run a marathon, learn French, and reorganize your entire life by February. I'm talking about the kind of goals that don't make you break out in a cold sweat every time you think about them.

You know what happens when we set crazy goals that have nothing to do with who we actually are? We overthink them to death. We lie awake at 2 a.m., wondering why we're not jogging at 5 a.m. like we said we would or why we haven't touched that guitar that's been collecting dust for three months.

Start With What Actually Matters to You

Before you even think about what you want to achieve, you need to get honest about what you care about. And I mean really care about, not what you think you should care about, because your sister's friend posted about it on Instagram. Sit down somewhere quiet (yes, the bathroom counts) and ask yourself, *What makes me feel good about myself?* Not accomplished or impressive—just good. Maybe it's making people laugh. Maybe it's having a clean kitchen. Maybe it's knowing random facts about penguins. Whatever it is, that's your starting point.

I spent years setting goals around being more "productive" because that seemed important. Turns out, I don't actually care about productivity. I care about having time to read weird books and take long walks. Once I figured that out, everything got easier.

Your values aren't a Pinterest board of inspirational quotes. They're the stuff that makes you feel like yourself when you're doing it.

Check Your Energy Account

Here's something they don't teach you in those goal-setting workshops: You can't spend energy you don't have. I know, revolutionary concept.

Think about your energy like a bank account. Some things make deposits; maybe that's time alone, or being outside, or talking to your best friend. Other things make withdrawals: difficult conversations, crowded places, or trying to adult before you've had coffee.

If you set a goal that requires more withdrawals than you've got deposits coming in, you're going to burn out. And then you're going to overthink why you can't stick to anything and what's wrong with you. (Spoiler alert: Nothing's wrong with you.) Look at your typical week. When do you feel energized? When do you feel drained? Don't try to force yourself into someone else's schedule. If you're not a morning person, stop setting goals that require you to be chipper at dawn. Work with what you've got, not against it.

Make Goals That Don't Stress You Out

Good goals should feel exciting, not terrifying. If thinking about your goal makes you want to take a nap, it's probably not the right goal for you right now.

Start smaller than you think you need to. Seriously. If you want to exercise more, don't commit to an hour at the gym every day. Commit to putting on your sneakers three times a week. That's it. You can always do more once you get there, but you can't do less than nothing.

The goal is to build momentum, not to impress anyone. I once set a goal to "drink more water" and started by just keeping a water bottle on my desk. Revolutionary? No. Sustainable? Absolutely.

Keep It Real With Yourself

Your goals need to fit your actual life, not the life you wish you had. If you've got three kids under five, your goal probably shouldn't be "meditate for an hour every morning." Maybe it's "Take three deep breaths before I lose my patience with someone."

This isn't about lowering your standards. It's about being smart about where you are right now. You can always adjust as things change, but you've got to start from reality.

Also, check in with yourself regularly. Not in a judgy way, but like you're checking in with a friend. How's this going? Does this still make sense? Do we need to switch things up?

The Overthinking Escape Hatch

When you start spiraling about whether you're doing enough or the right things, remember this: The perfect goal doesn't exist. There are just goals that work for you right now and goals that don't. If a goal is making you miserable, change it. You're not signing a contract with the universe. You're just trying stuff out to see what sticks.

Your goals should help you feel more like yourself, not less. If they're doing the opposite, it's time for a reset.

Chapter 13:

The Role of Gratitude and Positive Thinking

You've probably heard someone tell you to "have an attitude of gratitude," and chances are good you rolled your eyes so hard they nearly fell out of your head. I get it. I really do.

There's something about gratitude advice that makes it sound like it came straight from a motivational poster featuring a kitten hanging from a tree branch. It feels cheesy, forced, and about as helpful as being told to "just think positive" when you're having the worst day of your life.

But here's the thing, and I hate to be the bearer of news that sounds like it came from your overly optimistic aunt: There's actually some real wisdom buried under all that flowery language. Don't worry, I'm not about to tell you to start every morning by thanking the universe for your blessings while doing yoga in flowing white clothes.

The Great Mental U-Turn: How Gratitude Stops the Spiral

It's Tuesday, you're lying in bed at 2 a.m., and your brain decides now's the perfect time to replay that cringeworthy thing you said at work six months ago. Then it jumps to wondering if your boss thinks you're totally incompetent, which somehow spirals into imagining yourself getting fired, which ends up with you living in a cardboard box, eating ramen.

You know how it goes.

The Art of the Mental U-Turn

When your brain gets stuck in one of those loops, it's like a broken record that keeps skipping on the same terrible song. You keep hearing the same awful notes over and over, getting more frustrated each time, but you can't seem to make it stop.

Gratitude is like walking over and lifting the needle off that record. It doesn't fix the scratch, but at least you don't have to keep listening to the same depressing chorus on repeat. It's not magic, and it's not about ignoring your real problems. It's about giving your brain something else to chew on when it gets stuck replaying the same old disasters.

When you catch yourself going down one of those dark paths, instead of continuing the slide, you force yourself to change direction. If your brain is going "This presentation is going to bomb, and everyone will think I'm clueless," you jump in with, "Actually, I'm glad I get to talk about something I care about with people who might actually find it interesting."

It's not about fooling yourself. It's about showing your brain that the same situation can look completely different depending on where you focus.

Breaking the Worry Habit

Your brain loves doing the same thing over and over. It's like that friend who's been ordering chicken parmesan at every Italian restaurant for the past ten years because "I know I like it." Except in this case, what your brain "likes" is actually making you miserable; it's just familiar. When you worry about the same stuff repeatedly, you're teaching your brain to be a world-class worrier about that particular thing. It becomes your go-to response.

The boss wants to see you? Obviously, you're in trouble. Does your friend take a while to text back? They must be mad at you.

Gratitude works because it teaches your brain a different habit. Instead of jumping straight to the worst possible outcome, you train it to look around for something else first. It's like teaching your paranoid brain that not every creaky sound at night means someone's breaking in; sometimes it's just the house settling.

From What-If to What-Is

Your overthinking brain lives in what-if land. What if this goes wrong? What if they think I'm weird? What if I screw up? What if, what if, what if? It's like having a roommate who only talks about potential disasters.

Gratitude drags you back to right now. What's actually going okay today? What's working in your life at this moment? What do you have now that you were hoping for last year?

I'm not talking about forcing yourself to be grateful for stuff you genuinely hate. If your job sucks, you don't have to be thankful for it. But maybe you can be grateful that it pays for your morning coffee, or that your coworker makes you laugh, or that you learned something new this week.

The Confidence Connection

Here's something interesting: When you regularly practice looking for what's going right, you start to trust yourself more. It's like you're building a file in your brain labeled "Evidence That I Can Handle Things" instead of just the one labeled "All The Ways This Could Go Wrong." Every time you catch something you're grateful for, even tiny stuff like "I'm glad I remembered to charge my phone last night," you're basically building up evidence that says, "Hey, look, sometimes things actually work out okay. I'm not completely hopeless at this life thing."

This isn't about becoming annoyingly positive. It's about balance. If your brain spends all day looking for problems, of course, you're going to feel anxious and overwhelmed. But if you also spend some time noticing what's working, you start to feel more capable of handling whatever comes up.

Making It Real (Not Fake)

The key to using gratitude as a loop-breaker is keeping it real. Don't try to be grateful for things that genuinely upset you; that's just another form of lying to yourself. Instead, look for the small, true things that you actually do appreciate.

Maybe you're stressed about money, but you're grateful your friend listened to you vent about it. Maybe work is crazy, but you're glad you figured out how to use that new software.

Maybe your day was mostly lousy, but that sandwich you had for lunch was actually pretty great.

Small Moves, Big Changes: Your Daily Gratitude Toolkit

Let's talk about actually doing this gratitude thing instead of just thinking about it.

Start Before Your Feet Hit the Floor

Your brain is actually pretty mellow first thing in the morning, before it starts its daily freakout about everything you need to do. While you're still lying there dreading getting up, use this brief window of calm.

Think of five things you're grateful for. And I mean really simple stuff, not "I'm grateful for the gift of life," unless you genuinely feel that way. More like "I'm glad my bed is warm" or "I'm grateful I don't have to be anywhere for another twenty minutes."

Some days it might be, "I'm grateful my upstairs neighbor finally stopped playing music at 2 a.m." Other days it could be, "I'm glad I remembered to plug in my phone last night." The point isn't to find life-changing gratitude; it's to start your day noticing a few things that don't completely suck.

Write It Down (But Keep It Real)

Gratitude journals get a bad rap because people think they need to write beautiful, meaningful entries every day. Screw that. Your gratitude list can be a sticky note on your bathroom mirror or something you type into your phone.

Write down one thing that didn't suck about your day. Maybe your coffee was actually good for once. Maybe someone let you merge in traffic without honking. Maybe you found a parking spot right away. These tiny wins count just as much as the big stuff.

Notice the People Around You

This one's sneaky good for stopping overthinking because it pulls you out of your own head. When someone holds a door for you, actually make eye contact and say thanks. When the cleaning person at work does something nice, let them know you noticed.

It sounds tiny, but here's what happens: Instead of spending those moments stressing about your endless to-do list or replaying some cringey conversation, you're actually connecting with another person.

Your brain gets a break from running in circles. Plus, people remember when you actually see them. That cleaning person you thanked might be the one who helps you find your keys when you drop them later. The world feels a little less like everyone's just ignoring each other.

Get Outside Your Head (Literally)

When you're stuck spinning your wheels about something, go outside if you can. Not for some big nature moment, just step outside and notice one thing. How the light looks different than it did this morning.

How the air smells like rain or food from someone's kitchen. The fact that there are birds just doing their thing, completely unbothered by whatever's eating at you.

I'm not saying fresh air is going to fix everything. But it's hard to catastrophize about next week's meeting when you're watching a squirrel completely blow it trying to jump between trees. Sometimes you just need the reminder that the world is way bigger than whatever's bugging you.

Switch Up Your Phone Calls

Instead of calling someone to complain about how everything's going wrong (which we all do, and that's totally fine sometimes), try calling someone just to tell them something you like about them. It doesn't have to be deep. "Hey, I was just thinking about how you always remember to ask about my annoying boss situation," works perfectly.

This completely flips how your day feels. Instead of going over all your problems, you're actively hunting for good stuff to share. Your brain starts looking for positives instead of just scanning for disasters.

The Poetry Trick

You don't have to write good poetry. You don't even have to show it to anyone. But trying to put something you're grateful for into a few lines makes your brain actually focus on it instead of just breezing past.

"The coffee shop guy remembered my order / Made my Tuesday feel less like a chore" isn't going to win any awards, but it made me stop and actually think about how nice that moment was instead of rushing past it.

How Gratitude Rewires Your Overthinking Mind

Remember when your grandmother told you to "count your blessings?" Turns out, Grandma was right. She just didn't know she was giving you brain medicine.

The Overthinking Brain vs. The Grateful Brain

When you're stuck in overthinking mode, your brain looks like a traffic jam during rush hour. The prefrontal cortex, which is your thinking center, goes into overdrive, burning through mental energy like a gas-guzzling SUV. Meanwhile, your amygdala (the brain's alarm system) stays on high alert, convinced that thinking harder will somehow solve everything.

But here's where gratitude comes in like a traffic cop with a magic wand.

When you genuinely feel grateful, your brain does something cool. It dumps a bunch of feel-good chemicals: dopamine, serotonin, and oxytocin. These are like your brain's natural happy pills. Dopamine makes you feel good, serotonin lifts your mood, and oxytocin helps you chill out. This chemical rush does what your overthinking brain needs most; it makes everything stop for a minute.

The Default Mode Network: Your Brain's Screensaver

Scientists have discovered something called the default mode network (DMN) (Yeshurun et al., 2021). This is what your brain does when it's supposed to be "resting," except it's not really resting at all. It's ruminating, worrying, and running through scenarios like a broken record. For overthinkers, the DMN is like having a radio stuck between stations—lots of noise, no clear signal. Gratitude practices change how this network works. People who say "thank you" regularly have quieter minds. Less mental noise, fewer worry spirals, and actual calm.

Rewiring the Worry Highway

Your brain has neural pathways; think of them as well-worn hiking trails. The more you use a trail, the more established it becomes. Overthinkers have created superhighways for worry and rumination. Every time you spiral into "what if" thinking, you're strengthening those worry roads.

Gratitude creates new pathways. Each time you notice something you're thankful for, you're literally building new neural real estate. At first, these gratitude pathways are like tiny footpaths. But with practice, they become strong enough to redirect traffic away from the worry superhighway.

The Attention Hijack

Here's one of gratitude's best tricks: It steals your attention. Overthinking happens because your mind gets stuck on problems, spinning them around endlessly. Gratitude grabs your attention away from problems and points it toward what's actually okay.

This isn't about pretending problems don't exist. It's about giving your brain a breather so it can actually solve problems instead of just worrying about them.

The Stress Response Reboot

Chronic overthinking keeps your stress response system stuck in the "on" position. Your cortisol levels stay elevated, your nervous system remains activated, and your brain thinks you're constantly under threat.

Gratitude turns on your rest and digest mode. It's like switching your brain from panic mode back to normal. Your heart slows down, you breathe easier, and that tight feeling in your chest lets up.

Making It Stick

What I love about gratitude is that you can't mess it up. You don't need to feel thankful for huge, life-changing stuff every day. Sometimes it's just being glad your coffee didn't suck or that your dog did something adorable.

Your brain doesn't care if what you're grateful for is deep or silly. It just wants you building those new pathways, one "thanks" at a time.

Chapter 14:

Embracing the Flow of Life

Ever notice how some days just... work? You're crushing your to-do list, conversations feel effortless, and even traffic lights turn green as you approach. Then there are the other days, when you spill coffee on your shirt, forget your password for the seventeenth time, and every email feels like defusing a bomb.

The difference isn't luck. It's flow.

What the Hell Is "Flow" Anyway?

If "finding your flow" sounds like something your yoga teacher's yoga teacher would say while standing on her head and sipping kombucha, I get it. But stick with me here.

Remember that basketball game where you couldn't miss a shot? Or that work presentation where the words just came to you? Or even that road trip where four hours felt like twenty minutes because the conversation was so good? That's flow.

Flow is when you're so wrapped up in what you're doing that you forget to check your phone, worry about how you look, or mentally rehearse everything you need to do tomorrow. It's being completely here, now, doing this thing.

It is the sweet spot where your skills match the challenge perfectly, not so easy you're bored, not so hard you're freaking out. But I like to think of it as the mental equivalent of those perfect jeans that make your butt look amazing and are still comfortable enough to eat a burrito in.

The Overthinking Kryptonite

For those of us with brains that run on premium-grade anxiety, flow is like kryptonite to overthinking. When you're in flow, there's no mental bandwidth left for your greatest hits album of worries. Your internal narrator finally shuts the hell up.

Here's the beautiful irony: Flow happens precisely when you stop trying to control everything. It's surrendering to the current moment instead of frantically paddling upstream against it.

Take my friend Jake. He spent three months obsessing over asking for a raise, planning exactly what to say, and anticipating every possible objection his boss might have. When the big day came, he was so in his head that he tripped over his rehearsed script and left feeling like he'd bombed. Two weeks later, he had an impromptu conversation with the same boss about a successful project, wasn't overthinking it at all, and casually mentioned his contributions. Boom, got the raise on the spot.

The universe has a sick sense of humor that way.

Finding Your Flow (Without Moving to Bali)

So, how do you find this magical state without quitting your job to "find yourself" abroad? (Though if you can swing that financially, no judgment here.)

First, recognize that flow isn't one-size-fits-all. My flow state comes from writing or hiking. My partner finds it gaming. My mom gets it gardening. The activity doesn't matter; what matters is it's challenging enough to demand your full attention but familiar enough that you're not constantly stopping to figure out what to do next.

Here are some training wheels for your flow bicycle:

- **Physical stuff works wonders:** Running, swimming, yoga—anything that forces you to be in your body instead of just your head. I was skeptical until I tried lap swimming and realized I'd gone 30 minutes without a single thought about my work deadlines or that weird thing my friend said last week. Just me, counting laps, and trying not to drown. Bliss.

- **Set clear goals, but then forget about them:** Sounds contradictory, right? But flow needs direction without obsession. Know what you're aiming for, then focus on the process rather than constantly checking if you're "there yet," like a kid on a road trip.

- **Get familiar with the territory:** Flow happens more easily with tasks you know well enough to navigate confidently. That's why beginners rarely experience it; they're still at the "Wait, how do I hold this again?" stage. Stick with something long enough to get past the awkward phase.

- **Meditation isn't just for people who own singing bowls:** Even five minutes of focusing on your breath trains your brain to stay in the moment rather than time-traveling to past regrets or future catastrophes. And no, your thoughts won't magically stop. My meditation sessions still involve mentally redecorating my bathroom and remembering embarrassing moments from high school. The point isn't having zero thoughts; it's noticing when you're drifting and gently coming back.

- **Find your creative outlet:** Remember finger painting as a kid before you cared if it was "good"? Channel that energy. Write terrible poetry. Make ugly pottery. Cook experimental meals that sometimes fail spectacularly. Creating without judgment is flow's natural habitat.

Staying in Flow When Life Gets Stormy

"This is all great," you might be thinking, "but clearly you haven't met my boss/children/mortgage."

Fair point. Finding flow during life's highlight reel is one thing. Maintaining it when everything's falling apart is black-belt level.

But here's the secret: Challenging times are actually when flow becomes most valuable and, sometimes, most accessible.

When my dad was in the hospital last year, I found unexpected moments of flow sitting with him, just focusing on the rhythm of turning the pages in my book, the sound of his breathing, and the sunlight moving across the floor. Not because I was trying to escape reality, but because I was fully in it, without the added layer of anxious thoughts about what might happen next.

In crisis, our brains naturally narrow our focus to what's directly in front of us. The overthinking part gets temporarily sidelined by necessity. It's why people often report a strange clarity during emergencies.

You can cultivate this crisis-clarity without waiting for emergencies:

- **Bring it back to your body:** Feel your feet on the floor. Notice your breathing. Touch something and really feel its texture. Your body only exists in the present, so it's your anchor when your mind wants to time-travel.

- **Shrink the timeframe:** When everything feels overwhelming, focus on just the next hour, the next ten minutes, or even just the next breath. Flow doesn't require long stretches; it can happen in moments.

- **Embrace the suck:** Sometimes flow isn't about feeling good; it's about being fully present even with difficult emotions. Feeling the sadness or fear without adding a layer of thoughts about the feeling.

Flow isn't about having a perfect life. It's about being fully in the life you have, messy, uncertain, and occasionally wonderful. It's about trading the exhausting job of trying to control everything for the relief of riding whatever wave comes your way.

And for chronic overthinkers, that trade is the best deal going.

Chapter 15:

Living Your Life With Vitality

Remember that scene in The Wizard of Oz when everything suddenly shifts from black and white to Technicolor? That's what breaking free from overthinking feels like. The same life, but suddenly vibrant, dimensional, and way more interesting.

If you've stuck with me through fourteen chapters of untangling your mental knots, you're probably starting to experience some of those color bursts already. Maybe you've caught yourself actually enjoying a meal instead of mentally rehearsing tomorrow's meeting while you eat. Or perhaps you've gone a whole day without creating an elaborate disaster scenario based on a single ambiguous text message. Progress!

But here's the thing about overthinking: It's not just a mental habit. It's a whole-body experience that affects everything from your sleep to your digestion to that weird tension headache you get every Tuesday. The flip side is also true: When you calm your pinball-machine mind, your entire system benefits.

Let's talk about how all these pieces fit together and how to keep this momentum going long after you've used this book as a coaster for your third cup of coffee.

Your Brain and Body Are Actually Roommates

For years, we've treated physical health and mental health like they're living in separate apartments, maybe waving occasionally in the hallway. "Oh hey, anxiety! How's it going? Cool, cool. Well, I'm off to the cardiologist—see ya!" Turns out, they're actually sharing the same studio apartment and fighting over the thermostat.

My cousin Mark is a total health nut—he ran marathons, ate like he was auditioning for a kale commercial, and had the abs to prove it. But he was also the king of catastrophic thinking. Every minor work issue was the end of his career; every slight disagreement with his girlfriend was proof they were doomed.

Despite his peak physical condition, Mark developed chronic acid reflux, mysterious skin rashes, and insomnia that no amount of melatonin could touch. His doctor ran every test in the book before finally asking, "So... how's your stress level?"

Medical science is finally catching up to what our bodies have known all along: Your thoughts directly impact your physical health. When you're stuck in overthinking mode, your body is constantly flooded with stress hormones. Your heart works harder, your immune system gets suppressed, your digestion goes haywire, and your energy tanks faster than my phone battery on a road trip.

This isn't just woo-woo wellness talk. Hard-nosed cardiologists now routinely screen heart patients for anxiety and depression because the connection is that strong. One study found that people with high anxiety had a 48% higher risk of heart issues, about the same increased risk as being a heavy smoker (Roest et al., 2010). Yikes.

But before you start overthinking about your overthinking (meta-anxiety, anyone?), remember the reverse is also true: Reducing mental stress creates measurable physical benefits. Your blood pressure drops. Your sleep improves.

Your immune system perks up like a dog hearing the treat drawer open.

The Vitality Trifecta

Think of vitality as a three-legged stool: physical health, mental clarity, and emotional well-being. Kick out any leg, and you're going to have a hard time staying upright.

1. **Physical vitality** isn't just about having abs you could grate cheese on. It's about having enough energy to do the things that matter to you, whether that's chasing your kids around the yard or simply making it through a workday without mainlining caffeine. Basic stuff like moving your body regularly, eating food that doesn't make you feel like garbage, and getting enough sleep creates the foundation for everything else.

2. **Mental clarity** is what we've focused on throughout this book; the ability to think without your thoughts thinking you. It's recognizing when you're catastrophizing and being able to say, "Thanks, but no thanks" to that disaster movie your brain is trying to produce and direct.

3. **Emotional well-being** is perhaps the trickiest piece, allowing yourself to feel your feelings without drowning in them or stuffing them in the basement until they stage a midnight rebellion. It's the difference between "I'm feeling anxious" and "I am anxiety personified and doomed to eternal suffering."

When all three are working together, that's when life gets juicy. That's vitality.

From Surviving to Thriving: Your Owner's Manual

So, how do you maintain this delicate ecosystem once you've started to establish it?

Here's your no-BS maintenance guide:

- **Schedule worry-free zones:** Just like you might have a "no phones at dinner" rule, create pockets of your day that are overthinking-free. Maybe it's your morning shower, your commute, or the first cup of coffee. Train your brain that these times are sacred.

- **Move your meat suit daily:** Your body was designed to move, not hunch over a laptop for 10 hours. Find something that feels good—walking, dancing in your kitchen, chasing your dog around the yard, whatever—and do it regularly.

- **Feed yourself like you'd feed someone you actually like:** No, you don't need to become a clean-eating guru who makes their own nut milk. Just aim for food that gives you energy rather than making you want to nap under your desk. Your brain uses about 20% of your body's energy; it needs good fuel, not just whatever was available at the gas station.

- **Create a connection that doesn't require overthinking:** Some relationships feel like walking through an emotional minefield; one wrong word and boom. Other connections feel like coming home. Prioritize the people who don't require mental gymnastics just to have a conversation.

- **Remember that setbacks aren't failures:** You will absolutely have days when your mind goes full hurricane mode again. That doesn't mean you've failed or that this whole journey was pointless. It means you're human. The difference now is that you know how to find your way back to calm without getting lost for months.

When I finally broke my own overthinking habit, the most surprising change wasn't the improved sleep or even the reduction in those tension headaches that felt like wearing a too-tight headband. It was how much more room there was in my life. Room for spontaneous joy. Room for actual, deep-breath relaxation. Room for being present with the people I love instead of mentally preparing rebuttals to arguments that hadn't happened.

That's the real gift waiting on the other side of overthinking, not just the absence of mental chaos, but the presence of genuine vitality. Your life, in Technicolor.

Conclusion

So, here we are at the end of our little adventure together. If you've made it this far, you've probably dog-eared some pages, highlighted a few passages that hit too close to home, and maybe even tried some of the strategies we've talked about. Maybe you've caught yourself mid-spiral and thought, "Oh hey, I'm doing that overthinking thing again." Progress!

Let's be real: You're not going to close this book and suddenly transform into one of those mystical creatures who "just don't worry about things they can't control." Those people—do they even exist? Are they robots? The investigation continues.

Your brain isn't going to magically stop generating worst-case scenarios or replaying awkward conversations from 2014. That's not the goal here. The goal was never to stop thinking entirely, despite what my seventh-grade teacher suggested when she wrote "stop thinking so much" on my report card. Thanks, Mrs. Peterson, super helpful.

The actual goal is much simpler and much deeper: to stop being held hostage by those thoughts.

Remember where we started? With that familiar feeling of being trapped in a mental maze of your own creation. The exhaustion of rehearsing conversations that never happen. The physical tension of carrying tomorrow's problems in today's body. The relationships were strained because you were physically present but mentally lost in the labyrinth.

I'm not going to pretend that reading one book solves all that. No single tool or technique is a magic bullet. But what you have now is a toolbox.

Some days, you'll need the heavy-duty notice and name hammer for those persistent thought patterns. And some days, you'll forget the whole damn toolbox and find yourself three hours deep into an anxiety spiral about something someone might have implied about you at work.

That's not failure. That's being human.

The difference now is that you know the way back. You recognize the signs when your thoughts start to hijack your peace. You have practices to bring yourself back to the present moment. And most importantly, you understand that you are not your thoughts; you're the awareness behind them, the one who can choose whether to believe the stories your mind tells.

I still remember the first time I really got this. I was lying awake at 3 a.m., as one does, mentally drafting and redrafting an email to a client. I'd been at it for over an hour when suddenly I had this moment of clarity: "Wait, I'm not actually writing this email right now. I'm just torturing myself with hypothetical versions of it." I started laughing right there in the dark. The spell was broken.

Did I never overthink an email again? Please. I'm overthinking this very conclusion as I write it. But that moment changed something fundamental; I recognized the pattern. And once you can see the walls of the maze, you're already on your way out.

As you close this book and return to your life, with all its deadlines, relationships, and uncertainties, my hope for you isn't perfection. It's perspective. The ability to step back and see your thoughts as weather passing through the sky of your awareness, not as commands you must obey or truths you must believe. Your life is happening right now, not in the rehearsals and reviews your mind is staging.

It's in the taste of your morning coffee. The feeling of your kid's hand in yours. The satisfaction of solving a problem at work. The simple pleasure of a hot shower after a long day.

All the time you've spent overthinking isn't wasted if it led you here, to this new awareness. Think of it as the price of admission to a more present life. A life where you still think—deeply, creatively, meaningfully—but where thinking serves you rather than enslaves you.

Your thoughts will always be there, running commentary like an overenthusiastic sports announcer. But now you know you can turn down the volume, switch channels, or sometimes just mute the broadcast entirely and enjoy the game.

So, here's to fewer sleepless nights, less second-guessing, and more actually living the one wild and precious life you have.

Your overthinking mind brought you to this book. Your wiser self will take it from here.

Stop Your Stinking Overthinking
References

Ackerman, C. E. (2018, February 12). *Cognitive restructuring techniques for reframing thoughts.* Positive Psychology. https://positivepsychology.com/cbt-cognitive-restructuring-cognitive-distortions/#worksheets-cognitive-restructuring

Ackerman, C. E. (2024a, August 3). *23 amazing health benefits of mindfulness for body and brain.* Positive Psychology. https://positivepsychology.com/benefits-of-mindfulness/

Ackerman, C. E. (2024b, September 17). *Mindfulness-based stress reduction: The ultimate MBSR guide.* Positive Psychology. https://positivepsychology.com/mindfulness-based-stress-reduction-mbsr/

Anwar, Y. (2017, September 7). How many different human emotions are there? *Greater Good Magazine.* https://greatergood.berkeley.edu/article/item/how_many_different_human_emotions_are_there

Anxiety disorders—facts & statistics. (2022, October 28). Anxiety and Depression Association of America. https://adaa.org/understanding-anxiety/facts-statistics

Bardo, N. (2022, January 9). Silencing your inner critic: A beginner's guide. *It's All You Boo.* https://itsallyouboo.com/silencing-your-inner-critic/

Bernhard, T. (2011, June 6). 6 benefits of practicing mindfulness outside of meditation. *Psychology Today.* https://www.psychologytoday.com/us/blog/turning-straw-gold/201106/6-benefits-practicing-mindfulness-outside-meditation

Bernhard, T. (2014, June 5). 7 myths about mindfulness. *Psychology Today.* https://www.psychologytoday.com/us/blog/turning-straw-gold/201406/7-myths-about-mindfulness

Bhandari, T. (2023, April 19). Mind-body connection is built into brain. *ScienceDaily.* https://www.sciencedaily.com/releases/2023/04/230419125052.htm#google_vignette

Brown, H. (2024, July 26). *What is emotional intelligence? +18 ways to improve it* . Positive Psychology. https://positivepsychology.com/emotional-intelligence-eq/

Cash, E., Salmon, P., Weissbecker, I., Rebholz, W. N., Bayley-Veloso, R., Zimmaro, L., Floyd, A., Dedert, E., & Sephton, S. E. (2015). Mindfulness meditation alleviates fibromyalgia symptoms in women: Results of a randomized clinical trial. *Annals of Behavioral Medicine: A Publication of the Society of Behavioral Medicine*, *49*(3), 319–330. https://doi.org/10.1007/s12160-014-9665-0

Cassata, C. (2021, June 9). 10 areas that mindfulness & meditation make us better. *Psych Central*. https://psychcentral.com/blog/surprising-health-benefits-of-mindfulness-meditation

Ceruto, S. (2024, October 23). *How overthinking in relationships can destroy your connection & how to break the cycle.* MindLAB. https://mindlabneuroscience.com/overthinking-in-relationships-destroy-connection/

Challenging negative thinking. (n.d.). MindWell. https://www.mindwell-leeds.org.uk/myself/exploring-your-mental-health/depression/challenging-negative-thinking/

Cherry, K. (2022, September 2). *Benefits of mindfulness.* Verywell Mind. https://www.verywellmind.com/the-benefits-of-mindfulness-5205137

Cherry, K. (2024, July 14). *The 6 types of basic emotions and their effect on human behavior.* Verywell Mind. https://www.verywellmind.com/an-overview-of-the-types-of-emotions-4163976

Christian, K. (2021, September 16). *What is embodiment & how can we use it for self-care?* The Good Trade. https://www.thegoodtrade.com/features/embodiment-definition/

Claude Steiner biography. (2015, August 9). Eric Berne M.D. https://ericberne.com/claude-steiner-biography/

Cornyn-Selby, A. (n.d.). *Alyce Cornyn-Selby quotes.* A-Z Quotes. https://www.azquotes.com/author/64065-Alyce_Cornyn_Selby

Davidson, R. J., & Lutz, A. (2008). Buddha's brain: Neuroplasticity and meditation. *IEEE Signal Processing Magazine, 25*(1), 176–174. https://www.ncbi.nlm.nih.gov/pmc/articles/PMC2944261/

Dibdin, E. (2022a, March 29). Need to control everything? This may be why. *Psych Central.* https://psychcentral.com/blog/why-you-need-to-control-everything

Dibdin, E. (2022b, March 31). The mental health benefits of journaling. *Psych Central.*

https://psychcentral.com/lib/the-health-benefits-of-journaling

Dina. (2019, October 31). *10 surprising exercises to improve mindfulness.* HubPages. https://discover.hubpages.com/health/Mindfulness-Exercises-You-Never-Tried

Disney, W. (n.d.). *Walt Disney quotes.* A-Z Quotes. https://www.azquotes.com/author/4000-Walt_Disney/tag/imagination

Dostoyevsky, F., MacAndrew, A. R., & Marcus, B. (2004). *Notes from underground, White nights, The dream of a ridiculous man, and Selections from the house of the dead* (150th Anniversary Edition). Signet Classics. (Original work published 1862)

Dr. Amit Ray biography. (2023, April 3). Dr. Amit Ray. https://amitray.com/amitray-biography/

Dunham, W. (2023). Scientists identify mind-body nexus in human brain. *Reuters.* https://www.reuters.com/lifestyle/science/scientists-identify-mind-body-nexus-human-brain-2023-04-19/

Eddins, R. (2022, May 4). *Working with your inner critic.* Eddins Counseling Group. https://eddinscounseling.com/working-with-your-inner-critic/

The Editorial Team. (2022, November 29). *Daniel Goleman's emotional intelligence theory explained.* Resilient Educator. https://resilienteducator.com/classroom-resources/daniel-golemans-emotional-intelligence-theory-explained/

Einstein, A. (n.d.-a). *Albert Einstein quotes.* Quotation.io. https://quotation.io/quote/cant-solve-problems-using-kind-thinking

Einstein, A. (n.d.-b). *Albert Einstein quotes.* BrainyQuote. https://www.brainyquote.com/quotes/albert_einstein_121643

Eliaz, I. (2022, September 21). *Break free from chronic stress cycle—with nature's help.* Isaac Eliaz MD. https://dreliaz.org/break-free-from-the-chronic-stress-cycle-with-natures-most-powerful-herbs/

Emde, A. (2023, June 12). *How to write your goals for a balanced life.* Lifestyle Anytime. https://lifestyleanytime.com.au/how-to-write-down-your-goals-for-a-balanced-life/

Engebretson, P. (2021, February 12. How to stop overthinking everything: Close your open question loops - i'm busy being awesome. *I'm Busy Being Awesome.* https://imbusybeingawesome.com/open-question-loops/

Epictetus. (n.d.-a). *Epictetus quotes.* A-Z Quotes. https://www.azquotes.com/quote/90291?ref=communication

Epictetus. (n.d.-b). *Epictetus quotes.* Goodreads. https://www.goodreads.com/quotes/7588248-we-cannot-choose-our-external-circumstances-but-we-can-always

Estrada, J., & Lucas, C. (2024, May 17). *10 ways to regulate your nervous system, according to a brain and behavior experts.* Well+Good. https://www.wellandgood.com/regulate-your-nervous-system/

Fain, S., & Cahn, S. (1953). *You can fly! You can fly! You can fly!* Peter Pan Original Motion Picture Soundtrack. Walt Disney Records. https://genius.com/The-jud-conlon-chorus-you-can-fly-you-can-fly-you-can-fly-lyrics

Farris, M. (2022, July 13). How to manage difficult emotions. *Counseling Recovery.* https://www.counselingrecovery.com/blog-san-jose/-feel-your-feelings

Feldman Barrett, L. (2024, August 8). Simplistic "fight or flight" idea undervalues the brain's predictive powers. *Scientific American.* https://www.scientificamerican.com/article/simplistic-fight-or-flight-idea-undervalues-the-brains-predictive-powers/

Frontiers of the Mind. (2023, February 1). National Institute of Health National Library of Medicine. https://www.nlm.nih.gov/exhibition/emotions -and-disease/index.html#section6

Getting started with mindfulness. (n.d.). Mindful. https://www.mindful.org/meditation/mindfuln ess-getting-started/

Gibbons, E. (2023). The surprising benefit of meditative walks. *Nature.* https://doi.org/10.1038/d41586-023-01894-1

Gordon, E. M., Chauvin, R. J., Van, A. N., Rajesh, A., Nielsen, A., Newbold, D. J., Lynch, C. J., Seider, N. A., Krimmel, S. R., Scheidter, K. M., Monk, J., Miller, R. L., Metoki, A., Montez, D. F., Zheng, A., Elbau, I., Madison, T., Nishino, T., Myers, M. J., & Kaplan, S. (2023). A somato-cognitive action network alternates with effector regions in motor cortex. *Nature, 617*, 1–9. https://doi.org/10.1038/s41586-023-05964-2

Gould, W. R. (2024, March 7). *How to let go of the past and embrace your future.* Verywell Mind. https://www.verywellmind.com/how-to-let-go-of-the-past-8600268

Greenfield, K. (2020, January 4). The 4-7-8 breath technique and relaxation exercise. *The Joy Within.*

https://thejoywithin.org/breath-exercises/4-7-8-breath-technique-and-relaxation-exercise

Grover, S. (2018, July 11). Where do you store stress in your body? Top 10 secret areas. *Psychology Today*. https://www.psychologytoday.com/us/blog/when-kids-call-the-shots/201807/where-do-you-store-stress-in-your-body-top-10-secret-areas

Gupta, A. (2022, April 29). *Are you stuck in the vicious cycle of overthinking? It's risky, warns an expert.* Healthshots. https://www.healthshots.com/mind/mental-health/heres-how-overthinking-can-impact-your-overall-health/

Gupta, S. (2024, April 29). *Feeling anxious? Try the 5-4-3-2-1 grounding technique.* Verywell Mind. https://www.verywellmind.com/5-4-3-2-1-grounding-technique-8639390

Gura, S. (n.d.). *Stop struggling in your life and relationships.* Shira Gura. https://shiragura.com/

Hanh, T. N. (n.d.). *Thich Nhat Hanh quotes.* BrainyQuote. https://www.brainyquote.com/quotes/thich_nhat_hanh_591335

Harvard DCE Professional & Executive Development. (2024, January 9). How to improve your emotional intelligence. *Professional & Executive*

Development | *Harvard* *DCE*. https://professional.dce.harvard.edu/blog/how-to-improve-your-emotional-intelligence/

Heartwell, S. (2019, April 22). The art of conscious breathing: A powerful exercise to purify and rejuvenate the body and mind. *Conscious Lifestyle Magazine*. https://www.consciouslifestylemag.com/breathing-heal-exercises-body-mind/

Hendriksen, E. (2018, October 29). The 5 biggest myths of mindfulness. *Scientific American*. https://www.scientificamerican.com/article/the-5-biggest-myths-of-mindfulness/

Hoge, E. A., Bui, E., Mete, M., Dutton, M. A., Baker, A. W., & Simon, N. M. (2022). Mindfulness-based stress reduction vs escitalopram for the treatment of adults with anxiety disorders: A randomized clinical trial. *JAMA Psychiatry*, *80*(1), 13–21. https://doi.org/10.1001/jamapsychiatry.2022.3679

Hoshaw, C. (2021, February 9). *How to calm your nervous system*. Healthline. https://www.healthline.com/health/mind-body/give-your-nervous-system-a-break

How to practice gratitude. (n.d.). Mindful. https://www.mindful.org/an-introduction-to-mindful-gratitude/

Hurlburt, R. T., Alderson-Day, B., Kühn, S., & Fernyhough, C. (2016). Exploring the ecological validity of thinking on demand: Neural correlates of elicited vs. spontaneously occurring inner speech. *PLOS ONE, 11*(2), e0147932. https://doi.org/10.1371/journal.pone.0147932

Hutchison, C. (2023, September 4). How to journal | the ultimate guide. *Your Visual Journal.* https://yourvisualjournal.com/how-to-journal-the-ultimate-guide/

Inagaki, T. K., Bryne Haltom, K. E., Suzuki, S., Jevtic, I., Hornstein, E., Bower, J. E., & Eisenberger, N. I. (2016). The neurobiology of giving versus receiving support. *Psychosomatic Medicine, 78*(4), 443–453. https://doi.org/10.1097/psy.0000000000000302

Johanson, D. (2022, February 11). *The science of sadness.* Cosmos. https://cosmosmagazine.com/health/body-and-mind/the-science-of-sadness/

Jones, H. (2023, October 2). *10 exercises that help you stop overthinking.* Verywell Health.

https://www.verywellhealth.com/how-to-stop-overthinking-7570368

Kabat-Zinn, J. (2023, December 5). *Wherever you go, there you are: Mindfulness meditation in everyday life; 11th edition.* Hachette Go. https://a.co/d/bAEQMBe

Kaiser, B. N., Haroz, E. E., Kohrt, B. A., Bolton, P. A., Bass, J. K., & Hinton, D. E. (2015). "Thinking too much": A systematic review of a common idiom of distress. *Social Science & Medicine*, *147*, 170–183. https://doi.org/10.1016/j.socscimed.2015.10.044

Kane, R. (2024, February 19). *Jon Kabat-Zinn's 9 attitudes of mindfulness (+ PDF).* Mindfulness Box. https://mindfulnessbox.com/the-9-attitudes-of-mindfulness/

Killian, K. (2023, April 25). How inner monologues work, and who has them. *Psychology Today.* https://www.psychologytoday.com/us/blog/intersections/202304/inner-monologues-what-are-they-and-whos-having-them

Koehler, J. (2024, September 18). Achieving an equilibrium of the mind. *Psychology Today.* https://www.psychologytoday.com/sg/blog/beyond-school-walls/202306/achieving-an-equilibrium-of-the-mind

Kuyken, W., Hayes, R., Barrett, B., Byng, R., Dalgleish, T., Kessler, D., Lewis, G., Watkins, E., Brejcha, C., Cardy, J., Causley, A., Cowderoy, S., Evans, A., Gradinger, F., Kaur, S., Lanham, P., Morant, N., Richards, J., Shah, P., & Sutton, H. (2015). Effectiveness and cost-effectiveness of mindfulness-based cognitive therapy compared with maintenance antidepressant treatment in the prevention of depressive relapse or recurrence (PREVENT): a randomised controlled trial. *The Lancet*, *386*(9988), 63–73. https://doi.org/10.1016/s0140-6736(14)62222-4

Langshur, E., & Klemp, N. (2021, November 1). *How to make gratitude a daily habit*. Mindful. https://www.mindful.org/how-to-make-gratitude-a-daily-habit/

Lewandowski, G. (2023, March 7). How worrying and overthinking can ruin your relationship. *Psychology Today*. https://www.psychologytoday.com/us/blog/the-psychology-of-relationships/202303/how-worrying-and-overthinking-can-ruin-your

Lim, A. (2022, April 4). *Using Your Body to Express More Than Emotion*. Traditional Chinese Medicine World Foundation. https://www.tcmworld.org/using-your-body-express-more-than-emotion/

Lim, A. (2023, January 26). *The role of emotions in health and healing*. Traditional Chinese Medicine World Foundation. https://www.tcmworld.org/role-emotions-health-healing/

Lindberg, S. (2023, March 21). *How to let go of things from the past*. Healthline. https://www.healthline.com/health/how-to-let-go

Lonczak, H. S. (2020, November 17). *36 ways to find a silver lining during challenging times*. Positive Psychology. https://positivepsychology.com/find-a-silver-lining/#techniques

Mara. (2024, April 14). *How to effectively stop overthinking and enjoy life*. Important Enough. https://importantenough.com/how_to_stop_overthinking/

Marie, S. (2022, April 15). 10 mental health benefits of pets. *Psych Central*. https://psychcentral.com/health/pets-and-mental-health

Martins, I. L. (2020, July 6). How to practice positive self-talk. *Ivan Leal Martins*. https://www.ivanlealmartins.com/blog/how-to-practice-positive-self-talk

McAdam, E. (2021, July 9). *Skill #20 intrusive thoughts and overthinking: The skill of cognitive defusion - therapy in a nutshell.* Therapy in a Nutshell. https://therapyinanutshell.com/skill-20-intrusive-thoughts-and-overthinking-the-skill-of-cognitive-defusion/

McQuillan, S. (2024, June 28). What is your inner voice telling you? *Psychology Today.* https://www.psychologytoday.com/us/blog/cravings/202406/what-is-your-inner-voice-telling-you

Merriam-Webster. (n.d.-a). *Neuroplasticity.* In Merriam-Webster.com Dictionary. Retrieved October 5, 2024, from https://www.merriam-webster.com/dictionary/neuroplasticity

Merriam-Webster. (n.d.-b). *Plastic.* In Merriam-Webster.com Dictionary. Retrieved October 5, 2024, from https://www.merriam-webster.com/dictionary/plastic

Meyer, L. (2021, September 24). 5 mindful steps for self-observation. *Psychology Today.* https://www.psychologytoday.com/intl/blog/mindful-recovery/202109/5-mindful-steps-self-observation

Milbrand, L. (2023, June 29). *The 3-2-8 TikTok workout you might want to try.* Real Simple.

https://www.realsimple.com/the-3-2-8-tiktok-workout-you-might-want-to-try-7555470

Mind-body linkage is built into the structure of the brain, study reveals. (2023, April 17). *News-Medical.net.* https://www.news-medical.net/news/20230419/Mind-body-linkage-is-built-into-the-structure-of-the-brain-study-reveals.aspx

Mindfulness meditation: A research-proven way to reduce stress. (2019, October 30). American Psychological Association. https://www.apa.org/topics/mindfulness/meditation

Moe, K. (2021, June 4). 5 visualization techniques to help you reach your goals. *Betterup.* https://www.betterup.com/blog/visualization

Morin, A. (2023, November 3). *Healthy coping skills for uncomfortable emotions.* Verywell Mind. https://www.verywellmind.com/forty-healthy-coping-skills-4586742

Morin, A. (2024, June 16). *How to stop overthinking.* Verywell Mind. https://www.verywellmind.com/how-to-know-when-youre-overthinking-5077069

Most women think too much, overthinkers often drink too much. (2003, February 4). *University of*

Michigan News. https://news.umich.edu/most-women-think-too-much-overthinkers-often-drink-too-much/

Myler, C. (2024, June 4). *Stop overthinking now: 18 ways to control your mind again.* Science of People. https://www.scienceofpeople.com/stop-overthinking/

Nicks, S. (1977). *Dreams [Song]. On Rumours.* Warner Records. https://genius.com/Fleetwood-mac-dreams-lyrics

Nolen-Hoeksema, S. (2004). *Women who think too much.* Henry Holt and Company.

Online Etymology Dictionary. (n.d.). *Neuro.* In Online Etymology Dictionary. Retrieved October 5, 2024, from https://www.etymonline.com/search?q=neuro

The overthinking epidemic: Is modern society encouraging us to think too much? (2023, June 30). *A Life Well Lived.* https://www.alife-welllived.com/blog/theoverthinkingepidemic

Parker, M. (2023, May 20). *Stop overthinking: A practical guide to finding peace of mind and letting go.* OCBF Press. https://a.co/d/7ShS7iy

Parvez, H. (2024, July 13). *Cognitive behavioural theory explained.* PsychMechanics.

https://www.psychmechanics.com/cognitive-behavioural-theory-cbt-in/

Passaler, L. (2023, May 12). *Nervous system regulation: How to start regulating your nervous system*. Heal Your Nervous System. https://healyournervoussystem.com/nervous-system-regulation-how-to-start-regulating-your-nervous-system/

Pattemore, C. (2022, May 27). How to get started with practicing mindfulness. *Psych Central*. https://psychcentral.com/health/new-to-mindfulness-how-to-get-started

Pawula, S. (2021, June 13). A simple way to balance your emotions and revitalize your body. *Always Well Within*. https://always-well-within.squarespace.com/blog/2013/02/17/balance-your-emotions-and-body

Pelini, S. (2024, June 25). An age-by-age guide to helping kids manage emotions. *The Gottman Institute*. https://www.gottman.com/blog/age-age-guide-helping-kids-manage-emotions/

Ranganathan, V. K., Siemionow, V., Liu, J. Z., Sahgal, V., & Yue, G. H. (2004). From mental power to muscle power--gaining strength by using the mind. *Neuropsychologia*, *42*(7), 944–956. https://doi.org/10.1016/j.neuropsychologia.2003.11.018

Ray, A. (n.d.). *Amit Ray quotes*. Goodreads. https://www.goodreads.com/quotes/10112922 -overthinking-is-not-a-disease-it-is-due-to-the

Raypole, C. (2020, April 22). *7 emotion-focused coping techniques for uncertain times*. Healthline. https://www.healthline.com/health/emotion-focused-coping

Razdan, B. L. (2023, August 20). Training the brain to be happy. *Greater Kashmir*. https://www.greaterkashmir.com/opinion/trai ning-the-brain-to-be-happy/

Rebecca. (2023, July 19). 12 practical tips to help you deal with an overthinker. *Minimalism Made Simple*. https://www.minimalismmadesimple.com/ho me/how-to-deal-with-an-overthinker/

Reed, P. (2021, December 15). *Physical activity is good for the mind and the body*. U.S. Department of Health and Human Services. https://health.gov/news/202112/physical-activity-good-mind-and-body

Regan, S. (2021, January 18). *How to listen to your own inner voice & why it's so important*. Mindbodygreen. https://www.mindbodygreen.com/articles/liste n-to-your-inner-voice

Rice, A. (2021, October 26). Yoga for anxiety: 9 poses to try. *Psych Central*. https://psychcentral.com/anxiety/yoga-for-anxiety

Ridley, Y. (2024, February 5). How to grounded yourself: 6 grounding techniques. *Put the Kettle On*. https://putthekettleon.ca/how-to-stay-grounded-and-centered-in-life/

Russell, M. (2021, September 24). How to slow down: 20 simple ways to slow down & enjoy life. *Simple Lionheart Life*. https://simplelionheartlife.com/how-to-slow-down/

Sabater, V. (2023, June 7). *Naikan therapy: The healing art of self-reflection.* Exploring Your Mind. https://exploringyourmind.com/naikan-therapy-the-healing-art-of-self-reflection/

Sabater, V. (2024, April 8). *Seven Differences Between Mental and Emotional Health*. Exploring Your Mind. https://exploringyourmind.com/differences-between-mental-and-emotional-health/

Sander, V. (2022, November 9). How to stop overthinking social interaction (for introverts). *SocialSelf*. https://socialself.com/blog/stop-overthinking/

Santos-Longhurst, A. (2024, January 25). *What are the symptoms and causes of high cortisol levels?* Healthline. https://www.healthline.com/health/high-cortisol-symptoms#what-it-is

Schaffner, A. K. (2023, June 8). *Equanimity: The holy grail of calmness & grace?* Positive Psychology. https://positivepsychology.com/equanimity/

Schembra, C. (2024, September 5). Intelligent selfishness: How giving to others enriches your own life. *Rolling Stone.* https://www.rollingstone.com/culture-council/articles/intelligent-selfishness-giving-others-enriches-own-life-1235094815/

Schultz, J. (2020, July 24). *5 differences between mindfulness and meditation.* Positive Psychology. https://positivepsychology.com/differences-between-mindfulness-meditation/

Scott, E. (2023, October 23). *How to set and crush your goals with way less stress.* Verywell Mind. https://www.verywellmind.com/goal-setting-and-reaching-goals-3145004

Seaver, M. (2023, August 9). *What mindfulness does to your brain: The science of neuroplasticity.* Real Simple. https://www.realsimple.com/health/mind-mood/mindfulness-improves-brain-health-neuroplasticity

Seaver, M. (2024, April 26). *12 everyday habits to train your brain to be happier.* Real Simple. https://www.realsimple.com/how-to-be-happier-7485523

Shapero, B. G., Greenberg, J., Pedrelli, P., de Jong, M., & Desbordes, G. (2018). Mindfulness-Based interventions in psychiatry. *FOCUS*, *16*(1), 32–39. https://doi.org/10.1176/appi.focus.20170039

Stanborough, R. J. (2023, June 5). *How to change negative thinking with cognitive restructuring.* Healthline. https://www.healthline.com/health/cognitive-restructuring

Steffen, P. R., Austin, T., & DeBarros, A. (2016). Treating chronic stress to address the growing problem of depression and anxiety. *Policy Insights from the Behavioral and Brain Sciences*, *4*(1), 64–70. https://doi.org/10.1177/2372732216685333

Stone, J. (2024, October 22). Men and the hidden costs of overthinking. *Psychology Today.* https://www.psychologytoday.com/us/blog/the-souls-of-men/202409/men-and-the-hidden-costs-of-overthinking

Stress. (n.d.). Mind. https://www.mind.org.uk/information-support/types-of-mental-health-problems/stress/causes-of-stress/

Stress. (2024, May 20). Cleveland Clinic. https://my.clevelandclinic.org/health/diseases/11874-stress

Strick, M., Dijksterhuis, A., & van Baaren, R. B. (2010). Unconscious-thought effects take place off-line, not on-line. *Psychological Science, 21*(4), 484–488. https://doi.org/10.1177/0956797610363555

Therapy in a Nutshell. (2021). Intrusive thoughts and overthinking: The skill of cognitive defusion 20/30 [Video]. *YouTube.* https://www.youtube.com/watch?v=V3vhXQy48jo

Therapy in a Nutshell. (2022). Catastrophizing: How to stop making yourself depressed and anxious: Cognitive distortion skill #6 [Video]. *YouTube.* https://www.youtube.com/watch?v=bS2LPNlO07s

Therapy in a Nutshell. (2023a). Automatic negative thoughts - break the anxiety cycle 11/30 [Video]. *YouTube.* https://www.youtube.com/watch?v=lLZ-3TSoe9E

Therapy in a Nutshell. (2023b, November 9). *How to stop overthinking: Master the ACT skill of cognitive defusion 13/30* [Video]. YouTube. https://www.youtube.com/watch?v=OhNm7ZSiZls

Therapy in a Nutshell. (2024, January 4). *Emotional reasoning- the cognitive distortion that makes you emotionally reactive - anxiety 18/30* [Video]. YouTube. https://www.youtube.com/watch?v=YBzvkgA Rehg

Tsaousides, T. (2023, July 23). How many emotions can you feel? *Psychology Today.* https://www.psychologytoday.com/us/blog/s mashing-the-brainblocks/202307/how-many-emotions-are-there

U.S. Department of Health and Human Services. (2018). Physical activity guidelines for Americans 2nd edition. *U.S. Department of Health and Human Services* (pp. 8–10). https://health.gov/sites/default/files/2019-09/Physical_Activity_Guidelines_2nd_edition.p df

Vandervort, S. (2024, May 29). Get out of your head and into your body with these five practices. *The Local Mystic.* https://thelocalmystic.com/get-out-of-your-head-five-practices/

Viezzer, S. (2024, February 5). *How to improve emotional intelligence.* Simply Psychology. https://www.simplypsychology.org/how-to-improve-emotional-intelligence.html

Washington University School of Medicine. (2023, April 20). Hidden linkages: Scientists find mind-body connection is built into brain. *SciTechDaily*. https://scitechdaily.com/hidden-linkages-scientists-find-mind-body-connection-is-built-into-brain/

Wegner, D. (1990, June 1). *White bears and other unwanted thoughts: Suppression, obsession, and the psychology of mental control.* Penguin Books. https://a.co/d/iKczKER

Wegner, D. (2011, November). *Setting free the bears: Escape from thought suppression.* American Psychologist. https://dtg.sites.fas.harvard.edu/DANWEGNER/pub/Setting%20free%20the%20bears%202011.pdf

Wegner, D. M., & Schneider, D. J. (2003). The white bear story. *Psychological Inquiry, 14*(3/4), 326–329. https://www.jstor.org/stable/1449696

Weil, A. (2006, May 8). Richard Davidson. *TIME*. https://content.time.com/time/specials/packages/article/0,28804,1975813_1975844_1976433,00.html

Why laughing is good for you. (2024, August 29). Cleveland Clinic. https://health.clevelandclinic.org/is-laughing-good-for-you

Williams, C. (2022, July 4). *How to understand your inner voice and control your inner critic*. New Scientist. https://www.newscientist.com/article/mg2553 3941-100-how-to-understand-your-inner-voice-and-control-your-inner-critic/

Winzeler, M. (2020, May 27). *Calm your body and mind: A therapist's guide for nervous system regulation*. WellnessWinz. https://wellnesswinz.com/2020/05/27/calm-your-body-and-mind-a-therapists-guide-for-nervous-system-regulation/

Working out boosts brain health. (2020, March 4). American Psychological Association. https://www.apa.org/topics/exercise-fitness/stress

World Health Organization. (2022, March 2). *COVID-19 pandemic triggers 25% increase in prevalence of anxiety and depression worldwide*. World Health Organization. https://www.who.int/news/item/02-03-2022-covid-19-pandemic-triggers-25-increase-in-prevalence-of-anxiety-and-depression-worldwide

Yun, R. C., Fardghassemi, S., & Joffe, H. (2022). Thinking too much: How young people experience rumination in the context of

The Stinking Overthinking Trap References

Ackerman, C. E. (2018, February 12). *Cognitive restructuring techniques for reframing thoughts*. Positive Psychology. https://positivepsychology.com/cbt-cognitive-restructuring-cognitive-distortions/#worksheets-cognitive-restructuring

Ackerman, C. E. (2024a, August 3). *23 amazing health benefits of mindfulness for body and brain*. Positive Psychology. https://positivepsychology.com/benefits-of-mindfulness/

Ackerman, C. E. (2024b, September 17). *Mindfulness-based stress reduction: The ultimate MBSR guide*. Positive Psychology. https://positivepsychology.com/mindfulness-based-stress-reduction-mbsr/

Anwar, Y. (2017, September 7). *How many different human emotions are there?* Greater Good Magazine. https://greatergood.berkeley.edu/article/item/how_many_different_human_emotions_are_there

Anxiety disorders—facts & statistics. (2022, October 28). Anxiety and Depression Association of America. https://adaa.org/understanding-anxiety/facts-statistics

Bardo, N. (2022, January 9). *Silencing your inner critic: A beginner's guide*. It's All You Boo. https://itsallyouboo.com/silencing-your-inner-critic/

Bernhard, T. (2011, June 6). *6 benefits of practicing mindfulness outside of meditation.* Psychology Today. https://www.psychologytoday.com/us/blog/turnin g-straw-gold/201106/6-benefits-practicing-mindfulness-outside-meditation

Bernhard, T. (2014, June 5). *7 myths about mindfulness.* Psychology Today. https://www.psychologytoday.com/us/blog/turnin g-straw-gold/201406/7-myths-about-mindfulness

Bhandari, T. (2023, April 19). *Mind-body connection is built into brain.* ScienceDaily. https://www.sciencedaily.com/releases/2023/04/2 30419125052.htm#google_vignette

Brown, H. (2024, July 26). *What is emotional intelligence? +18 ways to improve it* . Positive Psychology. https://positivepsychology.com/emotional-intelligence-eq/

Cash, E., Salmon, P., Weissbecker, I., Rebholz, W. N., Bayley-Veloso, R., Zimmaro, L., Floyd, A., Dedert, E., & Sephton, S. E. (2015). Mindfulness meditation alleviates fibromyalgia symptoms in women: Results of a randomized clinical trial. *Annals of Behavioral Medicine: A Publication of the Society of Behavioral Medicine, 49*(3), 319–330. https://doi.org/10.1007/s12160-014-9665-0

Cassata, C. (2021, June 9). *10 areas that mindfulness & meditation make us better.* Psych Central. https://psychcentral.com/blog/surprising-health-benefits-of-mindfulness-meditation

Ceruto, S. (2024, October 23). *How overthinking in relationships can destroy your connection & how to break the cycle.* MindLAB. https://mindlabneuroscience.com/overthinking-in-relationships-destroy-connection/

Challenging negative thinking. (n.d.). MindWell. https://www.mindwell-leeds.org.uk/myself/exploring-your-mental-health/depression/challenging-negative-thinking/

Cherry, K. (2022, September 2). *Benefits of mindfulness.* Verywell Mind. https://www.verywellmind.com/the-benefits-of-mindfulness-5205137

Cherry, K. (2024, July 14). *The 6 types of basic emotions and their effect on human behavior.* Verywell Mind. https://www.verywellmind.com/an-overview-of-the-types-of-emotions-4163976

Christian, K. (2021, September 16). *What is embodiment & how can we use it for self-care?* The Good Trade. https://www.thegoodtrade.com/features/embodiment-definition/

Claude Steiner biography. (2015, August 9). Eric Berne M.D. https://ericberne.com/claude-steiner-biography/

Cleveland Clinic. (2022, May 15). *Overthinking disorder: Is it a mental illness?* Cleveland Clinic. https://health.clevelandclinic.org/is-overthinking-a-mental-illness

Cornyn-Selby, A. (n.d.). *Alyce Cornyn-Selby quotes*. A-Z Quotes. https://www.azquotes.com/author/64065-Alyce_Cornyn_Selby

Cox, J. (2022, November 15). *7 ways to overcome perfectionism*. Psych Central.

https://psychcentral.com/health/steps-to-conquer-perfectionism

Davidson, R. J., & Lutz, A. (2008). Buddha's brain: Neuroplasticity and meditation. *IEEE Signal Processing Magazine, 25*(1), 176–174. https://www.ncbi.nlm.nih.gov/pmc/articles/PMC2944261/

Davis, T. (2021, May 18). *9 ways to cultivate a positive mindset*. Psychology Today. https://www.psychologytoday.com/us/blog/click-here-for-happiness/202105/9-ways-to-cultivate-a-positive-mindset

Dibdin, E. (2022a, March 29). *Need to control everything? This may be why*. Psych Central. https://psychcentral.com/blog/why-you-need-to-control-everything

Dibdin, E. (2022b, March 31). *The mental health benefits of journaling*. Psych Central. https://psychcentral.com/lib/the-health-benefits-of-journaling

Dina. (2019, October 31). *10 surprising exercises to improve mindfulness*. HubPages.

https://discover.hubpages.com/health/Mindfulness
-Exercises-You-Never-Tried

Disney, W. (n.d.). *Walt Disney quotes*. A-Z Quotes. https://www.azquotes.com/author/4000-Walt_Disney/tag/imagination

Dostoyevsky, F., MacAndrew, A. R., & Marcus, B. (2004). *Notes from underground, White nights, The dream of a ridiculous man, and Selections from the house of the dead* (150th Anniversary Edition). Signet Classics. (Original work published 1862)

Dr. Amit Ray biography. (2023, April 3). Dr. Amit Ray. https://amitray.com/amitray-biography/

Dunham, W. (2023). Scientists identify mind-body nexus in human brain. In *Reuters*. https://www.reuters.com/lifestyle/science/scientists-identify-mind-body-nexus-human-brain-2023-04-19/

Eddins, R. (2022, May 4). *Working with your inner critic*. Eddins Counseling Group. https://eddinscounseling.com/working-with-your-inner-critic/

Einstein, A. (n.d.-a). *Albert Einstein quotes*. Quotation.io. https://quotation.io/quote/cant-solve-problems-using-kind-thinking

Einstein, A. (n.d.-b). *Albert Einstein quotes*. BrainyQuote. https://www.brainyquote.com/quotes/albert_einstein_121643

Eliaz, I. (2022, September 21). *Break free from chronic stress cycle—with nature's help*. Isaac Eliaz MD. https://dreliaz.org/break-free-from-the-chronic-stress-cycle-with-natures-most-powerful-herbs/

Emde, A. (2023, June 12). *How to write your goals for a balanced life*. Lifestyle Anytime. https://lifestyleanytime.com.au/how-to-write-down-your-goals-for-a-balanced-life/

Engebretson, P. (2021, February 12). *How to stop overthinking everything: Close your open question loops - i'm busy being awesome*. I'm Busy Being Awesome. https://imbusybeingawesome.com/open-question-loops/

Epictetus. (n.d.-a). *Epictetus quotes*. A-Z Quotes. https://www.azquotes.com/quote/90291?ref=communication

Epictetus. (n.d.-b). *Epictetus quotes*. Goodreads. https://www.goodreads.com/quotes/7588248-we-cannot-choose-our-external-circumstances-but-we-can-always

Estrada, J., & Lucas, C. (2024, May 17). *10 ways to regulate your nervous system, according to a brain and behavior experts*. Well+Good. https://www.wellandgood.com/regulate-your-nervous-system/

Evans, L. (2014, September 24). *You aren't imagining it: Email is making you more stressed out*. Fast Company. https://www.fastcompany.com/3036061/youarent-imagining-it-email-is-making-you-more-stressed-out

Expert Panel. (2022, April 29). 15 steps to get rid of negative thought patterns. *Forbes*. https://www.forbes.com/councils/forbescoachesco uncil/2022/04/28/15-steps-to-get-rid-of-negative-thought-patterns/

Fain, S., & Cahn, S. (1953). *You can fly! You can fly! You can fly!* Peter Pan Original Motion Picture Soundtrack. Walt Disney Records. https://genius.com/The-jud-conlon-chorus-you-can-fly-you-can-fly-you-can-fly-lyrics

Farris, M. (2022, July 13). *How to manage difficult emotions.* Counseling Recovery. https://www.counselingrecovery.com/blog-san-jose/-feel-your-feelings

Feldman Barrett, L. (2024, August 8). *Simplistic "fight or flight" idea undervalues the brain's predictive powers.* Scientific American. https://www.scientificamerican.com/article/simplis tic-fight-or-flight-idea-undervalues-the-brains-predictive-powers/

Forbes Coaches Council. (2021, December 10). 16 essential strategies to improve your decision-making skills. *Forbes*.

https://www.forbes.com/councils/forbescoachescouncil/20 20/05/28/16-essential-strategies-to-improve-your-decision-making-skills/

Frick, W. (2018, January 22). *3 ways to improve your decision making*. Harvard Business Review. https://hbr.org/2018/01/3-ways-to-improve-your-decision-making

Frontiers of the Mind. (2023, February 1). National Institute of Health National Library of Medicine. https://www.nlm.nih.gov/exhibition/emotions-and-disease/index.html#section6

Getting started with mindfulness. (n.d.). Mindful. https://www.mindful.org/meditation/mindfulness-getting-started/

Gibbons, E. (2023). The surprising benefit of meditative walks. *Nature*. https://doi.org/10.1038/d41586-023-01894-1

Godkin, S. (2020, April 5). *Self-Compassion or self-criticism: Which one motivates you more?* The Happiness Doctor. https://www.thehappinessdoctor.com/blog/self-compassion-or-self-criticism-motivation

Gordon, E. M., Chauvin, R. J., Van, A. N., Rajesh, A., Nielsen, A., Newbold, D. J., Lynch, C. J., Seider, N. A., Krimmel, S. R., Scheidter, K. M., Monk, J., Miller, R. L., Metoki, A., Montez, D. F., Zheng, A., Elbau, I., Madison, T., Nishino, T., Myers, M. J., & Kaplan, S. (2023). A somato-cognitive action network alternates with effector regions in motor cortex. *Nature*, *617*, 1–9. https://doi.org/10.1038/s41586-023-05964-2

Gould, W. R. (2024, March 7). *How to let go of the past and embrace your future.* Verywell Mind. https://www.verywellmind.com/how-to-let-go-of-the-past-8600268

Grande, D. (2024, June 26). *How to stop overthinking.* Psychology Today. https://www.psychologytoday.com/us/blog/in-it-together/202406/stop-overthinking

Greenfield, K. (2020, January 4). *The 4-7-8 breath technique and relaxation exercise.* The Joy Within. https://thejoywithin.org/breath-exercises/4-7-8-breath-technique-and-relaxation-exercise

Grover, S. (2018, July 11). *Where do you store stress in your body? Top 10 secret areas.* Psychology Today. https://www.psychologytoday.com/us/blog/when-kids-call-the-shots/201807/where-do-you-store-stress-in-your-body-top-10-secret-areas

Gupta, A. (2022, April 29). *Are you stuck in the vicious cycle of overthinking? It's risky, warns an expert.* Healthshots. https://www.healthshots.com/mind/mental-health/heres-how-overthinking-can-impact-your-overall-health/

Gupta, S. (2024, April 29). *Feeling anxious? Try the 5-4-3-2-1 grounding technique.* Verywell Mind. https://www.verywellmind.com/5-4-3-2-1-grounding-technique-8639390

Gura, S. (n.d.). *Stop struggling in your life and relationships.* Shira Gura. https://shiragura.com/

Hanh, T. N. (n.d.). *Thich Nhat Hanh quotes.* BrainyQuote. https://www.brainyquote.com/quotes/thich_nhat_ hanh_591335

Harvard DCE Professional & Executive Development. (2024, January 9). *How to improve your emotional intelligence.* Professional & Executive Development | Harvard DCE. https://professional.dce.harvard.edu/blog/how-to-improve-your-emotional-intelligence/

Heartwell, S. (2019, April 22). *The art of conscious breathing: A powerful exercise to purify and rejuvenate the body and mind.* Conscious Lifestyle Magazine. https://www.consciouslifestylemag.com/breathing-heal-exercises-body-mind/

Hendriksen, E. (2018, October 29). *The 5 biggest myths of mindfulness.* Scientific American. https://www.scientificamerican.com/article/the-5-biggest-myths-of-mindfulness/

Hoge, E. A., Bui, E., Mete, M., Dutton, M. A., Baker, A. W., & Simon, N. M. (2022). Mindfulness-based stress reduction vs escitalopram for the treatment of adults with anxiety disorders: A randomized clinical trial. *JAMA Psychiatry, 80*(1), 13–21. https://doi.org/10.1001/jamapsychiatry.2022.3679

Hoshaw, C. (2021, February 9). *How to calm your nervous system.* Healthline. https://www.healthline.com/health/mind-body/give-your-nervous-system-a-break

Hurlburt, R. T., Alderson-Day, B., Kühn, S., & Fernyhough, C. (2016). Exploring the ecological validity of thinking on demand: Neural correlates of elicited vs. spontaneously occurring inner speech. *PLOS ONE*, *11*(2), e0147932. https://doi.org/10.1371/journal.pone.0147932

Hutchison, C. (2023, September 4). *How to journal | the ultimate guide*. Your Visual Journal. https://yourvisualjournal.com/how-to-journal-the-ultimate-guide/

Inagaki, T. K., Bryne Haltom, K. E., Suzuki, S., Jevtic, I., Hornstein, E., Bower, J. E., & Eisenberger, N. I. (2016). The neurobiology of giving versus receiving support. *Psychosomatic Medicine*, *78*(4), 443–453. https://doi.org/10.1097/psy.0000000000000302

Indeed Editorial Team. (2024, July 2). *15 ways to improve your decision-making skills*. Indeed Career Guide. https://www.indeed.com/career-advice/career-development/how-to-improve-decision-making

Jaffe, A. (2024, December 9). *7 strategies for breaking habits that trigger relapse*. Psychology Today. https://www.psychologytoday.com/us/blog/all-about-addiction/202412/7-strategies-for-breaking-habits-that-trigger-relapse

Johanson, D. (2022, February 11). *The science of sadness*. Cosmos. https://cosmosmagazine.com/health/body-and-mind/the-science-of-sadness/

Jones, H. (2023, October 2). *10 exercises that help you stop overthinking.* Verywell Health. https://www.verywellhealth.com/how-to-stop-overthinking-7570368

Kabat-Zinn, J. (2023, December 5). *Wherever you go, there you are: Mindfulness meditation in everyday life; 11th edition.* Hachette Go. https://a.co/d/bAEQMBe

Kaiser, B. N., Haroz, E. E., Kohrt, B. A., Bolton, P. A., Bass, J. K., & Hinton, D. E. (2015). "Thinking too much": A systematic review of a common idiom of distress. *Social Science & Medicine, 147,* 170–183. https://doi.org/10.1016/j.socscimed.2015.10.044

Kane, R. (2024, February 19). *Jon Kabat-Zinn's 9 attitudes of mindfulness (+ PDF).* Mindfulness Box. https://mindfulnessbox.com/the-9-attitudes-of-mindfulness/

Killian, K. (2023, April 25). *How inner monologues work, and who has them.* Psychology Today. https://www.psychologytoday.com/us/blog/intersections/202304/inner-monologues-what-are-they-and-whos-having-them

Koehler, J. (2024, September 18). *Achieving an equilibrium of the mind.* Psychology Today. https://www.psychologytoday.com/sg/blog/beyond-school-walls/202306/achieving-an-equilibrium-of-the-mind

Kuyken, W., Hayes, R., Barrett, B., Byng, R., Dalgleish, T., Kessler, D., Lewis, G., Watkins, E., Brejcha, C.,

Cardy, J., Causley, A., Cowderoy, S., Evans, A., Gradinger, F., Kaur, S., Lanham, P., Morant, N., Richards, J., Shah, P., & Sutton, H. (2015). Effectiveness and cost-effectiveness of mindfulness-based cognitive therapy compared with maintenance antidepressant treatment in the prevention of depressive relapse or recurrence (PREVENT): a randomised controlled trial. *The Lancet*, *386*(9988), 63–73. https://doi.org/10.1016/s0140-6736(14)62222-4

Langshur, E., & Klemp, N. (2021, November 1). *How to make gratitude a daily habit*. Mindful. https://www.mindful.org/how-to-make-gratitude-a-daily-habit/

Leahy, R. (2021, April 11). *How to overcome perfectionism*. Psychology Today. https://www.psychologytoday.com/us/blog/anxiety-files/202104/how-to-overcome-perfectionism

Levine, G. N., Cohen, B. E., Commodore-Mensah, Y., Fleury, J., Huffman, J. C., Khalid, U., Labarthe, D. R., Lavretsky, H., Michos, E. D., Spatz, E. S., & Kubzansky, L. D. (2021). Psychological health, well-being, and the mind-heart-body connection: A scientific statement from the american heart association. *Circulation*, *143*(10). https://doi.org/10.1161/cir.0000000000000947

Lewandowski, G. (2023, March 7). *How worrying and overthinking can ruin your relationship*. Psychology Today. https://www.psychologytoday.com/us/blog/the-psychology-of-relationships/202303/how-worrying-and-overthinking-can-ruin-your

Lim, A. (2022, April 4). *Using Your Body to Express More Than Emotion*. Traditional Chinese Medicine World Foundation. https://www.tcmworld.org/using-your-body-express-more-than-emotion/

Lim, A. (2023, January 26). *The role of emotions in health and healing*. Traditional Chinese Medicine World Foundation. https://www.tcmworld.org/role-emotions-health-healing/

Lindberg, S. (2023, March 21). *How to let go of things from the past*. Healthline. https://www.healthline.com/health/how-to-let-go

Lonczak, H. S. (2020, November 17). *36 ways to find a silver lining during challenging times*. Positive Psychology. https://positivepsychology.com/find-a-silver-lining/#techniques

Lyon, R. A. (2024, October 17). *15 strategies to stop overthinking and find peace of mind*. Senior Fitness. https://www.seniorfitness.org/how-to-stop-overthinking/

Mara. (2024, April 14). *How to effectively stop overthinking and enjoy life*. Important Enough. https://importantenough.com/how_to_stop_overthinking/

Marie, S. (2022, April 15). *10 mental health benefits of pets*. Psych Central. https://psychcentral.com/health/pets-and-mental-health

Martins, I. L. (2020, July 6). *How to practice positive self-talk.*
Ivan Leal Martins.

https://www.ivanlealmartins.com/blog/how-to-practice-positive-self-talk

Marut, J. (2016, September 28). *4 ways to remain centered amid all of life's chaos.* Tiny Buddha. https://tinybuddha.com/blog/4-ways-to-remain-centered-amid-all-of-the-chaos/

McAdam, E. (2021, July 9). *Skill #20 intrusive thoughts and overthinking: The skill of cognitive defusion - therapy in a nutshell.* Therapy in a Nutshell. https://therapyinanutshell.com/skill-20-intrusive-thoughts-and-overthinking-the-skill-of-cognitive-defusion/

McCallum, K. (2021, April 12). *When overthinking becomes a problem & what you can do about it.* Houston Methodist. https://www.houstonmethodist.org/blog/articles/2021/apr/when-overthinking-becomes-a-problem-and-what-you-can-do-about-it/

McQuillan, S. (2024, June 28). *What is your inner voice telling you?* Psychology Today. https://www.psychologytoday.com/us/blog/cravings/202406/what-is-your-inner-voice-telling-you

Merriam-Webster. (n.d.-a). *Neuroplasticity.* In Merriam-Webster.com Dictionary. Retrieved October 5, 2024, from https://www.merriam-webster.com/dictionary/neuroplasticity

Merriam-Webster. (n.d.-b). *Plastic.* In Merriam-Webster.com Dictionary. Retrieved October 5, 2024, from https://www.merriam-webster.com/dictionary/plastic

Meyer, L. (2021, September 24). *5 mindful steps for self-observation.* Psychology Today. https://www.psychologytoday.com/intl/blog/mindful-recovery/202109/5-mindful-steps-self-observation

Milbrand, L. (2023, June 29). *The 3-2-8 TikTok workout you might want to try.* Real Simple. https://www.realsimple.com/the-3-2-8-tiktok-workout-you-might-want-to-try-7555470

Miller, K. (2020, March 13). *Building self-awareness: 16 activities and tools for meaningful change.* Positive Psychology. https://positivepsychology.com/building-self-awareness-activities/

Mind-body linkage is built into the structure of the brain, study reveals. (2023, April 17). News-Medical.net. https://www.news-medical.net/news/20230419/Mind-body-linkage-is-built-into-the-structure-of-the-brain-study-reveals.aspx

Mindful Staff. (2024, December 16). *How to practice gratitude.* Mindful. https://www.mindful.org/an-introduction-to-mindful-gratitude/

Mindfulness meditation: A research-proven way to reduce stress. (2019, October 30). American Psychological Association.

https://www.apa.org/topics/mindfulness/meditatio
n

Moe, K. (2021, June 4). *5 visualization techniques to help you reach your goals.* Betterup. https://www.betterup.com/blog/visualization

Moore, C. (2024, November 7). *What is flow in psychology? Definition and 10+ activities to induce flow.* Positive Psychology. https://positivepsychology.com/what-is-flow/

Morin, A. (2023, November 3). *Healthy coping skills for uncomfortable emotions.* Verywell Mind. https://www.verywellmind.com/forty-healthy-coping-skills-4586742

Morin, A. (2024a, February 21). *9 little habits that make you a better decision maker.* Verywell Mind. https://www.verywellmind.com/habits-for-better-decision-making-4153045

Morin, A. (2024b, June 16). *How to stop overthinking.* Verywell Mind. https://www.verywellmind.com/how-to-know-when-youre-overthinking-5077069

Most women think too much, overthinkers often drink too much. (2003, February 4). University of Michigan News. https://news.umich.edu/most-women-think-too-much-overthinkers-often-drink-too-much/

Myler, C. (2024, June 4). *Stop overthinking now: 18 ways to control your mind again.* Science of People. https://www.scienceofpeople.com/stop-overthinking/

Nicks, S. (1977). *Dreams [Song]. On Rumours*. Warner Records. https://genius.com/Fleetwood-mac-dreams-lyrics

Nolen-Hoeksema, S. (2004). *Women who think too much*. Henry Holt and Company.

Online Etymology Dictionary. (n.d.). *Neuro*. In Online Etymology Dictionary. Retrieved October 5, 2024, from https://www.etymonline.com/search?q=neuro

Oppland, M. (2016, December 16). *8 ways to create flow according to Mihaly Csikszentmihalyi*. Positive Psychology. https://positivepsychology.com/mihaly-csikszentmihalyi-father-of-flow/

Parker, M. (2023, May 20). *Stop overthinking: A practical guide to finding peace of mind and letting go*. OCBF Press. https://a.co/d/7ShS7iy

Parvez, H. (2024, July 13). *Cognitive behavioural theory explained*. PsychMechanics. https://www.psychmechanics.com/cognitive-behavioural-theory-cbt-in/

Passaler, L. (2023, May 12). *Nervous system regulation: How to start regulating your nervous system*. Heal Your Nervous System. https://healyournervoussystem.com/nervous-system-regulation-how-to-start-regulating-your-nervous-system/

Pattemore, C. (2022, May 27). *How to get started with practicing mindfulness.* Psych Central. https://psychcentral.com/health/new-to-mindfulness-how-to-get-started

Pawula, S. (2021, June 13). *A simple way to balance your emotions and revitalize your body.* Always Well Within. https://always-well-within.squarespace.com/blog/2013/02/17/balance-your-emotions-and-body

Pedersen, T. (2022, May 6). *7 tips for improving your self-awareness.* Psych Central. https://psychcentral.com/health/how-to-be-more-self-aware-and-why-its-important

Pelini, S. (2024, June 25). *An age-by-age guide to helping kids manage emotions.* The Gottman Institute. https://www.gottman.com/blog/age-age-guide-helping-kids-manage-emotions/

Positive Affirmations. (2023, October 4). *The art of mindfulness: How to stay calm and centered in a chaotic world.* Medium. https://medium.com/@positiveaffirmations91/the-art-of-mindfulness-how-to-stay-calm-and-centered-in-a-chaotic-world-7111ec455497

Ranganathan, V. K., Siemionow, V., Liu, J. Z., Sahgal, V., & Yue, G. H. (2004). From mental power to muscle power--gaining strength by using the mind. *Neuropsychologia, 42*(7), 944–956. https://doi.org/10.1016/j.neuropsychologia.2003.11.018

Ray, A. (n.d.). *Amit Ray quotes*. Goodreads. https://www.goodreads.com/quotes/10112922-overthinking-is-not-a-disease-it-is-due-to-the

Raypole, C. (2020, April 22). *7 emotion-focused coping techniques for uncertain times*.

Healthline. https://www.healthline.com/health/emotion-focused-coping

Razdan, B. L. (2023, August 20). *Training the brain to be happy*. Greater Kashmir. https://www.greaterkashmir.com/opinion/training-the-brain-to-be-happy/

Rebecca. (2023, July 19). *12 practical tips to help you deal with an overthinker*. Minimalism Made Simple. https://www.minimalismmadesimple.com/home/how-to-deal-with-an-overthinker/

Reed, P. (2021, December 15). *Physical activity is good for the mind and the body*. U.S. Department of Health and Human Services. https://health.gov/news/202112/physical-activity-good-mind-and-body

Regan, S. (2021, January 18). *How to listen to your own inner voice & why it's so important*. Mindbodygreen. https://www.mindbodygreen.com/articles/listen-to-your-inner-voice

Rice, A. (2021, October 26). *Yoga for anxiety: 9 poses to try*. Psych Central. https://psychcentral.com/anxiety/yoga-for-anxiety

Ridley, Y. (2024, February 5). *How to grounded yourself: 6 grounding techniques*. Put the Kettle On. https://putthekettleon.ca/how-to-stay-grounded-and-centered-in-life/

Roest, A. M., Martens, E. J., de Jonge, P., & Denollet, J. (2010). Anxiety and risk of incident coronary heart disease. *Journal of the American College of Cardiology*, *56*(1), 38–46. https://doi.org/10.1016/j.jacc.2010.03.034

Russell, M. (2021, September 24). *How to slow down: 20 simple ways to slow down & enjoy life*. Simple Lionheart Life. https://simplelionheartlife.com/how-to-slow-down/

Sabater, V. (2023, June 7). *Naikan therapy: The healing art of self-reflection*. Exploring Your Mind. https://exploringyourmind.com/naikan-therapy-the-healing-art-of-self-reflection/

Sabater, V. (2024, April 8). *Seven Differences Between Mental and Emotional Health*. Exploring Your Mind. https://exploringyourmind.com/differences-between-mental-and-emotional-health/

Sander, V. (2022, November 9). *How to stop overthinking social interaction (for introverts)*. SocialSelf. https://socialself.com/blog/stop-overthinking/

Santos-Longhurst, A. (2024, January 25). *What are the symptoms and causes of high cortisol levels?* Healthline. https://www.healthline.com/health/high-cortisol-symptoms#what-it-is

Schacht, E. (2021). Wellness tips nurturing a positive mindset. In *University of Iowa.*

https://medicine.uiowa.edu/md/sites/medicine.uiowa.edu.md/files/wysiwyg_uploads/Wellness%20Tips%20Mindset_052721.pdf

Schaffner, A. K. (2023, June 8). *Equanimity: The holy grail of calmness & grace?* Positive Psychology. https://positivepsychology.com/equanimity/

Schembra, C. (2024, September 5). *Intelligent selfishness: How giving to others enriches your own life.* Rolling Stone. https://www.rollingstone.com/culture-council/articles/intelligent-selfishness-giving-others-enriches-own-life-1235094815/

Schultz, J. (2020, July 24). *5 differences between mindfulness and meditation.* Positive Psychology. https://positivepsychology.com/differences-between-mindfulness-meditation/

Scott, E. (2023, October 23). *How to set and crush your goals with way less stress.* Verywell Mind. https://www.verywellmind.com/goal-setting-and-reaching-goals-3145004

Scott, E. (2024, April 2). *How to develop a healthier outlook and learn to be perfectly imperfect.* Verywell Mind. https://www.verywellmind.com/overcoming-perfectionism-how-to-work-past-perfectionism-3144700

Seaver, M. (2023, August 9). *What mindfulness does to your brain: The science of neuroplasticity.* Real Simple.

https://www.realsimple.com/health/mind-mood/mindfulness-improves-brain-health-neuroplasticity

Seaver, M. (2024, April 26). *12 everyday habits to train your brain to be happier*. Real Simple. https://www.realsimple.com/how-to-be-happier-7485523

Shapero, B. G., Greenberg, J., Pedrelli, P., de Jong, M., & Desbordes, G. (2018). Mindfulness-Based interventions in psychiatry. *FOCUS*, *16*(1), 32–39. https://doi.org/10.1176/appi.focus.20170039

Sowers, K. M., Rowe, W. S., & Clay, J. R. (2009). The intersection between physical health and mental health: A global perspective. *Journal of Evidence-Based Social Work*, *6*(1), 111–126. https://doi.org/10.1080/15433710802633734

Sperber, S. (n.d.). *Overthinking: Definition, causes, & how to stop*. The Berkeley Well-Being Institute. https://www.berkeleywellbeing.com/overthinking.html

Stanborough, R. J. (2023, June 5). *How to change negative thinking with cognitive restructuring*. Healthline. https://www.healthline.com/health/cognitive-restructuring

Steffen, P. R., Austin, T., & DeBarros, A. (2016). Treating chronic stress to address the growing problem of depression and anxiety. *Policy Insights from the*

Behavioral and Brain Sciences, *4*(1), 64–70. https://doi.org/10.1177/2372732216685333

Stone, J. (2024, October 22). *Men and the hidden costs of overthinking.* Psychology Today. https://www.psychologytoday.com/us/blog/the-souls-of-men/202409/men-and-the-hidden-costs-of-overthinking

Stress. (n.d.). Mind. https://www.mind.org.uk/information-support/types-of-mental-health-problems/stress/causes-of-stress/

Stress. (2024, May 20). Cleveland Clinic. https://my.clevelandclinic.org/health/diseases/11874-stress

Strick, M., Dijksterhuis, A., & van Baaren, R. B. (2010). Unconscious-thought effects take place off-line, not on-line. *Psychological Science*, *21*(4), 484–488. https://doi.org/10.1177/0956797610363555

Sutton, J. (2021, November 19). How to overcome perfectionism: 15 worksheets & resources. *Positive Psychology*. https://positivepsychology.com/how-to-overcome-perfectionism/

The Editorial Team. (2022, November 29). *Daniel Goleman's emotional intelligence theory explained.* Resilient Educator. https://resilienteducator.com/classroom-resources/daniel-golemans-emotional-intelligence-theory-explained/

The overthinking epidemic: Is modern society encouraging us to think too much? (2023, June 30). A Life Well Lived.

https://www.alife-
welllived.com/blog/theoverthinkingepidemic

Therapy in a Nutshell. (2021). Intrusive thoughts and overthinking: The skill of cognitive defusion 20/30 [video]. In *YouTube*. https://www.youtube.com/watch?v=V3vhXQy48j o

Therapy in a Nutshell. (2022). Catastrophizing: How to stop making yourself depressed and anxious: Cognitive distortion skill #6 [Video]. In *YouTube*. https://www.youtube.com/watch?v=bS2LPNlO07s

Therapy in a Nutshell. (2023a). Automatic negative thoughts - break the anxiety cycle 11/30 [Video]. In *YouTube*. https://www.youtube.com/watch?v=lLZ-3TSoe9E

Therapy in a Nutshell. (2023b, November 9). *How to stop overthinking: Master the*

ACT skill of cognitive defusion 13/30. YouTube. https://www.youtube.com/watch?v=OhNm7ZSiZl s

Therapy in a Nutshell. (2024, January 4). *Emotional reasoning- the cognitive distortion that makes you emotionally reactive - anxiety 18/30 [Video]*. YouTube. https://www.youtube.com/watch?v=YBzvkgAReh g

Tokeikyte, G. (2021, March 22). *Why we fall back into old habits when we're tired or stressed*. Psychology Today. https://www.psychologytoday.com/us/blog/yes-you-can/202103/why-we-fall-back-into-old-habits-when-were-tired-or-stressed

Tsaousides, T. (2023, July 23). *How many emotions can you feel?* Psychology Today. https://www.psychologytoday.com/us/blog/smashing-the-brainblocks/202307/how-many-emotions-are-there

Tsatiris, D. (2021, September 10). *Three practical tips to overcome perfectionism.* Psychology Today. https://www.psychologytoday.com/us/blog/anxiety-in-high-achievers/202109/three-practical-tips-to-overcome-perfectionism

U.S. Department of Health and Human Services. (2018). Physical activity guidelines for Americans 2nd edition. In *U.S. Department of Health and Human Services* (pp. 8–10). https://health.gov/sites/default/files/2019-09/Physical_Activity_Guidelines_2nd_edition.pdf

Vandervort, S. (2024, May 29). *Get out of your head and into your body with these five practices.* The Local Mystic. https://thelocalmystic.com/get-out-of-your-head-five-practices/

Viezzer, S. (2024, February 5). *How to improve emotional intelligence.* Simply Psychology. https://www.simplypsychology.org/how-to-improve-emotional-intelligence.html

Washington University School of Medicine. (2023, April 20). *Hidden linkages: Scientists find mind-body connection is built into*   *brain.*   SciTechDaily. https://scitechdaily.com/hidden-linkages-scientists-find-mind-body-connection-is-built-into-brain/

Wegner, D. (1990, June 1). *White bears and other unwanted thoughts: Suppression, obsession, and the psychology of mental control.* Penguin Books. https://a.co/d/iKczKER

Wegner, D. (2011, November). *Setting free the bears: Escape from thought suppression.* American Psychologist. https://dtg.sites.fas.harvard.edu/DANWEGNER/pub/Setting%20free%20the%20bears%202011.pdf

Wegner, D. M., & Schneider, D. J. (2003). The white bear story. *Psychological Inquiry, 14*(3/4), 326–329. https://www.jstor.org/stable/1449696

Weil, A. (2006, May 8). *Richard Davidson.* TIME. https://content.time.com/time/specials/packages/article/0,28804,1975813_1975844_1976433,00.html

Why laughing is good for you. (2024, August 29). Cleveland Clinic. https://health.clevelandclinic.org/is-laughing-good-for-you

Wignall, N. (2021, November 4). *10 simple ways to improve your self-awareness [with examples].* Nick Wignall. https://nickwignall.com/self-awareness/

Williams, C. (2022, July 4). *How to understand your inner voice and control your inner critic.* New Scientist. https://www.newscientist.com/article/mg25533941-100-how-to-understand-your-inner-voice-and-control-your-inner-critic/

Winzeler, M. (2020, May 27). *Calm your body and mind: A therapist's guide for nervous system regulation.* WellnessWinz. https://wellnesswinz.com/2020/05/27/calm-your-body-and-mind-a-therapists-guide-for-nervous-system-regulation/

Working out boosts brain health. (2020, March 4). American Psychological Association. https://www.apa.org/topics/exercise-fitness/stress

World Health Organization. (2022, March 2). *COVID-19 pandemic triggers 25% increase in prevalence of anxiety and depression worldwide.* World Health Organization. https://www.who.int/news/item/02-03-2022-covid-19-pandemic-triggers-25-increase-in-prevalence-of-anxiety-and-depression-worldwide

Yeshurun, Y., Nguyen, M., & Hasson, U. (2021). The default mode network: Where the idiosyncratic self meets the shared social world. *Nature Reviews Neuroscience, 22.* https://doi.org/10.1038/s41583-020-00420-w

Yun, R. C., Fardghassemi, S., & Joffe, H. (2022). Thinking too much: How young people experience rumination in the context of loneliness. *Journal of Community & Applied Social Psychology.* https://doi.org/10.1002/casp.2635